The Author

John Garang de Mabior was born in Southern Sudan in June 1945. He moved to the USA in the sixties to take a B.A. in Economics and in 1981 he gained his Doctorate. In the same year he was awarded the Gamma Sigma Honour Award for significant contributions to agricultural science. He has completed considerable research in the area of economic development in Southern Sudan.

He has also pursued a military career since joining Anyana in 1970. This culminated in his appointment as Deputy Director of Military Research Branch in the Sudan Army General headquarters in Khartoum. He is the founding member of the Sudan People's Liberation Movement (SPLM), and the Sudan People's Liberation Army (SPLA). He has been the Commander-in-Chief of the SPLA and the Chairman of the SPLM since their inception in 1983. He is married with three children.

The Editor

Dr Mansour Khalid is the Vice-Chairman of the World Commission on Environment and Development. The former Foreign Minister of Sudan, he was one of the first Northerners to join the Sudanese People's Liberation Movement (SPLM). He is the author of *Nimeiri and the Revolution of Dis-May* (1985) and *The Government They Deserve* (1990), both published by Kegan Paul International.

Dedication

To the memory of Congressman Mickey Leland who, on August 7, 1989, together with devoted colleagues and aides, lost their lives when their plane crashed in the highlands of Ethiopia as they tried to revisit the tragic victims of war and famine in Sudanese refugee camps. In the spirit of the dictum that "it is not the dead who suffer, it is those who cause their death, and those who watch them die," Congressman Leland and his companions chose to risk their lives in turbulent tropical weather rather than watch thousands of helpless men, women, and children die of starvation on the American television screens. May this book be a modest, but lasting symbol, of the cause for which they died.

The Call for Democracy in Sudan

by John Garang

Edited and Introduced by
MANSOUR KHALID

Kegan Paul International
London and New York

First published in 1987, as *John Garang Speaks*, by
Kegan Paul International Ltd

This enlarged and revised edition published in 1992 by
Kegan Paul International Ltd, PO Box 256,
London WC1B 3SW, England

Distributed by
John Wiley & Sons Ltd
Southern Cross Trading Estate
1 Oldlands Way, Bognor Regis,
West Sussex, PO22 9SA, England

Routledge, Chapman & Hall Inc
29 West 35th Street
New York, NY 10001, USA

© John Garang 1987 and 1992

Phototypeset by Intype, London
Printed in Great Britain by T. J. Press, Padstow

British Library Cataloguing in Publication Data
Garang, John, 1945–
  The call for democracy in Sudan.
  1. Sudan. Guerilla movements : Sudan people's Liberation
  Army & Sudan People's Liberation Movement
  I. Title II. Khalid, Mansour, 1931–
  322.4209624

  ISBN 0 7103 0401 3

Library of Congress Cataloging-in-Publication Data
Garang, John, 1945–
  The call for democracy in Sudan / John Garang : edited and
  introduced by Mansour Khalid. –2nd ed., rev. and enl.
    220 p. 21.6 cm.
    Rev. ed. of: John Garang speaks. 1987.
    ISBN 0–7103–0401–3
    1. Southern Region (Sudan)–Politics and government. 2. Sudan
  People's Liberation Movement. 3. Sudan–Politics and
  government–1956– I. Khālid, Mansūr, 1931– . II. Garang, John,
  1945– John Garang speaks. III. Title.
  DT159.6.S73G37 1992
  322.4′2′09624–dc20   92–46459
                                                              CIP

Contents

Preface:

SPLA/SPLM – Why, How and Whither

The aim of this book is to explain the genesis and objectives of the Sudan People's Liberation Movement (SPLM) and Sudan People's Liberation Army (SPLA) as well as the ways and means of achieving those objectives. It also endeavours to dispel misunderstandings about this Movement, some caused by ignorance, others by deliberate mystification.

The Sudanese and the world at large need to know what this political creature, the SPLM, stands for. Why was it fighting Nimeiri and why did it continue to fight those who succeeded him? To answer the second question one cannot but recall the history of disappointed hopes, broken promises and frustrated dreams of all Sudanese yearning for peace and unity for the last thirty years. Nimeiri's sins against humanity were many, but the creation of the so-called Southern problem was not one of them.

The book equally endeavours to lay bare evidence at hand, the claim that the SPLM has persistently refused to talk to other Sudanese political groups who were genuinely seeking a solution to the country's problems. The evidence adduced includes the following:

(a)   the first proclamation of the SPLM/SPLA defining the Movement's national character and objectives;

(b)   the series of speeches given by the Chairman of the Movement, before Nimeiri's downfall, placing the problem in its widest
political context and calling for a radical restructuring of power,
veritable nation formation, and an end to the conscious and subconscious prejudices that have marred Sudanese political life in
the last thirty years;

(c)   declarations by the Movement immediately after the fall of
Nimeiri outlining the Movement's interpretation of that event and
its vision of the way ahead;

(d)   exchanges between the SPLM leadership and the Khartoum
political forces and politicians after Nimeiri's downfall.

(e)   peace proposals put forward by the SPLM subsequent to the
nation's return to civilian rule;

(f)   policy statements and agreements with opposition groups following the military take-over by the National Islamic Front (NIF)
in June 1989.

All these facts were available for anybody who cared to make
an objective assessment of what the SPLM/SPLA stand for. For
this reason, accusations of secessionisn, callous aggression, ideological intransigence and perpetration of an ethnological coup
d'etat are not only fallacious but indeed an easy way to escape
from realities. They also reflect an absence of goodwill particularly
when purveyed by those who claim that they are conscious of the
injustice of the past but are now incensed by the horror of war;
goodwill presupposes a recognition of the bona fides of political
adversaries.

If more evidence is needed, the speech by Dr. John Garang
de Mabior, leader of the SPLM/SPLA, opening the Koka Dam
Conference, and his ensuing press conference, should have
answered all those questions. Surprisingly, that speech, recorded
in sound and vision, was never shown in Khartoum, while large
space was given in radio, television and the press, to statements
by political and intellectual nonentities who laboured hard to
abort the peace process. That happened at the same time as
Khartoum claimed that its public fora were open to the SPLM,
were the Movement to decide to use the media to make its case
known to the Sudanese people.

On the morrow of Nimeiri's downfall a large section of the

Sudanese people wanted to receive Dr. John Garang with open arms and give him a hero's welcome. The sentiment was universal and genuine. The prodigal son, however, elected not to return and many claimed that he has wasted a historic opportunity. But history, to paraphrase Ralph Waldo Emerson's saying, is not a shallow village tale, it is a dynamic process where past acts cannot be dismissed as of no current relevance. Critics of Garang's "historic" role never paused to ask themselves, "Why did the SPLM fight Nimeiri in the first place?" To many of them the question seemed immaterial. "If we say that Sudan has changed because of Nimeiri's departure, who is John Garang to say otherwise?" they most likely have said to themselves. Consequently, when the SPLM called the Transitional Military Council (TMC) Nimeiri II, some elements in Khartoum were infuriated. That the TMC was composed of the same army command that have executed Nimeiri's war in the South was again immaterial. If anything, this is further proof of the complete insensitivity of some Northern politicians and intellectuals to Southern sentiments. Those very politicians and intellectuals were most categoric in their damnation of Nimeiri's tool of terror in the North; they fought for, and achieved the total dismantling of the national security apparatus (down to the level of privates), because it represented the "ugly" face of Nimeirism – repression.

But Nimeirism had also its "ugly" face in the South, a face reflected by those in the military who accepted the role of the tyrant's drill sergeants to fight his unjust and unconstitutional war. The inadequacy of those pliant officers was highlighted by the bold stance of many of their comrades-in-arms who refused to participate in this unholy war. So when the SPLM expressed distrust in the *army command* (not the army rank and file), because of its role in prosecuting that unjust war and oppressing the South, they, themselves, became suspect. At no point did the SPLM condemn the national army, let alone demand its disbanding. The appeals by the SPLM/SPLA to the nation, before and after Nimeiri's downfall, were replete with calls to patriotic officers and men to join in fighting tyranny and oppression. This caveat is important, for often those who excel in twisting facts would ask, "Does the SPLM want the national army disbanded?" In a sense the message from Khartoum was that oppression in the North, however minimal, should not go unpunished but killings and maimings in the South were deemed to be mere statistics.

Those double standards have, understandably, enraged Southerners beyond tolerance.

This contumelious attitude towards the SPLM did not end at that. Current deprecations of the Movement go as follows: this continued war is humiliating the army, causing loss and suffering to the populace and *Northerners* cannot go on seeing their sons massacred without being infuriated and angered by the SPLM/SPLA. Those are not moanings of the feeble-hearted; in some instances they are a genuine expression of revulsion to violence, which the SPLM understands. However, when those sentiments are drummed up by politicians and some sectors of the media adding venom to anger they become nothing but a premeditated systemization of hatred between brother and brother, paradoxically in the name of patriotism. The SPLA has been fighting the same national army as that under Nimeiri, causing the same losses and yet was hailed as the army of salvation from Nimeirism. In other words the SPLA can fight the national army with impunity and be honoured and glorified as long as it is serving what Northern politicians consider to be a just cause, but when it fights for its own version of justice, which is national in character, it becomes treacherous.

Throughout its existence the SPLM has been speaking about the convergence of political action and armed struggle against oppression. Armed struggle, though tragic, is neither prompted by genocidal sadism nor is it an outburst of wanton cruelty. For this reason the SPLA has developed a code of behaviour for its combatants, imposing on them a large measure of discipline and self-restraint. When excesses happen and are traced miscreants are severely penalized. SPLA's children of war are trained to be the future soldiers of peace and development. On the other hand, throughout the last six years, national army soldiers who fell into the hands of the SPLA as prisoners of war were well treated and handed over to the government. Twenty soldiers of the national army were released in Malwal in 1984 and nineteen in Nasir in 1985. Some of the captured soldiers chose to remain with the SPLA and their names have been publicly announced: they include officers such as Colonel Salim Saeed the commander of Jekau, Colonel Abul Ela Yousif Jumaa and First Lieutenant Mohamed Mirghani, both of the Kurmuk garrison. These were joined in August of 1986 by Major Rasheed Sir el Khatem of the Tanks Unit. In contrast, neither during Nimeiri's war, nor later, has there been any record of a single prisoner of war from SPLA; they were all killed. Nimeiri's war in the South was not an act of last resort incited by desperation; it was an act of first resort to break the backbone of the South and make them knuckle under to the use of indiscriminate force. That is still the order of the day. However, despite several appeals by the SPLA to the government, in some instances through the ICRC or the National Alliance, for exchange of POWs the government remained wordless, embarrassed by the fact that it never kept prisoners of war; dead SPLA men were less of a bother. For the benefit of those concerned a list of those POWs, including 12 officers, is annexed.

Having shed their facile tears over loss of life, the purveyors of calumnies jump two questions on you: "What does John Garang want anyway?" and come to that, "Who does he think he is?" Those who genuinely wanted to come to terms with reality would have found the answer to the first question in all SPLM declarations. The second question is yet further evidence of the disdain with which Southerners are looked upon. There are also others who, brandishing their objectivity, would follow that question with another: "Where is Garang's programme?" The question is not above suspicion in a country where about forty political parties were disgorged after Nimeiri's downfall, and of which only half a dozen meant something to the Sudanese people; the rest were an amalgam of political adventures, foreign-inspired saboteurs, second-rate demogogues and third-rate opportunists. Nobody in Khartoum has questioned the political credentials of those parties, let alone their programme. Nonetheless what the SPLM stands for was there for those who cared to read.

A fourth question is blunt and devoid of discreet adornments: "does Garang 'really' want to rule Sudan?" The self-perceived virtues of some Northerners are limitless. Historically, we in the North have failed to reconcile ourselves with the fact that a Southerner, and worse still a Christian, could even dream of ruling the Sudan. This is the same Sudan whose successive constitutions have enunciated the principle of non-discrimination on the basis of race, religion or sex. The hypocrisy, indeed the shamelessness, in this question is telling. These questions and answers, often hushed, only go to prove SPLM's worst fears. The SPLM never sought to conquer power through the bayonet. What it is fighting for, and determined to achieve, is the creation of a new Sudan where such questions simply do not arise. Every Sudanese has the right to aspire to rule the Sudan as long as he is qualified to do so, in a society where all are equal, not a society of "so-called" equality with some more equal than others.

So what should the SPLM have done after the fall of Nimeiri? John Garang's speech in Koka, presented in this book, alluded to this. The April events as they have unfolded passed through two phases:

1 A popular revolution and civil disobedience which were, in essence, a popular explosion after many years of brewing discontent. Political parties, trade unions, individual politicians and army officers (those who challenged Nimeiri in 1982 and those who expressed their objection to the war in the South), all paved the way for that occurrence. Some of those were chased out of the country into exile, some were incarcerated in prisons and some paid with their blood.

2 An army coup, commonly described as the army's alignment with the people (in effect it was the army command bowing to the will of the people under pressure from the rank and file). This is not semantic hair-splitting, for if the Khartoum kingmakers decided to adopt the TMC because they had aligned themselves with the people against Nimeiri at the last hour, they should have equally realized that other soldiers took to arms and sided with the people, not on 5 April 1985, but since 1983. If only for that reason the SPLM should have been there, present at the creation, to explain its views on how power should be structured in a way that would achieve permanent peace for the Sudan.

Inviting John Garang to come to Khartoum, to bless what was decided for Sudan, and to take the place chosen for him, sounds like a repeat performance of what Nimeiri had done earlier: offering him the Vice-Presidency of Sudan and the right to choose six Southerners in the Cabinet. That political bribe was refused. In the words of Garang in his address to the Koka conference: "We are not priests to bless whatever Khartoum decides, we are politicians who want to participate in the decision-making."

Khartoum kingmakers argue that they were overtaken by events and, therefore, were not in a position to influence them. But who was masterminding the events then? This argument sums it all up. It belies the claim of the self-appointed makers of the 6 April events; those who strategize revolutions know beforehand what to do with them when they succeed. Why were the kingmakers not ready? The answer is simple, it was because of their dissension, sectionalism and personal squabbles, which Nimeiri knew and thoroughly exploited for sixteen years, that Khartoum found itself on the horns of a dilemma. This again gives credence to the SPLM claim that the country shall never be lifted from its fall without a clean break with the past, introspecting and subjecting to examination all the given assumptions which led to the cerebral paralysis of Sudan's body politic.

Following the formation of the TMC, Khartoum kingmakers decided to nominate two persons for the premiership: the presidents of the Doctors Union and of the Bar Association, given the leading role these two unions played, more than any other professional group, in triggering the April uprising. However, it did not dawn on one of those kingmakers that the leadership of the SPLM had equally contributed to Nimeiri's downfall, certainly more than the officers who were ensconced in power and possibly more than either of the two civilian aspirants. That the name of John Garang was not even considered for the post was not a coincidence, not even a deliberate exclusion through malice aforethought. Worse than that, it was a reflection of the given assumptions in power brokerage in Sudan. For some Northerners, with a bellyful of subconscious prejudice, it was simply unthinkable to countenance the idea of a Southerner as *primus*. Those are the hard realities which we in the North have to face up to, rather than pretend they do not exist.

My message here is addressed primarily to the public opinion moulders and those who aspire to national leadership. Forward-looking Northerners and Southerners of all hues and ranks can live with the prejudices of the average man and woman. Those prejudices are born out of ignorance and can only be weeded out through education and a long process of learning. The issue is not that of granting Southerners what is not due to them, given their demographic weight, but of recognizing the aspiration of every Sudanese citizen to any position, including the highest position in the land, without discrimination as to sex, race or religion.

Soon afterwards the Khartoum kingmakers proceeded to select members of the Cabinet: twelve Northerners of whom six came from one province, Gezira. The Prime Minister of the day called this a coincidence. Only after selecting those twelve ministers did the Cabinet attend to the selection of Southern ministers. The

South was, therefore, an afterthought, and only the South. In effect the absentees from the Cabinet were not only Southerners; elements from other marginalized areas and sections of the society were also absent, for example, the Fur, the Nuba, the Beja and women. This only goes to prove our claim that the Khartoum kingmakers, like their predecessors, subconsciously view the Sudan as their own corner of the country writ large. But why was it the South and not the equally marginalized West or East that was a matter of concern to the kingmakers? Was it not because the South has taken up arms to make the point? This is what gives credence to John Garang's assertion that the way to permanent peace is not through partial solutions to the problems of the disfranchised, but through a radical restructuring of power that takes into account the interests of all the marginalized regions, those who took to arms and those who groaned in silence.

Be that as it may, what did the kingmakers do next? They gladly left it to Southern politicians to choose three from their midst for the Cabinet; the selection of ministers for the "*national*" Cabinet has, thus, become a matter of concern for Southerners only. So who are the secessionists then? Khartoum kingmakers or John Garang who is championing the cause of the whole nation, refusing to be treated as the representative of the South and saying "No" to Nimeiri's offer to include seven Southerners in Nimeiri's Cabinet? "What about Darfur, the Beja and the Nuba? Do they have to take up arms before their place is recognized?" he asked Nimeiri. Evidently Nimeiri's "magnanimity" to the South was not because of his kindheartedness, but because of Southern armed and political resistance.

The inadequacy of the elitist professional leadership of Sudan is also reflected in their failure to find a place in the trade union ranks for leaders from those marginalized regions, particularly the South. Ministers for the transitional government were drawn from the different professions and chosen at random by a kitchen Cabinet. But it did not dawn on the kingmakers that there were also doctors, lawyers, judges, engineers and university professors, from the South, the West and the East. If they ever had such a national vision and accommodation they could have presented a more balanced Cabinet in a way that would make the issue of regional or ethnic representation a moot question. Precisely because of this, and admittedly, by way of reaction to it, many of the aspirants for power fell back on their ethnic and regional constituencies, leading to the emergence of several regionally based and possibly regionally biased political parties. Those parties eventually coalesced in what is known as the Alliance of Rural Forces. This Northern old-boy network is precisely what John Garang called the not-so-coincidental coincidences of always having power wielded by a certain group or groups from the North.

The Khartoum political forces, rather than facing this problem squarely, resorted to a "fuite en avant". "We are victims of an accident of history," they said. "There are more educated people in the North and, if we want quality, there is no way for power but to rest with Northerners." This facile argument lacks sincerity and has an alibi thin enough to see through. For one thing the struggle for power among Northern politicians, since Independence, has always been settled by compromises that took account of the interests of the major sects and parties; competence was seldom a factor in choosing rulers. That was the case yesterday, as it is today. On the other hand, the realities of cultural and ethnic diversity are universally accepted as determining factors in power sharing and apportionment. Even in a country as stable as the U.S.A., with over two hundred years of constitutional liberal democracy behind it, politicians can hardly ignore balancing conflicting ethnic interests, because of the country's heterogeneous ethnic origins. For example, Presidents are always careful to include in their Cabinets blacks, Catholics, Jews, southerners, westerners, Irish and lately those of hispanic origin and women.

With this record of intellectual and political failure and the disenchantment ensuing from it, any dialogue with those at the helm in Khartoum was doomed to be a dialogue of the deaf. The first contact between the SPLM and the kingmakers were nothing but public appeals over the airwaves, by the authorized and unauthorized alike. Typically, those appeals were accompanied by gossip in the Khartoum circle about the SPLM's reaction to those appeals, often emanating from unauthorized persons. This, manifestly, was not the professional way to do business. Governments have their channels of communications which were conspicuous only by their absence. Gossip, on the other hand, is the opiate of the idle. In effect, it would not have taken those who cared for peace and knew how to manage a crisis more than a one-hour flight from Khartoum either East or South to meet with the SPLM leadership. It took Khartoum political circles over six months to start this process seriously. In between, all that Khartoum had offered was megaphone diplomacy with the loudspeakers directed at full blast on the Khartoum audience, rather than on those to whom the message was addressed.

In this regard the first official communication between the SPLM and the authority in power came in June 1985, two months after the April uprising. In that communication the new Government offered nothing but the same old wine in the same old bottle. This official communication between John Garang and Dr. Gizouli Dafaalla, the Prime Minister, was revealing. The Prime Minister, who shouted as loud as anybody else calling for the dismantling of all vestiges of Nimeirism, had nothing to offer as a solution to the so-called problems of the South, other than the Addis Ababa Agreement – the seminal achievement of the Nimeiri era. But were Gizouli to do as Nimeiri and resurrect the Addis Ababa Agreement from the dead, he ought to have addressed the right person; John Garang never claimed to represent the South and often asserted that his concern is with power restructuring in the whole Sudan, the only way to achieve permanent peace in North and South alike.

Gizouli was echoing the incessant utterances from Khartoum referring to the SPLM as the champion of Southern Sudan. That the SPLM has kept saying that their concern is not only with the South but with the whole country seemed to be of no relevance. On the other hand, recalling the Addis Ababa Agreement did not only reflect a lack of will to face the real issue (power sharing and restructuring of power at both central and regional levels), but also a complete lack of imagination, if not intellectual stagnation. Khartoum officialdom inherited the Earth from Nimeiri and claimed that they knew better, however, their solution to Sudan's most serious problem was a leaf from Nimeiri's book. To their chagrin, Garang's answer to those fossilized solutions was understandably negative. Official Khartoum scarcely read the line, instead they essayed hard to read between the lines. If they had done, a meaningful dialogue could have commenced right there and then. However, having failed to rise to the challenge of a *national* movement that has it origin in the South and not the North, as things are conventionally assumed, they resorted to yet another Nimeiri trick. John Garang, they argued, is not a free agent, he must be a tool of somebody, and there were many masters: the Ethiopians, the Soviets, the Libyans, as well as the Christian Church which is "bent on destroying Islam". Some foul-mouthed media buffoons added, of late, Israel to the list, pushing Khartoum's efforts to besmear Garang's reputation beyond the limits of credulity.

So Khartoum slovenly neglected John Garang and decided to talk to his "masters and mentors". Some of those masters were the very people with whom Sudan was living in peace, having succeeded in achieving exemplary relations based on mutual respect of differing social systems and territorial integrity. This was the case with Ethiopia between 1973 and 1977, under both the imperial and Marxist regimes in that country. But if the South was handed on a silver platter to Ethiopia, at a time when Nimeiri was heaping abuse and scorn on its government and leadership, it was only the government of the day in Khartoum that was to blame. This is the game of politics at its ugliest in the real world and those who are engaged in that game should know it.

Equally, opposition to Nimeiri since 1969/1970 was first hatched in that same country by the late Sharif el Hindi who daily addressed the Sudanese from Radio Addis Ababa before moving later to Tripoli (the capital of the other master). Tripoli was used, it is to be recalled, as the springboard for an attack on Khartoum by the opposition. It is, therefore, the height of hypocrisy that the very people who hailed the leaders of the opposition to Nimeiri based in Tripoli and Addis Ababa, as heroic patriots who were entitled to cooperate with the devil for the sake of the country's salvation, could not find a better word to describe SPLM's cooperation with those countries than treacherous servility. There is also the accusation of Communist inspiration, as if all the public utterances by the SPLM were not enough proof to the contrary. Amazingly those accusations came from the very people who reconciled themselves with living with a Communist Party in Khartoum, the heart of Muslim Sudan; another Communist Party in Southern Sudan, the land of the "heathens" should not, one supposes, ruffle anybody's feathers.

The truth of the matter is that the SPLM has put Northern politicians off balance simply because it challenged conventional wisdom and slaughtered a few sacred cows. It has challenged a political hegemony that some people assumed was there to stay. It drove people to look inwards and identify what makes Sudanese of them all rather than look at Sudan from without, the way Arabs, Africans and Muslims think it is or would like it to be. It faced up to the ethnic, religious and cultural specificities as they are, rather than viewing them through distorting ideological lenses. It called for devising new political structures and institutions rather than repeating experiences that have outlived their usefulness – if they were ever useful. For Northerners to do all that, they need to exercise self-analysis if not self-criticism. Seemingly few are inclined to do this. The majority still indulge in the false comfort of contrived oblivion to reality. All our ills, they delude themselves, are caused by others.

This is precisely why some elements in Khartoum were shocked by the presence of some Northern elements within the ranks of the SPLM. To some this amounted to treason and they were not embarrassed to call it so. But they go on, nonetheless, masquerading as champions of a national unity that transcends race, region and religion. Those knaves would have preferred the SPLM to remain a Southern movement and to have dealt with it as such; all it would take for them to get out of the quagmire would be offering regional autonomy to the South and a few secure ministerial posts in Khartoum for Southern aspirants. This artless naivety is scarcely the way to ensure stability, let alone build a new Sudan. If history is to be our guide, such an approach is too primitive to address a problem so complex.

In effect, John Garang has rubbed salt into the wounds by calling a spade a spade. He did not mince his words when he talked about Northern hegemony and the disdain with which non-Arabicised ethnic groups are treated in Sudan. He was also prudent enough to say that the SPLM can live with the prejudices of the average person, which is a problem that time and education alone would solve. What he challenged was the harbouring of such ideas by those who have a claim to national leadership. In his Koka speech he drew a line between Arab culture and Arab racial supremacy. Arab culture "is our culture and Arabic is our language, and they are there to stay", he said. It is the racially biased hegemony that will have to go. Islam may be the religion of the majority but it should not be a stumbling-block in the way of non-Muslims to have full political rights, including the right to assume all political positions were they to seek them, nor should it, or any other religion for that matter, have a place in national politics. What the SPLM is challenging, therefore, is not Arabism as a cultural identity but as a political supremacy based on racial heredity. Also the recognition of ethnic diversity advocated by the SPLM is nothing but respect for cultural specificities rather than the perpetuation of ethnicity as a source of dissension.

Failing to face those issues within the context they were presented, some Khartoum politicians cried wolf all over the Arab and Islamic worlds, claiming that Arabism and Islamism were threatened by John Garang and his mentors: the Soviets (the very people who extend their defence umbrella over many Arab countries) or the Christian Church groups furnishing humanitarian aid to the SPLM (the very groups who are camping among the Muslims of the Red Sea hills and Darfur, extending similar aid to their famine-stricken and medical care to their emaciated women and children).

All these double standards, contradictions and deliberate ambiguities do not bode well for a genuine national dialogue on the real problems of Sudan. Historical prejudices, too, can only damage people's capacity for judgement. A better judgment requires from us all in the North to undergo an agonizing reappraisal. This time there is no easier route to peace. This appeal, I say again, is primarily made to the educated Sudanese, the pacesetters. One hopes, however, that this book will help dispel the wrong image created by those elements bent on sullying the reputation of the SPLM, as well as lay bare the confusion caused by the double talk of those who seek to mystify, and the simplistic interpretations of those whose minds are free from serious thought.

Mansour Khalid

Preface to the Second Edition

The first edition of this book appeared in the early part of 1987 under the title *John Garang Speaks*. Its purpose, at that stage, was to lay before the general reader the aims of the Sudan People's Liberation Movement (SPLM), its means to achieve those aims and thoughts of John Garang, its leader on those issues. At the time of writing, the SPLM was barely three years old, and it was, therefore, important to establish the movement for what it truly was, indeed what it remains to be today – a movement struggling for the establishment of a New Sudan to which all Sudanese voluntarily belong irrespective of ethnic origin, sex, religion or place of birth. Since that time, the role of the SPLM in the conflict taking place in Sudan has been accorded a great deal more attention by the world's media, if only because of its military successes and coherent political stances. Consistently the SPLM called for a radical socio-political restructuring in Sudan; a thesis that may have first shocked insular elements within the Northern Sudan, and they are many. Not so after the Koka-Dam Declaration to which all Sudanese political forces from the North and South have adhered save for the Democratic Unionist Party (DUP) and the National Islamic Front (NIF). Pursuant to that declaration the SPLM's call for a National Constitutional Conference to lay the foundations of a *New Democratic Sudan* united in justice and mutual respect was accepted by all. That call was made by Garang as early as 1983 and he has undeviatingly stood by it since that date.

Regrettably, some of those who affixed their signatures to the agreement failed to see its import or follow the logic of their commitment to it; Koka-Dam represented a watershed in Sudanese politics because it was meant to trigger fundamental changes. Indubitably it did not augur well for such a momentous agreement that some of its signatories failed to envisage its impact and the consequences of the processes it had initiated. Koka-Dam Declaration, on the other hand, was a package deal and, as such, every single word in it was studiously coined; consequently attempts by any political group, to tamper with the letter or spirit of that consensus document would not only put the accord in jeopardy; but it would also lend weight to the accusations, and summon old fears, about the perfidious nature of Northern partisan politics.

In constrast, the SPLM/SPLA chose to stick to the letter and spirit of the Koka-Dam Declaration it did so not because there was anything sacrosanct about it, but because it viewed it as the first serious step towards the creation of a *New Democratic Sudan*. Those who call for the creation of a *New Sudan* do not, by definition, recognize the viability of the status quo ante nor accept the claim that Sudan's ills would be cured by a return to the old system of rule, known as Sudan's "democracy". That is not to say that the SPLM has monopoly on wisdom or innate virtues to qualify it to set the national agenda; nor has any Sudanese government for that matter. However, what gives the SPLM more credibility is its consistent position that the national agenda can neither be set by the government, nor the Movement; not even by them together. It is only through a constitutional conference to which all legitimate representatives of Sudan's political forces, objectively defined, that major issues of national concern can be resolved.

It is for this reason that the present title, *The Call for Democracy*, seems, on today's reckoning, a far more apt description of the movement's pilgrim's progress; particularly when successive Khartoum governments have taken more and more aggressive stances against any kind of political reform within Sudan, including that to which some of them were publicly committed. The new material in this book aims to establish, through Garang's speeches and treatises, the strategic nature of that agreement and, thus, the SPLM's unyielding commitment of it. It also endeavours to establish the lack of seriousness on the part of those who strove to undo that agreement through wily tricks as well as the irresponsibility of those who were bent on torpedoing it and stopped at nothing in order to achieve their end.

The first edition of this book ended with a chapter entitled "Peace Around the Corner"; that was the measure of our optimism following the Koka-Dam Agreement. But soon thereafter things took a turn for the worse because of the quibbling of the Umma party, one of the major northern parties who signed it. As for the other major northern party, the Democratic Unionist Party (DUP), it was intially oblivious to the peace process and was, seemingly, wallowing in that complacent oblivion. Those are the two main leading parties in the North who, between them, controlled a government, that was destined to implement the Koka-Dam Agreement. Another important northern party in Parliament was the NIF, its attitude towards the agreement, from the start, was sheer repudiation. In these circumstances the return to hostilities was a foregone conclusion. The new material in this book traces developments since the failure of the Koka-Dam process and the responsibility of the traditional northern parties for the ensuing drama; the ground rules for peace-making were already established at Koka-Dam and any departure from, or obliviousness to them, would naturally have dire consequencies for peace.

With the return to hostilities also came the agonizing suffering of hundreds of thousands of innocent civilians caught in cross fire within the war zone. Accusations of using hunger as a weapon were traded between the parties in conflict, but hardly placed in their proper context. What was going on was war, and wars are not synchronous with the sanctity of human life. This is not an attempt to rationalize indifference to human life; only to emphasize the obvious. Consequently removing the malevolent sequels coincidental to war requires, from the warring parties, a serious effort to remove the causes that led to war in the first place, and those of them who are not in a hurry to achieve peace should be distrusted when they bemoan the sufferings of the hungry. Peace is obviously the ultimate solution but in the interim, emergency action would be needed and should be provided. In this second edition there is abundant material on the issue of emergency relief that would hopefully put the record straight and dispel the baseless charges that the SPLM/SPLA used hunger as a weapon, if anything it was the government agencies who were engaged in such a heartless exercise.

Needless to say, there was extensive confusion and mystery

surrounding the reasons behind the failure of Sudan's "democratic" regime to achieve peace and alleviate the suffering visited
on the Sudanese peoples because of the continuation of war.
Rather than coming to terms with bare-faced realities the delin-
quent government chose to camouflage its failure with conspiracy
theories and metahistorical explanations; the continuation of war
was attributed to everything on earth, except the most obvious
reason. Since the first edition of this book appeared in 1987, a
number of odious political changes have occurred in the country;
not the least amongst them was the military coup that toppled the
"democratic" government of Sadiq al Mahdi in July 1989 and
exploded the myth that democracy, as it was conceived and practised, was there to stay; the "democratic" system collapsed like a
house of cards. Coupled with this, the economic situation of Sudan
had worsened considerably, to the point that the country began
to lumber towards collapse. The connection between economic
deterioration and the failure of the peace process was not hard to
see except by the Sudanese leaders.

These have been years when the increasing irrelevance of many
of the alternative political "solutions" offered by the Khartoum
politicians, particularly the NIF and the Prime Minister Sadiq al
Mahdi, became so obvious to all concerned. A change in the
nature and content of politics was not only expected, but it was
also perceived to be long overdue. That the unfortunate outcome
of this was the installation of yet another military government,
despite the self-delusion of the political players in Khartoum that
the army was already consigned to oblivion, shows how far those
politicians had become caught in a trap of their own making. The
army had in fact been running affairs in many rural areas of Sudan
and its hold had become increasingly strong since the election of
Sadiq to the office of Prime Minister in 1986, mainly because of
the war situation and the cardinal role of the army in it.

Despite the turmoil of the times, the SPLM/SPLA has maintained a consistent position on the inevitability of the restructuring
of power and wealth if peace and real democracy were to be
established. In other words the SPLM's message was that it was
too late in the day to seek a settlement for Sudan's crisis through
legal artifices and political gimmicks as the NIF has tried to do in
what was known as the National Charter, or as Sadiq has earlier
ventured to do by drafting, single-handedly, a heavily loaded
document known as Sudan's Transitional Charter, intended to

pre-empt the Koka-Dam process. What the SPLM/SPLA has set off is a social revolution and revolutions are about justice, not power. In this respect the SPLM/SPLA's position has been outstanding, and all the more remarkable, in a period when Khartoum governments and parties, often hindered by the fanaticism of the NIF, were simply unable to make any cohesive effort towards the attainment of just peace, or indeed the establishment of any viable and broadly accepted policy that might speed up the process.

Probably the Prime Minister, whose party has signed the Koka-Dam declaration and reneged on it, has doubted the resolve of the SPLM/SPLA to stand behind the agreement. He may have also thought that he was capable of the impossible, fusing Koka-Dam's pardigm with the NIF's political pontifications. But those are, palpably, colliding postulates and strange bedfellows; religious fanaticism cannot cohabit with spiritual tolerance, ethnocentricity with cultural diversity and the SPLM's yearning for tomorrow's New Sudan with the NIF's call-back of Mecca's yesterday. This startling position of Sadiq led some to assume that the Prime Minister was essentially a fundamentalist, his constant solicitation to the NIF in the face of their almost universal isolation by all the political forces of the nation gave credence to the assumption. More so when it had become clear to the "democratically" elected Prime Minister that, given that obdurate position on the issue of religion and politics, the NIF was the last Sudanese political group to be committed to democracy and, therefore, the least qualified to be taken in confidence, let alone entrusted with the reins of power. Nonetheless Sadiq regularly saw to it that the NIF was kept in good humour till they were eventually incorporated in his government. For that reason there is no escaping the conclusion that the forcible seizure of power by the NIF in June 1989 was, partly, the making of those who courted them and accorded them unmerited political legitimization. The present nightmarish government in Khartoum, which shall remain a legend of wretchedness in Sudan's modern history, could not have been predicted three years ago by the most macabre crystal gazer.

Now that the unthinkable has become reality, the hope of every right-thinking Sudanese is that leaders have learned from their past mistakes and miscalculations and begun to recognize Sudan's problems for what they really are; fundamental problems that can only be resolved though radical solutions. That is why the SPLM/SPLA has elected to make it very clear, from the outset, that while it is now relentlessly fighting to rid the nation of the NIF incubus; that shall not be the end of the road, the road signs still point towards a New Sudan that is democratic, secular and united in diversity. This assertion had to be made so that the movement should not be faced later on with the insidious question: now that al Beshir is gone what is the SPLM fighting for?

What is this "New Sudan" to which the SPLM yearns and struggles to bring about; the second edition of *John Garang Speaks* throws some light on this question through some of the major speeches, public declarations, correspondence and press interviews made in the periods prior, and subsequent, to the conference at Koka-Dam in 1986. It would also be gleaned from the SPLM's reaction to the charter adopted by the National Democratic Forum (NDF), an amalgam of political parties, trade unions and army officers who are spearheading the resistance against the Junta. The chosen documents outline Garang's political vision for the country and the SPLM's position on a range of issues such as: democracy, economic reform, the place of religion in society and the much confused issue of nationalities.

To those merely seeking a narrative history of events in the Sudan in recent years, some of those statements may appear repetitive, even though the major speeches that appeared in the first edition are fairly condensed in this edition. However, the idea behind the book was not merely to retell events, but to make available to researchers and serious students of Sudanese affairs textual resources that are badly needed on a subject that is often misrepresented, misunderstood and deliberately maligned.

Introduction

For a political movement that is only six years old, the impact of the SPLM/SPLA, both inside and outside Sudan, is indeed remarkable. Outside, the SPLM has succeeded in focusing the world's attention, as never before, on Sudan's indentity crisis. Within the Sudan, it succeeded in sharpening the awareness of many Sudanese of this indentity crisis, albeit intimidating those who believed in their ethnic superiority and shaped their politics accordingly. But even among those who had a lot of time for the SPLM, feelings towards the Movement have oscillated between adulation, during the last two years of Jaafar Nimeiri's rule, and anger, after his fall. In the mind of those all would have been "milk and honey" had John Garang de Mabior, leader of the SPLM/SPLA, made it to Khartoum on 6 April 1985, following Nimeiri's removal. We have to ask ourselves the question: why has there been this change of heart about the SPLM/SPLA and its leader? The answer will lead us to a better understanding of the way the Northern Sudan perceives the Southern Sudan, and, for that matter, the other marginalized regions of the country, in the West and East.

Sudan, since self-government in the early 1950s, has witnessed several insurrections in the South, but nothing as intensive and far-reaching as that achieved by the SPLM, after only six years of action. Why has the SPLM become such a formidable force? And why has the Northern admiration of SPLM/SPLA during Nimeiri's rule turned into disapprobation by some and mistrust by others after his demise? Again, these questions can only be answered by looking at the way Northerners perceive Southerners

1

and in particular, the way they take Southern Sudanese for granted. By "Notherners" we mean, primarily, politicized elements living in the urban and semi-urban centres of the Northern and Central Sudan in Khartoum, White Nile, Gezira and Kordofan Provinces.

Northern Sudanese have, traditionally, dismissed all legitimate grievances expressed by the marginalized regions of the country as racist or secessionist causes although those grievances were championed by respectable regional politicians and political parties acting within the bounds of the established system such as SANU in the South, the Beja Congress in the East and the Nuba Mountain Union in the Centre West. Those regional movements that pleaded for justice and equality were, invariably, depicted by Northerners as fractious racial movements conjuring up hatred between non-Arabs and Arabs. The distinction between Arab and non-Arab is based on a distorted vision of the ethnic composition of the Sudan. This distortion is not only a brainchild of the misinformed foreign press, who often divide Sudanese into Arabs and Africans, but also a myth assiduously cultivated by those Sudanese who want to reach down to their racial roots only to distinguish themselves from others, us and them, the racially superior and the racially inferior. The articulators of this retrograde concept of Sudanism are not only encumbered by a mighty feudal intellectual baggage that weighs heavily on their thinking, also the bottom line in this way of thinking is politico-economic dominance by the North versus politico-economic servitude in the marginalized regions which are mainly inhabited by Sudanese of non-Arab stock including those who are culturally arabicized, e.g. the Fur and the Beja.

This, in essence, is the endemic disease of Sudanese politics that existed long before Nimeiri assumed power, albeit aggravated by his arrogance and high-handedness. The basic problem of the Sudan, now as at Independence, is how to achieve political unity in such a culturally diverse country and to achieve equitable socio-economic development in a country (like many others in the Third World) where the urban populace predominates the economy to the detriment of the rural. Those two basic problems have never been successfully tackled in Sudan, certainly not by the British colonialists who made a policy of dividing the country in half, nor by the various regimes of the parties paralysed by their own myopia and divisiveness nor by the military rule of General

Abboud between 1958 and 1964, which tried to substitute brute force for the workings of democratic process.[1]

The Sudan, anthropologically, is not a country of Arabs and Africans but that of Arabicized Africans or Africanized Arabs and pure Africans; racial purity is alien to it. On the other hand the pre-eminence of Arab culture has never been challenged by the non-Arabs, except those driven by reactive inferiority complexes, like the secessionists of Anyanya I and Anyanya II. In fact the entrenchment of Arabo-Islamic culture in the Sudan was the great achievement of two purely African Sudanese kingdoms: the Funj and the Fur.[2] However, the bottom line, we argued, is political and economic power and political phenomena cannot be explained away by anthropology, less so by zoology.

It is precisely this insidious racialism that accentuated Southern reaction to Northerners, the extreme expression of which was the call for secession. Those who have called for secession in the past have been prompted by a sense of despair, rather than a desire to see their country divided. Theirs was a reaction against what they viewed as Northern intransigence and neglect, leading to economic deprivation and powerlessness.

The political kingmakers and moulders of public opinion in the North, more than anybody else, are the ones to blame for turning genuine regional claims into racial conflict. This situation still obtains; the term *harakat unsurya* (i.e. racist movements) still recurs whenever a regional group organizes itself to call for power-sharing as an alternative to the prevailing end to historical injustices. At best this is a reflection of political ignorance; unawareness of alternatives is the height of political ignorance. At worst it is a manifestation of unenlightened self-interest that seeks to mobilize "Arabs" against non-Arabs only to perpetuate a privileged status at a very high cost to all.

By making a *casus belli* of the race issue those Northern

1 For further views see "A Plea for Pluralism" by the author, *Africa Report*, July-August 1985, and "The Sudan: What Went Wrong and the Way Ahead", by the same author (speech delivered to the Royal Institute of International Affairs at Chatham House, London, April 1985).
2 See "Cultural Diversity and Political Unity", by the editor (speech delivered to the Essex University Cross-Cultural Conference in July 1985).

3

elements have simply fuelled rebellion and widened the breach. What they did not realize was that at the end of the day they would be hoist with their own petard. This is the background against which the SPLM was born. There are basic factors (alluded to above) and immediate reasons that triggered off the rebellion, specifically those decisions taken by Nimeiri to play the South against the North, to divide the South itself and completely to overturn the constitutional settlement of the Southern question as laid down in the Addis Ababa Agreement.

The basic factors, however, are the ones that led John Garang to plead for a nationwide self-analysis, denounce secessionism and call, in the first place, for the mobilization of the historically aggrieved, while opening the door wide for the adhesion of all Sudanese who are seeking a genuine and lasting peace based on justice and equality. In his thinking, that is the only way to build a new Sudan that can play the role Sudan is destined to play, not as an appendage of the Arab world, nor as a half-hearted African country apologetic about its Africanity (despite all the lip service to pan-Africanism). This way the Arabo-African and Afro-Arab identities of the country can be harnessed as a source of strength, not a factor of division.

On a personal level, I joined the ranks of the SPLM in mid-1984 for very objective reasons. Firstly, because of the seriousness of the Movement in its opposition to Nimeiri, the SPLM was undistracted by the bickerings and personal squabbles that characterized northern-based opposition groups. Secondly, because I could see that the SPLM was determined to face squarely the root causes of the Sudanese crisis which revolve around issues of identity, unity in diversity, nation building, development and a foreign policy designed to serve national interest rather than view the Sudan from the outside through the prism of others. SPLM's opposition to Nimeiri was concerned with what was to follow Nimeiri in essence and not in structural forms. My views, in this respect, were reiterated in public declarations on television and radio, both before and after the demise of Nimeiri and both inside and outside the Sudan. Those views were also expounded in speeches delivered to the Royal Institute of International Affairs at Chatham House, London, and to Essex University in England, and before Nimeiri's departure the same views were presented in a book entitled *Nimeiri and the Revolution of Dis-may*. Throughout the last two years of Nimeiri's rule, I aligned myself with a movement which was hailed by all Sudanese up to April 1985 not only because of what it stood for but also because of what it was doing to achieve its ends; armed struggle.

In reality, the SPLM was admired in the North only as long as it worked within the limits set for it by Northerners as a Southern movement with no claim to have a say as to what happens beyond the boundaries of the South. All the same, any Northern-based party could claim national character and vocation, and have a say in how the South, the East and West should be run. This is revealed in the questions brazenly posed in Khartoum: "What has John Garang got to do with the Nuba, Beja and other non-Southern groups? Why is he upset by the *Sharia* as long as it is not going to be applied to the South? Why does he not settle for the solution of the problem of the South?" Constant appeals were made to John Garang to help solve the problem of the South, often by the same people who asserted that Garang, after all, was not the authorized spokesman of the South. John Garang earned golden opinions in 1983/1984 only because of a convergence of interests, namely, the defeat of Nimeiri.

The fact that the SPLM was fighting for certain goals of which the removal of Nimeiri was only one, was immaterial to its critics in the North. Those goals transcended the South; but once Nimeiri was deposed and the aspirations of the North satisfied (or so they naively thought), the SPLM were expected to put arms aside and bless whatever was decided for the Sudan by those who considered themselves the arbiters of the nation's destiny. Even the interim government's recognition of the SPLM's role in the fight against Nimeiri was measured. For example, a letter written by Dr. Gizouli to John Garang, on 1 June 1985, had this to say: "You did your bit in *paving the way for the revolution* by the means available to you, and the nation appreciated that," as though armed struggle for two years was not revolution enough.

Few people cared to look back and see how the SPLM/SPLA had started and what were its objectives. On 3 March 1984 John Garang appealed to the Sudanese people (to all Sudanese people) on the founding of the Movement. In that appeal he charted the way to the future and referred to the history of oppression in Sudan, before and during the Nimeiri era: "To this end the oppressor had divided the Sudanese people into Northerners and Southerners; Westerners and Easterners, Halfawin and the so-called Awlad al Balad, who have hitherto wielded political power in Khartoum; while in the South, people have been politicized along tribal lines . . . The oppressor has also divided us into Muslims and Christians, and into Arabs and Africans." So when it came to the definition of oppression and its root causes, the vision of the SPLM was clear: Nimeiri was only one in a row.

The onslaught of John Garang on secessionist and national chauvinist tendencies which developed at different times and jeopardized the unity of the people was vehement. His proclamation dealt with the crisis of the Nimeiri regime and called for a vanguard movement to liberate the whole Sudanese people. People who keep asking the question "liberation from whom?" have missed the point; the question should have been "liberation from what?"

By incidence of history and geography, this Movement originated in the South. Its aim was, and still is, to create a new, united Sudan under: ". . . a socialist system that affords democratic and human rights to all nationalities [ethnic groups] and guarantees freedom to all religions, beliefs and outlooks." According to the appeal: ". . . the content of our socialism cannot be determined mechanically and equated with Communism, as Nimeiri would like the Western world to believe. The conceptualization and particularization of socialism in the Sudan shall unfold as the armed struggle proceeds and as socio-economic development programmes are implemented during and after the war according to Sudanese local and objective conditions." A glance at the biography of John Garang may help to divine some of the man's political and intellectual sources of inspiration.

It is therefore self-evident that the SPLM is:

(a)   National not regional;
(b)   Unitarian not secessionist;
(c)   Socialist not Communist;
(d)   Pragmatic not dogmatic in its approach to socialism.

However, like Nimeiri, the Khartoum media and many of its politicians continued to harp on the same string, repeating accusations of secessionism, Communism and ideological dogmatism. This is the measure of their failure to stand up to the political challenge presented by a Southern-based Movement that took them off guard.

How did the movement start? Dr. John Garang, in his March appeal, outlined the history of the SPLM and the immediate factors that triggered off the rebellion; these were: the dismantling of the Addis Ababa Agreement by Nimeiri's singlehanded dissolution of the regional government and assembly in 1980, 1981 and 1983; changing the boundaries of the Southern provinces; division of the South into three regions, and, finally (the last straw) the decision to transfer to Khartoum Southern soldiers (old Anyanya) who were absorbed into the national Army after the Addis Ababa Agreement and according to its agreed terms. Nimeiri, rather than allowing the process of military integration to continue, aborted it and ended by bloodying his nose.

The army in the South witnessed several mutinies after the Addis Ababa Agreement. Those mutinies were dismissed at the time as mere "teething problems". The first mutiny, in Akobo in 1975, led to the creation of Anyanya II. The remnants of those mutineers are the very forces used by the government today against the SPLA. At that time, the men involved in the mutiny were disarmed, paradoxically, by officers and men including John Garang himself, then an officer in the national army. Other mutinies followed and were controlled mainly by Southern officers. For example. the mutiny in Wau in 1976; in Ariath in 1983; in Bor and Pibor in 1983. Nimeiri had no reason to fear the presence of Southern officers and men in the South, and his decision in 1983 to transfer them to the North was a result of his panic after his assault on the Addis Ababa Agreement and fright that those forces might rebel against his misdeed. That was a self-fulfilling prophecy.

Again, at a personal level, if there was one thing that made me go the additional mile in my opposition to Nimeiri, it was his dismantling of the Addis Ababa Agreement and abortion of the process of national integration. That agreement, with all its limitations, was our greatest achievement. It was the cornerstone of national unity in diversity, paving the way for permanent peace. The process, though stifled in its infancy, has gone some way, within its historical context, in recognizing the root cause of the North/South conflict. To me, who was present at the creation of that Agreement and participated fully in its formulation, Nimeiri's decision was the deepest cut of all; it was not only a demolition of a dream, also an undoing of a laboriously stitched national unity. Nimeiri would not have survived as long as he did, or received as much international recognition and support, without that achievement. So more than anyone I could understand why the Southerners have taken to arms again, and dismissed all patriotic exhortations coming from Khartoum as sheer humbug.

Many of my Northern compatriots could not countenance the presence of one of their number in the ranks of the SPLM. Those are a heterogeneous bunch; some of them were driven by spite, others by genuine bafflement: how could a "senior" Northerner accept the leadership of a Southerner? Southerners are only to be led or to lead their like. The former, because of their lack of extrinsicality are irrelevant to the main issue and deserve no attention, those who fail to segregate the subjective from the objective in a time of crisis shall never see it all. One's problem is with the latter, those who contemptuously condemn the SPLM (a movement with a declared national vocation) to being only Southern or at best negroid and shamelessly view Northerners cooperating with it as nothing but traitors. Such thinking, with its transparent racial undertones, almost suggests that a sector of the population is genetically flawed and as such has no place but the back seat. No legislation or constitutional embellishment can hide those ugly undertones. Neither would assertions of respect for human rights enshrined in national charters. Those shall remain political vacuities as long as the central issue of power-sharing on the basis of equality and participation at all levels of government as of right, is addressed. Political power is the only guarantee against the excesses of bigotry and the intemperance of fanaticism.

The concept of a linear order of rank is not only limited to the North. In the South also it applies to the so-called master tribes. Garang was the first Southerner to recognize this pernicious phenomenon and to seek to demolish it. The task is hard, since this master mentality is not only limited to a fringe of the tribal order; as in the North, there are also educated Southerners who believe in tribal mastery. That is why SPLM's first onslaught was on tribalism and secessionism in the South; its failure in checking this superiority syndrome in the South, would have made it as politically inadequate as some of its adversaries in the North, particularly as lack of logic has always been a tragic inevitability in Sudanese politics.

Accusations against the SPLM continue pell-mell, even after the breakthrough at Koka-Dam (i.e. acceptance by the SPLM of national debate on the Sudan question, the holding of a constitutional conference to take place *in Sudan in June 1986*, the setting of the agenda for the conference, the creation of a joint coordinating mechanism and the establishment of a time frame for the work of that coordinating mechanism). Those accusations were heaped on the SPLM, notwithstanding the fact that the follow-up meetings envisaged in that declaration were, invariably, postponed on the request of the Khartoum interlocutors – probably with reason. Sometimes the reason was the necessity to await the results of parliamentary elections; at others it was awaiting the formation of the new government and its policy declaration on the so-called Southern Sudan problem. The SPLM was also kept on hold pending the fulfilment by Khartoum of the agreed upon prerequisites for holding the national constitutional conference, that is, abolition of the September laws (*Sharia*) and of military pacts with Egypt (Nimeiri's) and Libya (TMC's). Surprisingly, the call for the abolition of both came from the majority of Sudanese political forces in the North.

Some of the Khartoum critics bent over backwards to assail the "treachery" of the SPLM/SPLA who continued fighting while those talks were going on, although both parties have agreed at Koka Dam to delay the question of ceasefire until the ground is set for the constitutional conference. This was yet another aspect of what one calls the inevitable illogicality of Sudanese politics; people stand condemned for reneging on what they explicitly or implicitly agreed upon and not for what they expressly debarred. Having posed the question and answered it without consulting their source books the Khartoum media went on to aggravate the situation by drumming up hatred. In that they were joined by insensitive politicians, soldiers with injured pride and the raw fascists of the Islamic fundamentalist fringe who were not loath to see the Sudan dismembered if that was the only way to establish God's kingdom in the Sudan. Unity of the Sudan was not on their agenda.

The intimidation and hate campaign was so permeating that even those who seemed to be addressing the real issue in Khartoum did not feel comfortable enough to make their position known on the issue without, first, enumerating the wrongdoings of John Garang. If anything, this only went to show that it was Garang who was uppermost in people's thinking rather than the situation that made Garang possible. This is a sad commentary on the way things were perceived in Khartoum. Garang, like all mortals, is transient and he is not the first Southerner to take up arms against the central authority; not will he be the last if the tragic situation persists. Southerners have never been driven to war because of their contumacy; there are reasons. For this reason one hopes and prays that the pacesetters would be bold enough to strip the facts naked thus correcting the Sudanese defective vision of their own identity crisis, for the half-convinced can never be convincing. What the Sudan needs is not only originality of mind but also courage of conviction.

Garang's challenge was that, rather than going into a cocoon calling for secession, he addressed the central issue: if all the ills of the Sudan, before and during Nimeiri's era, were caused by the way Khartoum is run, then it is the power structure in Khartoum that should be changed. For thirty years, because of myopia, Northern leaders have failed to address the root cause of the problem and resorted instead to policies of divide and rule.

The original sin was the removal from the interim constitution of 1956 of the provision giving Southerners the right to opt for federation, as if federalism was tantamount to treason. Countries as vast and diversified as Sudan, like India, Yugoslavia and Brazil, could not have been ruled effectively except in that way. Also Northern leadership never had the charity of thought to realize that in countries where sectors of the society were subjected to injustices, real or imagined, or where regions were historically neglected, those sectors and regions must be given special attention. In India, for example, only about ten per cent of the population are Muslim, and yet India has had, since independence, two Muslim presidents. President Tito could not have created a strong united Yugoslavia without recognizing and living with that country's diversity. Yugoslavia today has six republics, three religions and five languages. President Sokarno of Indonesia created a united republic out of one hundred and fifty thousand islands inhabited by millions of people professing different religions and speaking different languages. He chose the language of the smallest of those islands as the national language and isolated religion from politics including his own Islam; the religion of the majority.

Sudanese politicians were in the lucky position of not having to choose a langauge different from that of the majority, since Arabic language and culture were accepted by Arabs and non-Arabs alike as part of the cultural patrimoney of the whole nation. Those who called for federation in the early 1950s were not seeking to dismember the country, they were advocating a decentralization that would enable the disfranchised to do most with least. Freedom of creed was equally never challenged; what was and is still challenged is politicized religion as it is interpreted by the fundamentalists, and recently as it has been practised in 1983 and 1984, including the inculcation in the constitution of certain concepts that are inimical to basic human rights. That version of Islam leads to a stratification of society in such a way that certain categories of citizens like non-Muslims and women, become condemned to second-class citizenship in Sudan's godly commonwealth.

Sudan, since independence, has lacked a leadership with the vision and intellectual fecundity of the Nehrus and Titos, who turned deep cleavage into harmonious integration only because they saw their countries for what they are, an ethnic kaleidoscope. Our leadership has obstinately refused to see the Sudan for what it is, and, therefore, continued to grasp at shadows. When Jaafar Nimeiri went one step in this direction in 1972, Southerners thought that was a change of heart, not a policy drawn out of a hat, which is how Nimeiri saw the Addis Ababa Agreement. Ten years later his greatest achievement became the cause of his damnation.

With the benefit of hindsight we can see that Nimeiri only wanted to use the South as a countervailing force against the North. He also wanted to win Africa's support and to present himself to the world as the peacemaker, but he was never willing to follow through his decisions to their logical conclusions. By 1982 he showed his real colours, particularly when the democratic process in the South began to work. This is what Garang called the unconstitutional dismissal of regional governments and parliaments in three successive years.

In all those cases Nimeiri was faced either by non-compliant regional legislators or by politicians who were reluctant to forfeit their self-respect and constitutional rights. Consequently he resorted to divide and rule tactics, extending patronage to Southern elites while playing the one of them against the other. Some have fallen prey to those tactics, and this is what John Garang called the betrayal of the Southern elite. Those concerned with political advancement quickly began to jockey for position and power and scramble for Nimeiri's favour. The few who did not were made to pay through their noses. Inevitably, this led to disenchantment among a new generation of Southerners. But if some of the elite have failed to stand up to Nimeiri's machinations, those who did not equally failed to produce a new agenda for change; they chose to play the political game according to the rules set for them by others. This way they lost their political base.

Like some of their counterparts in the North they did not have a synoptic view of the country's problems, only fragmented vision. Representatives of regional groups, we mentioned earlier, have always worked in unison during successive parliaments, since 1956. Together, they called for an end to historical inequities. This is why John Garang's appeal in March 1984 was directly made to those marginalized masses, an appeal dictated by prudential motives and political expediency. While doing so the SPLM leader also extended his appeal to all Sudanese seeking a genuine end to fratricidal conflict; the history of the last thirty years should have taught us that the global problems of the Sudan are more than the sum total of their parts.

The betrayal was not only that of the Southern elite. Many in the North were in cahoots with Nimeiri in his trampling over the constitution and the Addis Ababa Agreement; castrated political organizations and acquiescing trade unions, parliament and officers. Nimeiri's action was unconstitutional, and those who vowed an oath of allegiance to that constitution should have been the first to challenge its breach. Also, those who were made to pay with their blood for Nimeiri's folly (the army) should have challenged that unjust war. Worse still, when Nimeiri was eventually challenged for his excesses by his Minister of Defence, General Abdel Magid Khalil and twenty-one senior officers, the rest of the army command came to Nimeiri's rescue, and those who did not cowed down and accepted the ignominious dismissal of the twenty-one courageous officers. This was the same army leadership that assumed power on 6 April 1985, and John Garang's position towards them should be seen in this light.

Having destroyed his institutions in the North and South and emaciated the army, Nimeiri's tricks caught up with him, so he resorted to religion, the last resort of scoundrels. In the course of his sixteen-year rule, Nimeiri has used and abused all ideologies, only religion was left for him. He, thus, conjured up his so-called Islamic laws and ambushed the unsuspecting nation with the September decrees. In those laws there was nothing but terror. With the Muslim Brothers behind him all the way, he did not take it badly that those laws were contrary to some principles enunciated in the country's constitution. By so doing, they have deepened the rift already existing in the country. Religion was not the real issue; it was a tool for political ends, terror, intimidation and blackmail.

So if Nimeiri, the only Northern politician who was presumed to have understood the real problem of the country and found a solution to it, was capable of going to the extent of destroying his greatest achievement, Southerners must have come to the conclusion that the only Northern politician to be trusted is a dead one. And it is in this light that Northerners should view the radicalization of the new Southern generation. The answer to this radicalization lies neither in the vacuous assumptions that the war is a result of foreign machinations nor in resorting to a policy of divide and rule through inciting tribal and regional hatred. Those are lame and empty conclusions. Rather than hiding behind our fingers, we in the North should ask ourselves the questions: "Why do young educated Southerners and others (e.g. the Nuba and Ingassena) gravitate towards the SPLM? Why was Garang able to attract them? Why did Southern university lecturers, judges, parliamentarians, teachers, doctors, students and commissioned officers opt for the risks and hardships of an armed opposition rather than the comfort and privilege of a post in Khartoum?" Those are the questions that must be asked and answered if Northerners are to discover what has gone wrong.

Effectively, John Garang took to arms with an important difference: his belief that Northern politicians needed shock therapy to awaken them to the reality of the Sudanese condition. He thought that policies towards the South and other marginalized regions, were, partly, the result of prejudices, some conscious, others, beyond the threshold of consciousness. But if previous movements in the South were driven by a sense of inferiority vis-à-vis the North, leading to calls for the secession or begging for acceptance, the SPLM will challenge this conventional wisdom. Khartoum belongs to all Sudanese, and the marginalized Sudanese have as much right to influence its policies as those who traditionally monopolized power.

To this end the SPLM began as an all-embracing national movement, open to all Sudanese, and particularly those of the marginalized regions of the country: Nuba, Beja, Fur and Ingassena. All those ethnic groups happen to be of non-Arab stock. Instead of taking this all-embracing approach as evidence of SPLM's national vocation, it was taken as yet another proof of the SPLM's "racism". It is not the fault of the marginalized that they were all of non-Arab stock. What those critics want to say, and dare not utter, is that the political ascension of those groups poses a threat to Northern hegemony over the whole country; a typical reaction of an insecure privileged group.

This racial differentiation, between Arabs and non-Arabs, by definition, breeds contempt. In fact not only the coalescence of the so-called "non-Arab" Sudanese to fight for their rights is considered anti-Arab "racism" but their very presence around urban centres in the North is viewed with suspicion. For example, Northern city-dwellers often depict the presence of the unemployed from the West and South in the shanty towns mushrooming around those cities as a "black" cordon meant to suffocate the cities and dilute their racial purity. Man's capacity for self-delusion being infinite, this "black" presence is often described as a conspiracy hatched by some weird foreign power against Arabism. The candidates are many: some African governments, the Christian Church and even Zionism. Those who do not know the Sudan would conclude that those shantymen must have descended from Ruritania and are not authentic Sudanese, whose right to move within their own country is as good as any. This is not narrow-minded self-assertion, it is pretentious self-deceit at its worst.

Charitably, one could blame all this on the ignorance of those outdated people of the socio-economic dynamics of human settlements in a developing country. However, when those very narrow-minded elements bewail the injustices suffered by Southern tribes at the hands of the Dinka (John Garang's "master" tribe) at the very time they are taking for granted the mastery of one region over the whole country, one scents something rotten in the state of Denmark. This bewailing is nothing but a pretext to sow discord among Southern tribes in order to divide and rule. Surprisingly, among those elements in the South incited against the Dinka were the very secessionists who mutinied in Akobo and became Anyanya II. When the SPLM/SPLA fought them because of their call for secession, they changed colours and aligned themselves with Nimeiri, and were later used by the Transitional Military Council (TMC). The Sudan has known policies of divide and rule since Wingate Pasha, and now those policies are turning up again like a bad penny.

In the same vein of double bluff, some Northern politicians would tell you that the marginalized regions are not economically worse off than some areas in the North itself. This is a half-truth, if not an economy of truth, since the question at issue is not only that of economic underdevelopment but also of political powerlessness and condemnation to second-class citizenship. As a result of these factors the SPLM took up arms to ensure that there is a more balanced economic development and a more equitable distribution of the fruits of development. It is power restructuring that is at issue, and without resolving this issue there will be no lasting peace in Sudan.

What the Khartoum power brokers are still to learn is that both the South and the other marginalized regions of Sudan have crossed a critical threshold since March 1984. Surely it is thanks to the SPLM that Northern political parties have moved to redress the balance in political promotion to ministerial posts; the government of Sadiq el Mahdi was an example, since for the first time in Sudan's parliamentary history a deliberate attempt was made to recruit ministers from the Nuba, the Fur and the Beja. But the double talk continued with some arguing that the SPLM/SPLA, by continuing the war, was, objectively, frustrating the democratic process. Democracy, however, can only survive when people agree on fundamentals. Among those fundamentals is the recognition that there should be no constitutionally entrenched privileged position, no exclusions subjectively decided and no divine rights implicit or explicit. This is the only framework within which people can compete democratically for power, otherwise democracy is but a procedure.

The failure of several democratic experiences in the Sudan is proof enough. To say that democracy has only failed in Sudan because it was frustrated by the army is begging the question. Any democracy that collapses under the heels of a dozen officers and a few tanks is intrinsically inadequate and, by definition, a failure. On the other hand, agreement on those fundamentals can only be achieved through open and frank dialogue involving all Sudanese. Without this the Sudan will continue writhing in bloody agony – all the Sudan and not only the South. Those who mistake the SPLM's fight as an attempt to impose its will and, therefore, call by way of answering it for a more formidable force to destroy it, also miss the point. Nothing short of annihilation would enable either party to establish supremacy.

15

Sudan's transitional government has wasted precious time. It has got its priorities upside down, was wanting in its articulation of the problem and was eventually caught up in petty altercations by lesser talents who were big on rhetoric but short on specifics. By mid-term, it was disowned by its own constituency and had to overstay its welcome. What the Sudan needed yesterday and needs today is a new vision, an ability to articulate the problems and a courage to convey the message to those to whom the message is to be addressed, especially those who need to be saved from themselves, the master races and the master tribes. The responsibility for this lies squarely on the educated Sudanese, particularly those among them who claim or aspire to national leadership. Education, in essence, is the ability to abstract, analyse and synthesize; people are not educated simply because they have gone through the process of accumulating inert facts. Leadership. on the other hand, had its ethical dimension reflected in intellectual honesty and moral courage. Those traits are not to be confused with political prowess, they belong to the universe of morality where values are absolute.

Mansour Khalid

Chapter One:

The Genesis of the SPLM

Jong Garang de Mabior has many times described the origins and objectives of the SPLM/SPLA, but never more clearly than in his appeal to the Sudanese people on the founding of the SPLM/SPLA, given on 3 March 1984. This appeal should not be read out of context; it came at a time when the SPLM/SPLA was the only political movement in the country that concluded that it was only through the convergence of political and military action that Nimeiri could be destroyed. The tyrant, through his divide and rule tactics, had succeeded in 1978 in cajoling even those who took up arms against him from the start and dragged them into a spurious national reconciliation. Having disarmed the armed opposition in the North and sowed discord within its ranks Nimeiri turned to the South. That was a sufficient lesson to the SPLM not to be duped by the tricks of Nimeiri's trade; there is only one language which tyrants understand and that is force. By 1983 the SPLM/SPLA, by all counts, was the only effective resistance against Nimeiri and its leader had, therefore, every justification in calling it the vanguard of that resistance.[*]

The March 1984 appeal was followed by an important policy statement by Dr. Garang on 22 March 1985, a few days before Nimeiri's collapse. In that statement the SPLM leader reiterated the national objectives of the Movement and, in the process, tore to pieces the North/South polarization. He also announced the adherence of some Northern elements to the ranks of the SPLM

17

and prophesied the imminent downfall of Nimeiri. Both speeches read together describe the national crisis afflicting Sudan since Independence as a crisis of identity emanating from the inability of the Sudanese to reconcile themselves with the cultural and ethnic realities that make of them a nation.

Though no one doubts the role of colonialism in fanning into a blaze the differences that exist between the North and South, Sudan's problems have since transcended the North/South divide. Thirty years after Independence the giant country (the largest in Africa) still wandered, battered and bruised, in the political wilderness. In those thirty years the culprits were many: insular politicians whose judgement was constantly dimmed by parochialism, militarists who because of their "déformation professionelle" sought the ultimate solution in cutting corners and a deliberately misinforming media who plaintively wailed at how the North was wronged by those whom the North has first injured.

Out of all this torment the SPLM/SPLA was born as a movement initially composed of the historically injured who sought to put an end to injustice, restructure power and achieve peace and equality for all. This politico-military movement, though born in the South, claimed, from its inception, a national character because it has evolved as a result of Sudan's national crisis. Garang described why this national movement began life in the South. The reasons are clear when seen in the context of thirty years of inequitable development and neglect of the outlying regions of the Sudan, in particular the South. The objectives of the SPLM/SPLA were clearly spelled out in that speech; they are permanent peace, unity and progress. The message is that SPLM/SPLA is not only national (i.e. not secessionist), but also a movement committed to the birth of a new Sudan, the only way to achieve lasting peace. The statement also dispels all ideas that the SPLM/SPLA is a Communist Party with a rigid ideological outlook. It makes clear that the SPLM/SPLA is a socialist movement, with a pragmatic outlook which, from the very beginning, has been and remains dedicated to the peaceful and equitable development of the nation's resources within a framework of political unity and national independence.

Following are excerpts of the main features of Garang's appeal to the Sudanese people on the founding of the SPLM/SPLA, made on 3 March 1984, and of his speech on 22 March 1985, delivered shortly before Nimeiri's downfall.

Speech by John Garang, 3 March 1984

Divide and Misrule
The history of the Sudanese people from time immemorial has been the struggle of the masses of the people against internal and external oppression. The oppressor has time and again employed various policies and methods of destroying or weakening the just struggle of our people, including the most notorious policy of "divide and rule". To this end the oppressor has divided the Sudanese people into Northerners and Southerners; Westerners and Easterners, Halfawin and the so-called Awlad et Balad who have hitherto wielded political power in Khartoum; while in the South, people have been politicized along tribal lines resulting in such ridiculous slogans as "Dinka Unity", "Great Equatoria", "Bari Speakers", "Luo Unity" and so forth.

The oppressor has also divided us into Muslims and Christians, and into Arabs and Africans. Tomorrow when these divisions become outdated, the oppressor will contrive other ingenious schemes for keeping the Sudanese people and their just struggle divided and weak.

It was therefore natural that secessionist movements and chauvinistic tendencies developed in different periods in different areas of the Sudan thereby jeopardizing the unity of the people and prolonging their suffering and struggle. The Sudan People's Liberation Army (SPLA) has been founded to spearhead armed resistance against Nimeiri's one-man system dictatorship and to organize the whole Sudanese people under the Sudan People's Liberation Movement (SPLM), through revolutionary protracted armed struggle waged by the SPLA and political support.

Crisis of the Nimeiri Regime
The neo-colonial system that has developed in our country since 1956 and was represetned by Nimeirism since 1969 is a regime in which a few people have amassed great wealth at the expense of the majority. This injustice has resulted in profound crises and distortions in our economy, politics, ethics and even religion which Nimeiri has perverted into an article of trade. A few of the system crisis problems include:

(a) The general fall in production and productivity especially of essential commodities such as dura, wheat and sugar

(b) The mounting rate of unemployment that has resulted in social instability and emigration

(c) Hyper-inflation, currency problems and foreign indebtedness amounting to US10 billion dollars and the consequent entrenchment of dependency relations

(d) An acute inadequacy and deterioration of social services in the whole country and particularly in rural areas

(e) The general social and moral bankruptcy that is reflected in the institutionalization of corruption and bribery, the daily fear by any Sudanese of being apprehended by agents of the State Security Organization, and the absurd institution of "Kacha".[1]

These crises and many others have plunged the overwhelming majority of the people throughout the country into an abysmal ocean of poverty and suffering from which no land can be sighted unless and until this one-man system of Nimeiri that threatens to drown the nation is destroyed in its entirety.

The Plight of the South

The general exploitation, oppression and neglect of the Sudanese people by successive Khartoum clique regimes took peculiar forms in the Southern third of our country. Firstly, racial and religious segregation was much more intensely meted out and felt in Southern Sudan than in other parts of the country. Secondly, development plans in the South such as the Melut and Mongalla sugar industries, Tonj Kenaf, Wau Brewery, Nzara and Mongalla textiles etc. remained on paper as development funds were embezzled in Khartoum while Southern Regional Governments watched on in impotence or participated in the looting. Development Schemes that were implemented in the South were those that did not benefit the local population, such as the extraction of oil from

---

1 Kacha refers to the huddling of thousands of young men and women, mainly Southerners and Westerners, from the Khartoum market place and the shanty towns around it to be sent back to their homes of origin in the rural areas, as if Khartoum is not the national capital that belongs to all Sudanese. The Kacha was always accompanied by a severe dose of bias against the southerners and "gharaba" i.e. Westerners who are sustaining life in the capital by providing most of the manual labour.

Bentiu via the Chevron projects and extraction of water via the Jonglei Canal. Socio-political neglect, economic backwardness and general underdevelopment therefore became intensified and exacerbated in the South.

The burden and incidence of neglect and oppression by successive Khartoum clique regimes has traditionally fallen more on the South than on other parts of the country. Under these circustances the marginal cost of rebellion in the South became very small, zero or negative; that is, in the South it pays to rebel. Nevertheless, your mad President Nimeiri and his habitually lying Vice-President Omer Mohammed al Tayeb have openly aggressed and agitated Southern Sudanese into rebellion and civil war. The following provocations precipitated renewed civil war in the Sudan:

(a) Nimeiri systematically started to dismantle his Addis Ababa Agreement. He singlehandedly and unconstitutionally dissolved Southern Assemblies and Governments one after the other in 1980, 1981 and 1983.

(b) He signed an unconstitutional Integration Treaty with Egypt to protect himself against insurrection in the South or any other parts of the Sudan.

(c) He unconstitutionally and unsuccessfully tried to change the boundaries of the Southern Region via his 1980 People's Regional Government Act. In this way he wanted to deprive the South of mineral rich or prime agricultural land such as Hofrat el Nhas, Kafia Kingi, Northern Upper Nile, Bentiu etc. *Natural resources, wherever they are found in the Sudan, belong to the whole Sudanese people.* The location of these resources in the South should not register any negative connotation and suspicions in the mind of a true Sudanese patriot and nationalist. But Nimeiri felt sufficiently agitated to the extent of attempting to legislate the formal exclusion of these areas from the South. Such behaviour can only be explained by Nimeiri's halfhearted belief in Sudan unity, his belief in the hegemony of clique chauvinism and his mistrust of South Sudanese.

(d) Again, when Chevron Company discovered oil in 1978 Nimeiri started to talk about oil finds 450 miles southwest of Khartoum instead of telling the truth that the oil was in Bentiu in Southern Sudan and that it belongs to the whole Sudanese people. He continued to hatch more transparent tricks when he talked about carving out his so-called "Unity Province" to include Bentiu, Abyei and Kadugli with himself the "Oil Governor". When this failed he came up with another scheme to build the refinery in Kosti instead of Bentiu. Finally, he ended up deciding that all the oil was to be piped out of the country at Port Sudan against the interest of the Sudanese people whether in the South or the North.

(e) Nimeiri completed the abrogation of his Addis Ababa Agreement by agitating for the division of South Sudan into three mini-regions, consistent with his policy of divide and rule. In this way Nimeiri unilaterally proclaimed redivision of the South in June 1983 to the consternation of even his foreign sympathizers.

(f) In all these provocations there was an important catch for Nimeiri. As the old adage says, thieves and rogues end up outwitting themselves. In 1972 Nimeiri agreed to absorb 6,000 Anyanya guerillas into his Army, to be stationed in the South. The absorbed Anyanya had opposed Nimeiri's policies since 1972 and they were increasingly becoming an obstacle to his schemes. He therefore decided to crush the absorbed Anyanya forces by summarily transferring them to the North where they would be neutralized. In this Nimeiri was an utter failure. He failed to deceive the South into abandoning armed resistance.

Nimeiri's provocations, recklessness and stupidities in the South resulted in the Akobo mutiny of 1975 which triggered off the Anyanya II Movement; in the Wau mutiny of 1976; in numerous grenade-throwing incidents in which lives were lost; in the Ariath incident of January 1983; the Bor, Pibor and Fashalla clashes of May 1983; in the Malout clash of the same month; the Ayod and Waat clashes of June and July 1983; in the Buma capture of hostages; in the guerilla warfare in Abyei and Bentiu and, finally, in the birth of the Sudan People's Liberation Army and the Sudan People's Liberation Movement as the most advaced form of armed and political struggle in the Sudan.

SPLM, Vanguard Movement for All Sudanese
From all that I have said, it is clear that a vanguard movement for the liberation of the whole Sudanese people had to have its origins in the South Sudan. Any armed struggle must have as its

point of departure the immediate and genuine needs and demands of the masses of the people. This was the case in the South in 1955. At that time the armed struggle was led by reactionaries and it ended in a reactionary revolution in 1972. Again, such was the case in the South in 1975 and again it was led by reactionaries in the form of Anyanya II. Again, such was the case in the South in 1983, but this time the insurrection is led by revolutionaries fighting as the vanguard of the whole Sudanese people. Because of the oneness of the Sudanese people and the unity and integrity of Sudan, the armed struggle in the South must of necessity eventually engulf the whole Sudan.

The anarchy in production, the separatist tendencies in the various regions of our beloved country, the moral decay and all the ills that I have enumerated *can only be solved within the context of a united Sudan under a socialist system that affords democratic and human rights to all nationalities and guarantees freedom to all relgions, beliefs and outlooks.* A united and Socialist Sudan can be achieved only through protracted revolutionary armed struggle. Peaceful struggle has always been met with ruthless suppression and callous killing of our beloved people.

In pursuance of protracted revolutionary armed struggle the SPLA has been organized and has already achieved significant victories. In the first offensive after 16 May 1983, it was the SPLA that captured and destroyed Malual Gahoth on 17 November 1983. At Malual Gahoth the enemy suffered 120 killed, 60 wounded and 1 helicopter shot down, while SPLA forces lost 12 killed and 30 wounded. Omer Mohammed Al Tayeb lied that the SPLA lost 480 killed. Any soldier would know that this could not be true; what, for example, could have been the size of the attacking force? Malual Gohoth is a small garrison where it is not possible to deploy even 200 men in an attck. Our attack force at Malual Gohoth was only 150 men. After Malual Gahoth, beginning from 12 December 1983, SPLA forces occupied for seven days the eastern half of Nasir, capital of the new Sobat Province. In Nasir the enemy suffered 267 killed, 173 wounded, 3 helicopters shot down, 3 river boats destroyed, 1 armoured personnel carrier and the Commander's Land Rover knocked out. The SPLA lost only 4 killed and 9 wounded in Nasir. Nimeiri and Omer hid these facts but they are true. The man in the street in Khartoum believes the SPLA from the funeral ceremonies of officers and soldiers held in the Three Towns. As Commander-in-Chief, I commanded and directed the battles of Malual Gahoth and Nasir. These important and successful battles heralded the victories of the Sudanese people that the SPLA was soon to achieve.

In its second offensive, beginning on 8 February 1984, and ending with the bombardment of Malakal on 22 February 1984, SPLA units under Lt. Col. Kerubino Kuanyin Bol, Lt. Col. William Nyuon Bany and Lt. Col. Kawae Makuei, attacked and overran all of Ayod, CCI Camp at Kilo 215 on the Jonglei Canel, CCI HQ at the Sobat Mouth and a Nile "Busta" Steamer at Wathkei. In its second offensive the SPLA inflicted untold and immeasurable havoc on Nimeiri's regime. In only two weeks Nimeiri's army suffered 1,069 killed and 490 wounded to SPLA 30 killed and 59 wounded. The SPLA destroyed 9 T55 tanks, 8 APCs, 8 Magirus army trucks, 1 civilian CCI truck, 2 small Cesna planes, 2 bulldozers, 2 steamers, 2 fuel stations, 1 big winch, a large quantity of medicines and 2 long-range signal sets. The magnitude of these operations and the impotence of Nimeiri's army forced CCI to stop digging the Jonglei Canal and Chevron Company to close down all its oil operations in the South. Hereafter, Nimeiri can no longer deceive the Sudanese people that prosperity, through exploitation of oil and water, is just around the corner. When the SPLA liberates our country under SPLM government, these two precious liquids shall be developed and used *for the benefit of the whole Sudanese people.*

The SPLA will continue to destroy *Nimeirism or any other minority clique regime in Khartoum until genuine Sudanese unity is achieved* and the SPLM transfuses the correct socialist blood into Nimeiri's Sudanese Socialist Union (SSU). Like he does with Islam, Nimeiri has also turned socialism into an article of trade. He correctly sees socialism as the genuine demand of the Sudanese people and uses the SSU to deceive the people that he is implementing socialism while in reality he and his gang pillage and loot the country.

We are aware that by declaring the SPLA/SPLM as a socialist movement, Nimeiri will depict us as Communists. This is only another cheap propaganda Nimeiri will use to beg sympathy, money and material assistance from the Western world. Nimeiri himself says he is a socialist by virtue of his membership and presidency of the Sudanese Socialist Union. Is he therefore a Communist?

The content of *our socialism cannot be determined mechanically and equated with Communism as Nimeiri would like the Western world* to believe. The conceptualization and particularization of socialism in the Sudan shall unfold as the armed struggle proceeds and as socio-economic development programmes are implemented during and after the war and *according to Sudanese local and objective conditions.*

It is not the first time that Nimeiri and other minority clique regimes in Khartoum have attempted to slander and blackmail a Sudanese movement in South Sudan. In the first civil war, the false propaganda and slander was that the Anyanya Movement was "imperialist inspired" and its leaders stooges of the Western world. This was because at that time Nimeiri's opportunism took him to Moscow. Today the accusation is that the SPLA/SPLM is "Communist inspired" and its leaders stooges of the Eastern world and/or Libya. This is because this time Nimeiri's opportunism has taken him to Washington. But in all this false propaganda, we want to underline the truth that Nimeiri and past clique regimes in Khartoum are directly responsible and accountable for all the civil wars in the Sudan.

We conclude by reiterating that the slogans of the SPLA are "National Unity", "Socialism", *"Autonomy", where and when necessary*, and "Religious Freedom". Our belief in and commitment to these slogans are irrevocable. *The SPLA welcomes and embraces all Sudanese nationalists, patriots and socialists*; in short, the movement belongs to the whole Sudanese people and will fight tirelessly for their unity, peace and progress.

Speech by John Garang, 22 March 1985

The SPLM/SPLA Two Years Later
In March of last year, I appealed to you on the founding of the Sudan People's Liberation Army (SPLA). In that appeal I outlined the principles and objectives of the Movement. Some of the points contained in that appeal are worth repeating and reiterating because the test of time has proved that our understanding of the fundamental problems of our country is correct, while at the same time the enemy, *the oppressor in Khartoum*, represented *at present* by Nimeiri's minority one-man-no-system dictatorship, has tried all means, all foul, to distort our principles and objectives in order

25

to distract and divert the Sudanese people from the true path of liberation that the SPLA/SPLM has charted since 16 May 1983.

The objectives of the SPLA/SPLM were proclaimed in the manifesto of the Sudan People's Liberation Movement, issued in July 1983. In summary:

1   We are committed to the liberation of the whole Sudan, and to the unity of its people and its territorial integrity.

2   We are committed to the establishment of a NEW and *democratic* Sudan in which eqality, freedom, economic and social justice and respect for human rights are not mere slogans but concrete realities we should promote, cherish and protect.

3   We are committed to solving national and religious questions to the satisfaction of all the Sudanese people and *within a democratic and secular context* and in accordance with the objective realities of our country.

4   We stand for genuine *autonomous or federal governments* for the various regions of the Sudan, a form of regionalism that will enable the masses, not the regional elites, to exercise real power for economic and social development and the promotion and development of their cultures.

5   We are committed to a *radical restructuring of the power of the central government* in a manner that will end, once and for all, the monopoly of power by any group of self-seeking individuals *whatever their background*, whether they come in the uniform of *political parties, family dynasties, religious sects or army officers*.

6   We firmly stand for putting to an end the circumstances and policies that have led to the present uneven development of the Sudan, a state of affairs in which vast regions of the *East, South, West and the far North* find themselves as undeveloped peripheries to the relatively developed central regions of our country.

7   We are committed to fight racism which various minority regimes have found useful to institutionalize, and that has often been reflected in various forms and colours, such as the apartheid-like "Kacha", a policy under which many poor and unemployed have been forcibly driven en masse to their regions of origin, mainly Western and Southern parts of the country, for the simple reason that they do not "belong" to Khartoum which the ruling

clique think is their home alone and not for all the Sudanese people. A similar obnoxious attitude of the ruling clique is the often repeated agitation to label *any attempted coup d'etat by soldiers from Western and/or Southern Sudan as racist*, while similar action by members of the regular armed forces who originate from other areas is never so described!

8   We are dedicated to the eradication of "tribalism", sectionalism and provincialism, which have of late been fanned by the regime and other self-seeking politicians to divide and weaken the Sudanese struggle.

9   We are committed to the rapid transformation of our country from its present state of helplessness, backwardness, underdevelopment, bankruptcy, dependency and retrogression to an industrial and agro-industrial society where the Sudan shall never again be the sickly and degenerate dwarf of the Arab World nor the starving bastard child of Africa. We have sufficient natural resources, bountiful agricultural land, water and minerals, skilled manpower and national will to realize this socio-economic transformation of our society.

In proclaiming and pursuing the objectives I have just mentioned, we have no illusions about the abhorrent nature of the regime we are fighting. We are fighting a one-man rule, a dictator who is clinging to power by means of use of savage repression, torture, unlawful detention, harassment and murder of innocent citizens by the security apparatus. We are aware that our objectives can neither be asked from nor negotiated with the minority and decaying regime in Khartoum. We are mentally and physically prepared to *fight a long war* in order to completely destroy all the institutions of oppression that have been evolved in Khartoum to oppress the masses of the Sudanese people. The history of the Sudanese people since time immemorial has been the struggle against internal and external oppression. The SPLA/SPLM represents the highest form of this historical struggle of the masses, and in this connection, I assure the Sudanese people that the SPLA/SPLM shall never let them down in their just struggle for real freedom, democracy, human dignity and economic and social justice for all.

Ending the North–South Myth

The Movement's great military and political achievements within a relatively short period of only twenty-two months of revolutionary armed struggle have thrown the oppressor in Khartoum into complete disarray. Nimeiri's May regime has lost its bearings and is tottering, senile, and is moving towards its final collapse. The regime is like a patient at a terminal stage of illness. This state of affairs did not just come about by chance. As the revolutionary upsurge and action grow, the fortunes of the unpopular system dwindle by the hour, with the result that the system and those who benefit from it become desperate and are ready to do anything and everything including selling national sovereignty, if by so doing they could delay the inevitable victory of the people and their revolution spearheaded by the SPLA/SPLM. When a buffalo is seriously wounded, it becomes most dangerous a little before it releases its last breath of life. Nimeirism is just like a wounded buffalo and it is prepared to plunge the country into total chaos in its vain attempts to hold on to power even by holding on to red-hot iron nails. In this connection, Nimeiri has desperately tried all means to apply his time-tested weapon of deceiving and dividing the Sudanese people to make them fight among themselves in order to continue to rule them.

In my last appeal, I had warned you that the oppressor has time and again employed various policies and methods of destroying or weakening the just struggle of our people, and that this notorious policy of "divide and rule" has been widely and frequently used as a weapon by Nimeiri against the people's struggle. The oppressor has always divided the Sudanese people into Northerners and Southerners, into Arabs and Africans, Muslims and Christians, and so forth. In the North itself our people have been categorized into Westerners, Fallatas, Arabs, Easterners and the so-called "Awlad el Balad"; while in the South the enemy has attempted to politicize the people along tribal lines and tribes into sections.

The SPLA/SPLM has fought consistently and resolutely against all attempts aimed at dividing the Sudanese people, and the regime in Khartoum is genuinely disturbed and confused by our unshakable stand and commitment to the cause of our people, the cause of all the Sudanese people everywhere. Nimeiri is angry, disturbed and in a state of helplessless because the SPLA/SPLM calls for the unity of the Sudan and denounces all forms of secession. The regime has fought hard to pin the label of separatism on the SPLA/SPLM, but we have fought this lie relentlessly, and we have won because what we say is what we believe and practise. Today our people everywere – in the South, West, East, North, Centre and abroad no longer believe that the SPLA/SPLM is a separatist or Southern organization. They have come to believe the fact that we are a national Movement because of our principles and deeds. The SPLA/SPLM has indeed torn into pieces the North–South polarization. It is because we are sincere and have never wavered on the question of unity that people believe us. It is why patriots from what used to be called "the North" have joined the Movement. Among prominent "Northerners" who have become members of the Movement are patriots like Brother Yusuf Kuo, who until he left last year was the deputy leader of the Sudanese Socialist Union (SSU) Assembly Body for Kordofan People's Regional Assembly, Brother Daniel Kodi, who until three weeks ago was a member of the People's National Assembly for Southern Kordofan, and First Lt. Rahma, who recently destroyed several enemy vehicles in Bentiu, fighting as a company commander in Tumsah Battalion. Several other prominent politicians and army officers from the "North" are already talking with SPLA/SPLM leadership and announcements will soon be forthcoming welcoming them into the Movement. The idea of the South and North being traditional enemies has been destroyed and buried for good in less than two years of sincere and persistent education of our troops and by the open-mindedness shown by our people from both North and South. Understandably, the May Regime is bitter with this development which has blown their reactionary foundations. It means a loss of one of its weapons aimed at destroying the unity of the people. But this sudden destruction of the North–South Divide shall remain as one of the great achievements of the SPLA/SPLM.

The SPLM and Tribalism

Seeing that the Movement has won the battle against Nimeiri's claim that it is separatist, seeing the North–South divide crumble, the regime found another weapon in "tribalism". The regime openly conducted a morbid campaign of hate and distortion, projecting the SPLA/SPLM, not only as a separatist Southern Movement, but as a tribal organization of the Dinka. Proceeding from this obnoxious reasoning, the regime has tried all means to play tribes against one another with the hope of destroying the Movement. Separatists, such as William Abdhala Chuol, became the friends of the regime in this anti-Unity, anti-Sudan policy of the dictator. These separatists were armed to fight the SPLA. Stooges like Daniel Koat Mathews were incited and given money and guns to arm their innocent tribesmen to fight the SPLA for reasons these simple people did not understand. Then the enemies of the SPLA went on dreaming to see the coming into the open of an alleged Dinka/Nuer conflict which they hoped would disintegrate the Movement. But the consciousness of our people stood between our goal and the evil intentions and wishes of the enemy. Nimeiri's attempts to use tribalism as an instrument to rend the Movement asunder, although they have failed, have been responsible for the destruction of lives and properties of innocent citizens who fell victim to the tools and stooges like William Abdhala Chuol and D. K. Mathews, who allowed themselves to be used to promote Nimeiri's crazy schemes. The use of trialism by the enemy could not succeed because the SPLA/SPLM from the very beginning has always been consistent in its principles, and has fought against this weapon of tribalism patiently, resolutely, firmly and responsibly, always making careful distinction between those on the payroll of the enemy and avoiding harm to those innocent citizens who unwittingly mixed with hostile elements. The people, the common folk in the villages, showed more maturity than the DMs. The villagers were quick to identify the real enemy, as witnessed by the recent battle at Jekow on 3 March 1985, when the Gajek Nuer fought the battalion of Colonel Abdrahaman Ahmed el Ba'laa 15 miles before they could reach SPLA positions. Failing to use the weapon of tribalism against the Movement in Upper Nile and Bahr el Ghazal, the regime came to realize too late that nothing could stop the Movement from moving to other regions of the Sudan. So, the regime shifted gears to Equatoria to develop other weapons to isolate the SPLA. When SPLA started operations in Equatoria late last year, the Tumburas and the Wajos were told that the SPLA was there to fight against Equatoria, not even against Nimeiri's system, but against Equatoria region; a very absurd agitation indeed. The regime was so agitated about using regionalism against the SPLA that it shifted Radio Juba programmes to 1500 hours, Sudan Local Time, in order to counter Radio SPLA that start its programmes at this time; and the old and discredited sentiments of "kokoro" or division (to which SPLA was never a party) were fanned up once again. But the people of Equatoria knew that the SPLA was not and is not a party to the local Juba politics of that time. The people of Equatoria, except for a few elite opportunists, acknowledge that the SPLA/SPLM was formed before "kokoro" was decreed. The people of Equatoria believe that the Movement is fighting to liberate the whole of the Sudan and that Equatoria must make its rightful contribution to this noble objective of liberating the Sudan. This is why the people of Equatoria have joined the SPLA in thousands; and they have already distinguished themselves and made the ultimate sacrifice in the field of combat as men and women who have the interests of the Sudanese people at heart.

The Proximate Causes of the War

The regime in Khartoum has fought very hard to isolate the Movement from the Sudanese masses by depicting the SPLA as what they call Communist, and blaming all difficulties in the South on alleged foreign conspiracies emanating from Moscow, Addis Ababa or Tripoli. But the Sudanese people and the Sudanese army see the war in War Zone No. 1, not as communist-inspired, but on the contrary as caused and kept alive by Nimeiri himself. The Sudanese people and the Sudanese army know that.

1 It was Nimeiri, not SPLM, that tore up the Addis Ababa Agreement in June 1983, in violation of his own constitution and laws.

2 It was Nimeiri, not SPLM, that started the unlawful policy of removing troops from the South to the North, again in contravention of the Addis Ababa Agreement.

3 It was Nimeiri, not the SPLM, that sabotaged the democratic process in the South by dissolving legally elected regional governments for the South in 1980, 1981 and 1983, again in violation of the Addis Ababa Agreement.

4 It was Nimeiri's regime, not the SPLM, that failed to execute the Central Government projects in the South, like Tonj Kenaf, Melut and Mongalla Sugar Projects, Wau Brewery, Kapoeta Cement Factory, Malakal Pulp and Paper Factory, Beden Electrical Plant, and so on. The failure of the Central Government to execute these and other projects in the South at a time when

31

similar projects were completed in the North was confirmation of the Central Government's neglect and indifference to the social and economic development of the South.

5 It was Nimeiri, not the SPLM or some foreign country that started the present war. It was Nimeiri who attacked his own garrisons. He ordered attacks on Battalion 105 garrisons at Bor, Pibor and Fashalla on 16 May 1983. The Sudanese Army knows these facts, so do the Sudanese people, and that is why they call the present war "Nimeiri's War". Only Nimeiri and his clique invoke "Communism" to beg material assistance from the West and to blackmail the SPLA and divide the Sudanese people. But this charge has outlived its usefulness. The people know that the only declaration of policy we have affirmed publicly is that the SPLA/SPLM is a socialist organization, but so is Nimeiri's Sudanese Socialist Union (SSU).

Again, the regime has gone to great lengths to depict the Movement as racist. But this is not new. The regime has always depicted national movements from the less developed regions of our country as racist. The regime is essentially incapable of correctly solving the nationalities' problem because a correct solution would deprive the clique of its privileges.

Nimeiri's bag of tricks is almost empty. All the various schemes the regime has employed to divide and weaken the people's just struggle have all failed and the SPLA marches on. The North–South divide has crumbled and only those myopic Southerners and Northerners who cannot see the dawn of the New Sudan still cling to it. The charge of separatism has died along with the North–South divide, while the charge of "Communism" against the SPLM has been discredited. The Movement is no longer seen by most Muslims as anti-Islam, because we have many Muslims in the ranks of the Movement, while the charge of racialism makes no sense since all Sudanese nationalities are to be found in the Movement, and no nationality in the Movement claims to be any more Sudanese than the others. The fanning up of "tribalism" and "Equatorianism" in the South have all failed to impede the progress of the Movement. However, it is a general essential character of all parasitic regimes, such as the one of Nimeiri, to always look for new slogans to divide the people for otherwise if the people are united the regime would surely collapse. Thus the regime must, of necessity, as a matter of survival, develop new ways to divide and weaken the struggle. In my last appeal, one year ago, I warned you that the oppressor has time and again employed various policies and methods for destroying or weakening the just struggle of our people including that notorious policy of "divide and rule", and I emphasized that tomorrow when these divisions become outdated the oppressor will contrive other ingenious schemes for keeping the Sudanese people and their just struggle divided and weak.

Negotiations with Nimeiri Regime!

It is in this context of the regime devising new methods of division that the recent pronouncements by Nimeiri about dialogue, negotiations and ceasefire must be viewed. The minority regime in Khartoum is determined to use new plots in the place of those which we have defeated. The new weapon is for Nimeiri to tantalize the Sudanese people with the prospect of peace, because he knows that he has terrorized and bankrupted the nation sufficiently long enough for the people to be buoyed by fake promises of peace and prosperity being just around the corner. In this respect, since the middle of last year, Nimeiri has posed as the "peacemaker" while portraying the SPLA/SPLM as intransigent and the "warmonger". Using this new ploy Nimeiri and his system have made moves to deceive the Sudanese people and the Western world that this murderer, one-time "Communist" and now "Imam", can bring real peace to the Sudan. Let us concretely analyze the absurdity of how Nimeiri plans to bring about peace to the Sudan. It consists of the following highlights:

1   Nimeiri started his "peace offensive" in February, 1984 when he started arming the bandit gang of Gai Tut/Akuot Atem/William Abdhala Chuol to fight the SPLA, while at the same time appearing to negotiate with them. This concoction was doomed to fail as it did, although after causing suffering to lots of innocent people. It is absurd for Nimeiri to claim to negotiate with people with whom he never fought and whom he himself armed to fight the SPLA. But the ploy gained some points for Nimeiri as a "peacemaker" in the eyes of his foreign friends, and he was encouraged to fabricate more tricks in the direction of his type of "peace negotiations".

2   So the regime concocted more false negotiations to improve Nimeiri's image as a "peacemaker". Attempts were made to nego-

tiate with some imaginary five groups of Anyanya II in Bentiu area. But this ill-fated ploy ended in an embarrassment that would have forced leaders of other countries to resign, but Nimeiri bore it without the slightest shame. His peace delegation, consisting of twenty-one members, headed by his commissioner of the so-called Unity Province (Bentui), all defected to the SPLA on finding that Nimeiri had deceived them just to build his peace image. The delegation found no such five groups of Anyanya II. All Anyanya II in Bentiu had long since joined the SPLA.

3   Left with nobody and nothing else to use, Nimeiri on 3 March 1985 declared a unilateral ceasefire with what he termed "outlaws", meaning SPLA. While Nimeiri was announcing his ceasefire at 3 p.m., his forces under Col. Ba'laa arrived and attacked SPLA positions in Jekow area. The SPLA dealt a crushing defeat to this force, dispersing it and killing Col. Ba'laa. Four days later on 7 March 1985, Nimeiri violated his own ceasefire and sent two companies of paratroopers to attack not even SPLA but his own army garrison at Kajo Kaji, alleging that the garrison commander, Major Martin Manyiel, was a rebel and a member of the SPLA. It is clear from these incidents that the idea of ceasefire was and is not genuine. It is for external and domestic consumption only, that is, to present Nimeiri as a "peacemaker". In military terms, if the SPLA accepts this so-called ceasefire, Nimeiri would use the three months left of the dry season to stock his remote and besieged garrisons with food and ammunition.

4   Nimeiri followed up his cease fire declaration with the formation of a so-called High Committee for Peace to find what Nimeiri calls "the final solution to the Southern problem". In this, Nimeiri is essentially telling the Sudanese people and the world at large that his 1972 Addis Ababa Peace Agreement was a temporary solution! The aim of this ploy was to please the American Vice-President as the announcement of the so-called peace committee was made immediately after the end of the visit of Mr. George Bush. Otherwise there is nothing that would make Nimeiri's 1985 "peace agreement" any more peaceful or permanent a solution than his 1972 agreement.

Nimeiri's slogans of dialogue, negotiations, ceasefire, the so-called High Committee for Peace and a "final solution to the Southern Problem" are hollow and despicable attempts to win foreign friends and to divide the Sudanese people into those who want peace and those who allegedly do not want peace. There are of course still some Southerners who think in terms of a "Southern problem" and who believe that the SPLA has made sufficient pressure and who are apparently convinced that *now* is the time for the South to get the best possible concessions from the North. Similarly, there are Northerners who believe that *now* is the time to give Southerners their *reasonable* demands. Nimeiri is trying to use these Southern opportunists and Northern chauvinists to present himself as a "peacemaker" as he did in 1972.

The SPLA/SPLM totally rejects Nimeiri's so called dialogue and negotiations. Nimeiri has different meanings for these words and concepts. The Sudanese people know very well what Nimeiri means by dialogue, negotiations and agreements, and this is shown by his deeds over the last sixteen years of his rule. The following are a few examples:

1 In 1969 Nimeiri was a Communist who, in his own words, said he was going to turn the Sudan into what he termed "the Cuba of Africa". At that time Nimeiri came into agreement with the Sudan Communist Party and other elements to seize power, but this marriage of convenience ended in the massacre of large numbers of members and leadership of the Communist Party.

2 In 1969 Nimeiri made a pact with the Republican Brothers and executed their 76-year-old leader, Mahmoud Mohammed Taha, in 1985.

3 In 1972 Nimeiri signed the Addis Ababa Agreement with Major General Joseph Lagu of the Anyanya and abrogated it in 1983.

4 In 1977 Nimeiri made an agreement with Sadig el Mahdi and imprisoned him in 1983.

5 1983 saw the emergence of the Muslim Brotherhood as Nimeiri's political allies, while 1985 saw their dismissal and imprisonment of their leadership; and so forth for other acts of deception and insincerity.

The above are but few of the experiences of the Sudanese people with Nimeiri's peace initiatives. In a nutshell, Nimeiri is a man who initiates dialogue, negotiations and agreements with the sole purpose of destroying them along, of course, with his adversaries.

Our masses must never again be deceived and listen to lies, plots and intrigues in Khartoum. The SPLA/SPLM will never betray the Sudanese people and negotiate with their oppressor, the regime of Jaafar Nimeiri, or any other similar minority government in Khartoum. The SPLA is determined to fight for a democratic and new Sudan where social justice, freedom and human dignity for all flourish. We fight for a new democratic Sudan in which the nationality question is correctly solved. We fight for a Sudan in which the problem of uneven development is solved such that all the regions of the country, especially the most neglected areas, receive a fair and accelerated socio-economic development. We fight for a Sudan free from racism; a Sudan in which power is vested in the masses, exercised by them and in their interests; a Sudan in which there is no monopoly of power by any group whether ethnic, religious or regional. We are committed to the liberation of the Sudan, and to us liberation is a continuous process involving not only political and economic liberation, but also liberation of the mind, so that the Sudanese are proud of their identity, their heritage, history, values and their historic struggle. We are committed to wrest power from the minority clique in Khartoum and give it to the masses. Finally, I would like to reiterate that the SPLA/SPLM is a genuine Sudanese Movement that is not interested in concessions for the South, but a Movement that is open to all people of the Sudan to join and participate in the building of the new and democratic Sudan.

Appeal to the Sudanese Army

I end by appealing to the Sudanese army to start talking directly with the SPLA in War Zone No. 1, not through the dictator. You form your own committees in your garrisons in order to form joint commands with the SPLA so that a New Sudan and its corresponding New Army are born. The dictator Nimeiri has nothing new to offer. Forget about him and all those generals and bourgeoisified elite around him who have bled our country for the last sixteen years. You form your own committees in your respective garrisons and contact the nearest SPLA unit to convey your views to SPLA GHQs. *We envisage a national congress to be organized by the SPLA, progressive and patriotic elements in the Sudanese Army and other democratic forces in the country to discuss the essence and programme for formation of a New Sudan and its New Army consistent with its particularity.*

Chapter Two:

The SPLM's Fight for Peace

For the first two years of the life of the SPLA/SPLM Northern Sudanese sang hymns of praise to the Movement's valiant struggle against Nimeiri. That struggle, if ever people cared to trace its history, was not against a man but against a system and against policies that have ended in tears and bloodshed. On the other hand, Nimeiri was not fighting the Southern war alone; he had his cohorts and supporters who conspired with him by either silence or bovine acquiescence. Nimeiri's methods, to win that support, in the South and North were brutal force, intimidation and bribery but his fall did not mean the end of those policies. The vestiges of Nimerism remained, after him, in the entangled and distorted perception of the Sudanese ruling elite who still saw the country's problem in terms of North/South polarization, rather than one of reconciliation of interests and recognition of rights of all the marginalized regions in a united Sudan. Those at the helm in Khartoum who assumed that all would be "milk and honey" once Nimeiri was out of the way, failed to realize that Nimeiri was our own Frankenstein. In their condescension, they saw no reason why the SPLM should not agree with their perception and stop its struggle once Nimeiri, the man, was gone. But the SPLM had a different vision of what has gone wrong in Sudan and how to move forward. With the fall of Nimeiri it remained consistent in what it stood for, hailing the April Revolution as a victory of the Sudanese people but seeing the military takeover by the TMC for what it was: a tactical regrouping on the part of some elitist groups.

The SPLA/SPLM is dedicated to achieving genuine and permanent peace, not a makeshift peace. This peace can neither be realized through a formalistic tinkering with power nor by political handouts; it can only be achieved through restructuring of power and dialogue among the Sudanese on the fundamentals and a prior identification of those fundamentals. To this end the leader of the SPLM addressed the nation on 9 April 1985 following the fall of Nimeiri. Less than two months later John Garang addressed the nation on the occasion of the second anniversary of the Bor, Pibor and Fashalla resistance on two consecutive days (26 and 27 May). Khartoum, in the course of those months, continued to be oblivious to the calls of the SPLM/SPLA for the creation of a bold, new and united Sudan, instead it still addressed itself to the so-called problem of the South.

The point that had to be hammered in was that Sudan's crisis is one of national identity that can only be resolved through dialogue and national democratic consensus. The 26 and 27 May speech was meant to spell out clearly how the SPLM envisions this consensus and extends its hand to all those elements in the Sudan who were ready and willing to face up to the realities of this country.

Speech by John Garang, 9 April 1985, following the downfall of Nimeiri

Since my speech on 22 March 1985 and repeated on 23 March on Radio SPLA many things have happened. Nimeiri has been forced out of power by your revolutionary action in the streets of Khartoum and other cities, and Nimeiri's Minister of Defence and General Staff have assumed power. I am obliged by responsibilities and duties to the nation and people to give a statement to outline the stand of the SPLA/SPLM on the current and prospective events in our country.

Fall of Nimeiri, a First Round
The events that erupted starting from 27 March were and are a popular uprising against Nimeiri's system as a whole. The mass

of the Sudanese people rose up to tell the dictator and his clique in Khartoum that enough was enough. And in this historic confrontation the people have won the first round in their just struggle. Congratulations! This a great and historic victory that will, like October, be admired and honoured by all posterity. The SPLA, being the armed vanguard of the Sudanese revolutionary struggle, has contributed effectively to this *first round* in the overthrow of Nimeiri and his system. In effect, the SPLA/SPLM has been the moving central force behind the people's uprising in Khartoum and other cities as embodied by the people in their slogans when they shouted, "Down, down with Nimeiri; we want the urgent return of Dr. John Garang." The brilliant military victories by the SPLA against Nimeiri's army, the closure of Chevron Oil, the stoppage of the Jonglei Canal, the establishment of Radio SPLA and many other victories – all these systematically weakened Nimeiri's regime and strengthened the people's resolve and confidence that the regime is vulnerable. I take the opportunity to congratulate the SPLA for this great contribution to round no. 1 of the destruction of Nimeirism, and the establishment of a just society.

The SPLA/SPLM wholeheartedly supports the popular uprising. It is abundantly clear, as shown by the current events in the Sudan, that popular uprising is complementary to revolutionary armed struggle (as waged by SPLA in the Sudan). The masses of the people in the streets of the capital and other cities, organized, agitated and led by the workers, professionals, trades and students unions and the SPLA in the bushes of the South are the ones who, through their determined action and sacrifice, overthrew dictator Nimeiri. But as you all know, on the morning of 6 April 1985, Nimeiri's Minister of Defence and senior army officers told the Sudanese people over Radio Omdurman that the dictator Nimeiri had been overthrown – this, the people knew because they are the ones who overthrew Nimeiri. However, the generals told the people that they did not know and did not expect – that it was they, the generals and not the people, who had taken over power from Nimeiri! Since that time these generals have been making a series of statements relating to the dismantling of the May regime. They have also been taking very uncertain and reluctant measures in this direction. The ugly shadow of Nimeiri looms ominously over the military administration in Khartoum.

Why the Generals?

The military seizure of power in our country raises many questions. Among them: Why did the military decide to take over power when the people had already succeeded in overthrowing Nimeiri's regime? Why cannot the transition from Nimeiri to the people be direct without the military as was the case in the October 1964 revolution? What is it that the military can do and which the people cannot do during this so-called "interim period"? What has motivated the generals to take power from the people at this stage? Why is it that it is Nimeiri's closest associates who claim that they are on the side of the people? Why have these generals been on the side of Nimeiri for the last sixteen years? Why was it that it was the masses who stormed Kober prison to release political prisoners? Why did the new regime not do it, or might it be that some of these generals were a party to the arrest of those who opposed Nimeiri?

Furthermore, why did it have to take a lot of pressure from the people to convince the generals to disband the infamous State Security Organization (SSO)? Why did the shooting of innocent citizens continue even after the military takeover? What role has international and local reaction played in this fake transfer of power from Nimeiri to Nimeiri's Minister of Defence? Why did not the junta ask for the unconditional and immediate extradition of Nimeiri from Egypt to face a real people's court, or does the junta think that Nimeiri is not a criminal? Why did Nimeiri yesterday send Swar al Dahab a message of support from Egypt wishing his Defence Minister good luck and success in his new job and expressing understanding and sympathy for the takeover?! Has there really been a change or is this just Nimeiri's regime without Nimeiri? *In the bush we had something called Anyanya II*, could the *new government in Khartoum be May II regime of Nimeiri*?

The answers to these and many other similar questions clearly show that the *April coup d'etat and the popular uprising are two different political phenomena* with diametrically opposed objectives. The popular uprising, led by the workers, professionals, trades and students unions and encouraged by the SPLA has completely different political objectives from those of the May II regime. The masses want a popular government not another military administration, which in this case is Nimeiri's regime in a different uniform.

The army officers who treacherously stole your victory and

power have never participated in the people's struggle against Nimeiri. Instead, they have contributed to your oppression and exploitation during Nimeiri's rule which they staunchly defended against you, and of which they are an inseparable part. These officers, with instruction from outside the homeland, have aborted and stolen the victory of the masses. These officers were and are part of Nimeiri's rule and were actually his power base. They will not hand over power to the people. What qualifications do they have to hand over power to the people? Why did they not do this before you took to the streets? No, all these generals who now claim to be on the side of the people actually stood in their way, and they were the real repressive arm and body of Nimeiri. You, the people, in your popular uprising succeeded in cutting off the monster's head, but the lifeless body continues to deceive you that the monster is still dangerous. No, it is not! Having cut off the monster's head, it is your sacred duty to push down the monster's body, not stand in fear of it.

The contradictions between the military junta and the people have already emerged and will continue to grow. The junta, as to be expected, has isolated the leaders of the popular uprising. The workers, professional, trade and student unions who dealt the final blow to Nimeiri are now isolated from their revolution and are threatened with arrest and repression by the new military regime with the same intimidation and arrogance as they did in the old military regime. This is concrete proof that the people's revolution has been stolen by a gang of four generals whose interests are more in common with international and local reaction than with the broad masses of the Sudanese people who, ironically, brought them to power.

We are aware that this junta already started its first day by making contacts with the reactionary and discredited old political parties. The junta even contacted some of Nimeiri's own ministers by virtue of their membership in these parties! These are the very parties that contributed so much to the aggravation of suffering and misery in the country, and to divisions among the Sudanese people as most of these parties are based on serving sectarian interests of race, religion or family dynasty. Swar al Dahab, the head of the present military administration, being an affiliate of the Khatmiya sect, is expected to be more inclined to the reactionary political parties – that is why he has and will continue to ignore the broad masses who actually overthrew Nimeiri. Now these parties and the junta are conniving to steal the people's revolution and to take over their power from the military junta. They should not wait for the junta to hand over power to them because they will definitely not – who gave the junta the right to give power to the people? No, the people must seize, not be given, power.

There is no difference between this military junta and that of Nimeiri. It is the same Nimeiri regime minus the excesses of Nimeiri such as the chopping off of limbs, the public floggings and so forth. No matter what clothes a hyena puts on, it remains a hyena. Swar al Dahab's administration is simply a continuation of May. It is the May II regime of Nimeiri. This is not your revolution, dear citizens. This junta was planned outside the Sudan and with full participation of Nimeiri himself. The execution of the plan was carried out by the gang of four. The Sudanese people must know that their revolution has been taken away and that international and local reaction conspired against the popular revolution of 6 April.

We shall not support the Generals
In the light of all that I have said, I here assure all the Sudanese people that the SPLA/SPLM cannot and will not support a system that will continue oppressing and exploiting them. The SPLA/SPLM will never betray you in your just struggle. I therefore call on the Sudanese people to continue the war in the streets of our cities and in the bushes and sands of our great country.

We will continue to fight to liberate the Sudanese people from any oppressive and exploitative system in Khartoum. We will continue to fight to liberate the whole Sudan, so that the unity of its people and its territorial integrity are achieved and maintained. *We shall continue to fight to establish a new Sudan, a democratic Sudan in which equality, freedom, economic and social justice and respect for human rights are not mere slogans but concrete realities* we should promote, cherish and protect.

We will continue to fight to solve the nationality and religious questions to the satisfaction of all citizens and within a democratic and secular context and in accordance with the objective realities of our country, so that never again shall anyone be discriminated against because he is a Nuba, a Southerner, a Darfuri, a Beja or a Halabi; so that the Sudan belongs equally to all of us irrespective of race, religion, family background, or any other sectarian considerations. We shall continue to fight in order to achieve a radical restructuring of the power of the central government in a manner that will end once and for all the monopolization of this power by any self-appointed gang of thieves and criminals, whatever their backgrounds, whether they come in the form of political parties, family dynasties, religious sects, or army officers such as the present gang of four generals of Swar al Dahab.

We shall continue to fight so that genuine autonomous or federal governments are established for the various regions of the Sudan, that is, to realize a form of regionalism (federalism) that will enable the masses, and not the elites from the regions, to exercise real power for economic and social development of their regions. We will continue to fight to put to an end the circumstances and policies that have led to the present uneven development of the Sudan, a state of affairs in which vast regions of the Sudan (South, West, East and Far North) find themselves as underdeveloped peripheries to the relatively developed central parts of our country. We will continue to fight to end racism and religious bigotry that various minority regimes in Khartoum have found useful to institutionalize.

We will continue to fight to develop on our own our vast natural and human resources; our 200 million acres of agricultural land, our vast mineral wealth of oil, iron, gold, copper, uranium and much more, our vast water, fish and forest resources, and above all our precious and creative Sudanese people. We will continue to fight, through our own directed development, to put an end to the vicious circle of the external debt, now standing at 10 billion US dollars, so that never again shall we be forced to borrow new loans in order to pay off old loans that are due, as was the case with Nimeiri's regime and will be the case with the neo-Nimeiri regime of General Swar al Dahab.

A War to end War

We will continue to struggle until those objectives are achieved. But let nobody think that we are warmongers. On the contrary, we fight to bring about genuine and permanent peace so that the nation does not oscillate between war and peace as happened in our thirty years of independence and misrule by the reactionary political parties and the military. We are for genuine peace, but this peace must not be at the expense of the real interests and aspirations of the Sudanese people. It is the junta that is warmongering. The junta's high command made it clear in its fourth public statement that it intends to open the road and river transport and to start work on the development projects such as Chevron's and Khashoggi's oil projects in Bentiu and the digging of the Jonglei Canal in the South. The intentions of the junta are clear. The new rulers want to use force to open up the routes. All indications are that the new junta is preparing to launch an offensive against the SPLA in their mistaken belief that this will divert the Sudanese masses from seizing power from this gang of military rulers.

Lest they forget, because they are in power, let the generals of Nimeiri's new regime be reminded that:

(a)   These generals were the ones directing Nimeiri's war when the SPLA destroyed the railway bridge on the Lol River, and thereby cut all rail transport to the South. This bridge will cost the generals 12 million US dollars to rebuild.

(b)   These generals were the ones directing the war when the SPLA destroyed and sank four steamers on the River Nile, and thereby stopped all river transport to the South. The River Nile transport corporations will surely be more cautious than the generals.

(c)   These generals were the ones directing the war when the SPLA shot down 8 helicopters, 2 Buffalo transport planes, 1 C–130 Hercules and 2 F–5 jet fighters, and thereby made air transport hazardous. We believe the Sudanese Air Force will be more cautious than the generals in Khartoum.

(d)   These generals were the ones directing Nimeiri's war when the SPLA closed down Chevron Oil in Bentiu, and thereby stopped the oil from being used by Nimeriri and his clique to oppress the Sudanese people.

(e)   These generals were the ones directing the war when the SPLA stopped construction of the Jonglei Canal and held four CCI workers captive for twelve months. We do not believe that the CCI or any other foreign company will agree to restart digging the Jonglei Canal unless the SPLA gives the green light.

(f)   We remind the generals to look into their financial books. They will find that the war is costing the nation 3 million Sudanese pounds each day, that is 125,000 pounds every hour, night and day!

(g)   We remind the generals that they were directing the war when the SPLA attacked and destroyed thirty-two military garrisons in the South.

(h)   We remind the generals that it was SPLA's military victories that weakened Nimeiri's regime considerably and contributed greatly to Nimeiri's downfall and that, therefore, it was the SPLA that ironically brought the generals to power.

We remind the generals of all these, and we assure them that unless they hand over power to the people immediately we shall fight and bring them down in the same way that we brought down their former boss, Nimeiri. We assure the generals that oil will not flow; water will not flow in the Jonglei Canal; vehicles will not move in War Zone No. 1; the air will continue to be dangerous for air transport; and we shall paralyse and frustrate their neo-Nimeiri regime until the SPLA and the people take over power. It is advisable for the generals to hand over power now before the Sudanese people take it by force and hang them. I assure the generals that the Sudanese people will not leave them like they have left Nimeiri and his ministers. The Sudanese people will most certainly bring them to trial.

Invitation to Dialogue with the Army

Because we do not want war, because we want genuine and permanent peace, I appealed in my last speech to the Sudanese people on 22 March 1985 to garrisons of the Sudanese army in the South to initiate talks directly with the SPLA and to ignore Nimeiri and his generals in Khartoum because they cannot bring about genuine peace. This appeal of 22 March was before Nimeiri fell and his generals took over on 6 April. This call and offer to the Sudanese army in War Zone No. 1 to start talking with the SPLA still stands. The SPLA is ready to talk with the Sudanese army garrisons in the field of combat in War Zone No. 1 (in the South) and to ignore Swar al Dahab and his generals in Khartoum. The generals do not know what is going on in the field of combat in War Zone No. 1. *It is the Sudanese army soldiers and the SPLA soldiers who are fighting and dying in the field, not the generals in Khartoum.* And *it is the soldiers on both sides*, not the generals

who can honestly contribute to bringing real peace to the country.
So we have rejected any negotiations with Nimeiri, or, in the
present case, with his Minister of Defence and General Chiefs of
Staff. On the same principle our forces will continue contact with
Sudan army garrisons in the South. So far the response from
Sudan garrisons in the South has been positive and encouraging.
We repeat the pledge. We shall not talk with Swar al Dahab's
Nimeiri regime of May II, but we shall continue the talks which
we initiated with the garrisons in the South before Nimeiri's fall,
so that junior officers, NCOs and men of the Sudanese army
contribute positively in the process of taking over power by the
people instead of dying unnecessarily for a gang of thieves in
Khartoum.

The SPLA/SPLM again *reiterates its solidarity with the popular
uprising in Khartoum and other cities and towns of our country.*
We support and encourage these uprisings. The SPLA/SPLM
being the armed vanguard of the Sudanese revolution will continue the struggle until power is taken by the representatives of
the people.

I end this statement by presenting the following programme of
action to you:

1 I call on General Swar al Dahab to immediately transfer power
to the people. *The generals must resign and hand over power to
the people within seven days from today.* Within this period the
SPLA will suspend operations, except for moving military targets,
whether by road, river or air. The people are capable of doing
whatever the generals can do during the so-called interim period.
The generals are unnecessary and their usurpation of power is
harmful to the nation. If the generals do not hand over power to
the people within seven days, the SPLA will be obliged to continue the war in order to ensure that the people take over power.

2 I call on the workers, professionals, trades and students unions
to continue the strikes and demonstrations until the generals hand
over power to the people. The SPLA is solidly and wholeheartedly
with you, the people, and we are prepared to talk with you, but
never to the "second republic" of Nimeiri under the "gang of
four".

3 The popular uprising was hijacked by the generals *because the
people did not prepare an instrument to take over power* and

therefore there was no effective coordination with the SPLA for this purpose. I therefore call on the workers, professionals, trades and students unions to form agitational steering committees to continue the uprising and a general steering committee composed from all the workers, professional, trades and students unions to take over power from the generals. The SPLA/SPLM is prepared to talk with such a body, nay, the SPLA/SPLM is prepared to be part of such a body in the process of taking over power, and in this connection we assure you that we will never betray you and talk with Nimeiri's "second republic" of Swar al Dahab, or any similar regime.

4   I call on junior officers, NCOs and men in the Sudanese army, police and prisons to be on the side of the people and not stand in the way of the people's march to victory. Instead, you form your own steering committees in your units to enable you to participate effectively in the current revolutionary process. Do not listen to the generals, they are taking you to Nimeiri's unnecessary war and it is you and the SPLA soldiers, not the generals, who will die – you will die to maintain the system of the generals and we to change it.

Finally, I end by reiterating and underlining this very fundamental truth to the Sudanese people: the SPLA/SPLM fights for genuine and permanent peace, and genuine and permanent peace can and will be brought about under our present conditions by the following three forces:

1   the SPLA/SPLM,
2   the masses, organized and represented by the workers, professionals, trades and students unions; and
3   revolutionary and patriotic junior officers, NCOs and men in the army, police, prisons, game wardens and fire fighters force.

These are the forces that have real interest in real permanent peace. I appeal to these forces not to postpone their legitimate victory by compromising with the gang-of-four generals, or with the reactionary and sectarian political parties, who together with the army generals have been responsible for seventeen years of war, for the present war, and who have bankrupted the country to the tune of 10 billion US dollars in external debts.

These forces have already scored significant victories and they should not doubt their strength. Among these victories are the following:

1 These forces have thrown out Nimeiri,
2 These forces have disbanded the hated State Security Organization (SSO) and arrested its director, General Omer Mohammed al Tayeb,
3 These forces have disbanded the corrupt so-called Sudanese Socialist Union (SSU); and
4 These forces stormed the hated Kober prison and released all prisoners without approval from the gang of four.

These forces will continue to score victories until they seize power for the people. The road is clearly leading to a people's victory, and so why do we stop halfway and thereby allow our enemies to place more obstacles on victory's road and make that victory costly when we achieve it, which without doubt we will? I thank you very much for your attention. I am confident that you will do your part. I assure you that we in the SPLA/SPLM will do our part and we will abide by our promise.

Statement by John Garang on 26 and 27 May 1985, on the Second Anniversary of the Bor, Pibor and Fashalla resistance and Ayod revolt

Fifty Days Later
Among the many things that have happened, I call your attention to the following:
The gang of four has increased its number to a junta of fifteen generals;
A toothless and clawless civilian government has been formed under the junta;
The military junta has been in power today exactly fifty days and it has revealed its true colour, every day becoming indistinguishable from Nimeiri's regime. I do not have to tell you again that this junta is indeed the May II regime which we exposed on 9 April. You, yourselves, have seen from the actions and pronouncements of the junta that it is in reality Nimeiri's second republic;
Like Nimeiri, the junta has declared a unilateral ceasefire while they prepare for war;

Like Nimeiri, the junta has made a lot of noise and lies about negotiations with the SPLA including unfounded fabrication that Col. Dr. John Garang was at one point on his way to Khartoum; The junta has implemented Nimeiri's turn-around and reunited the South into a sort of "super region" with three mini-regions, and put the South under a mini-military council similar to that in Khartoum, and similarly a Gazouli-type mini-civilian cabinet has been formed under the mini-Southern military council.

For reasons totally unconnected with concern for the people, the junta declared the South a famine-stricken disaster area and has appealed to the SPLA to open up the roads and rivers for the alleged famine, shamelessly insinuated that the SPLA will be held responsible for the alleged famine if we do not open up the roads and rivers.

However, despite the continuation of Nimeirism in a different uniform, there have been positive aspects in the change of guards from Nimeiri to his Minister of Defence and Chiefs of General Staff. Among these positive aspects:

You, the massses, have *restored some of your rights and as a result there are now forty political parties and ninety trade and professional unions* that are able for the first time in sixteen years to hold rallies and air their views in a new breeze of freedom. You have regained your ability to fight and bring down an unpopular regime, which is a necessary prelude to realizing the necessity to establish your own regime to safeguard your gains. Favourable conditions have been created for the struggle waged by SPLA to converge with *democratic forces* in other parts of the country beyond the birthplace of the SPLA/SPLM.

As an affirmation of this convergence of *democratic forces* the *Free Officer's Movement* has pledged their *solidarity* and *unity* with the SPLA and have symbolized this *solidarity* by electing the Commander-in-Chief of SPLA as their commander.

Finally, an event of singular importance has just passed. The SPLA/SPLM is celebrating this month the end of two years of revolutionary armed struggle. Before I discuss the issues I have enumerated, I take your permission to address SPLA/SPLM troops in the field, together with the masses on this great and historic occasion, the second anniversary of the founding of the SPLA/SPLM! Thank you for the permission.

No to Simplistic Solutions

Two years ago Nimeiri and his generals, that now rule the Sudan on his behalf, decided to attack Battalions 105 and 104 at Bor, Pibor, Fashalla and Ayod. The attacks were carried out on 16 May and 6 June, 1983. These events triggered off the formation of the SPLA and SPLM to spearhead a genuine Sudanese revolutionary armed struggle that is bound to have a far-reaching impact on the country and in the region. For the last one week Radio SPLA and the Sudanese people have been celebrating the second anniversary of the resistance in Bor and Ayod and the subsequent formation of the SPLA/SPLM.

It is necessary to be well informed and to appreciate the objective reality of our situation correctly and concretely so that you, the masses, are not deceived by simplistic solutions hastily and opportunistically hatched by the generals or any other forces of reaction in Khartoum, and so that your hopes are not raised deceptively and unnecessarily. I sincerely believe that the SPLA/S-PLM belongs to all the masses of the Sudanese people, that it mutated and developed from the *fundamental contradictions* of our society, and that its impact on the Sudan is incalculable. It is therefore necessary to put you, the masses, in the correct perspective towards the essential character of the SPLA/SPLM in order to more fully appreciate the Movement's perception of genuine solutions to the many difficult problems that confront our great country and people.

The attack and resistance in Bor and Ayod signalled the stage of eruption reached by the contradictions inherent in the Addis Ababa Agreement. As correctly analyzed in chapter 4 of our Manifesto, issued in July 1983, the Addis Ababa Agreement was in reality a deal between the Southern and Northern bourgeosified and bureaucratic elites. The Northern elite dictated the terms, while the Southern elite compromised the interests of the masses in return for jobs which had long been denied them during Sudanization in the 1950s. These jobs were given to them in 1972 in Addis Ababa at a cost of about one and a half million lives lost during the seventeen years of war. Clearly then, the Agreement was bound to collapse, as it ignored the real interests of the masses of the people who paid dearly for it. The Southern elite used the Agreement as a means to enrich and entrench themselves and this brought them into contradiction with the people, while the Northern elite, having removed the armed component at Addis

Ababa, tried to return the country to the pre–1972 status quo, when they were dominant in both North and South, and this brought them into contradiction with the Southern bureaucratic elite. It took eleven years for these contradictions (the ones between the Southern elite and the Northern elite) to develop to a stage of antagonism and eruption. Whereas many minor eruptions had occurred during the eleven years of the Agreement, the major eruption occurred on 16 May 1983 at Bor when Nimeiri, Swar al Dahab and Siddiq al Banna decided to attack Battalion 105 garrisons.

The unwise and inexpedient decision to attack Battalion 105 was taken against the considered advice of the majority of Nimeiri's Chiefs of General Staff as well as other patriotic senior officers at General Headquarters. As you recall, at that time Nimeiri's Chiefs of Staff consisted of three Generals, respectively: General Swar al Dahab, the Deputy Commander-in-Chief and Chief of Staff for Logistics; Lt. General Yousif Ahmed Yousif, Chief of Staff for Administration; and Lt. General Towfik Salih Abu Kadok, Chief of Operations. Generals Yousif and Abu Kadok advised against attack on Battalion 105 and they were summarily dismissed by Nimeiri for their wise counsel. They now stay in their homes with dignity, satisfied that they acted patriotically. Nimeiri dismissed these patriotic officers as he did many other patriotic and efficient officers, like Abdel Magid Hamid Khalil and the group of twenty-two officers, who dared to give the dictator correct advice in the national interest. Swar al Dahab managed to remain in the army and is today the inheritor of May II. In the case of Bor, like in many other cases, Swar al Dahab buried his head in the sand and allied himself with petty traders like the retired Major General Siddiq al Banna, a known coffee smuggler and elephant poacher, who played a great role in agitating Nimeiri to attack Bor. As some of you may recall, Siddiq al Banna was at that time openly telling people in Juba that he was going to attack Bor, a state of emergency would be declared in the South and that Nimeiri would appoint him military governor of the South. Siddiq al Banna even consulted some opportunistic Southerners with the view to forming an emergency cabinet. At that time Omer Mohammed al Tayeb was also agitating Southerners to take to rebellion, telling Southerners in rallies that they could rebel and go to the bush to join wild animals, if they so wished, and that the Government did not care since such a rebellion would be crushed. Our heroic Jarad Division now sing a verse that says "Faturna Tumbakna", that is, "our Breakfast is our Tobacco", in retort and challenge to Omer's warning that those who contemplated rebellion would starve in the bush. I take this opportunity to congratulate each and every SPLA soldier for proving wrong these petty thieves and criminals who masqueraded in Khartoum as the national government and who thought they were invincible. All reactionary and clique regimes in Khartoum must know that when the people are united and resolved they can dig out a mountain with shovels, let alone the May II regime which is much weaker than May I.

Birth and Evolution of the SPLA/SPLM

The attacks on Bor, Pibor and Fashalla, the subsequent redivision of the South on 5 June 1983 and the revolt at Ayod on 6 June 1983, as I said earlier, represented the crisis point, the eruption of the grave contradictions between the Northern and Southern bureaucratic and bourgeoisified elites and between these two elites as a group and the masses of the Sudanese people. These events buried the Addis Ababa Agreement for good, but as you all know Nimeiri tried in vain to resuscitate the lifeless Agreement. At the present Swar al Dahab, not learning from futile attempts by his master, is also trying again to solve what he calls the "Southern problem" by reviving the Addis Ababa Agreement. The generals fail to understand that the Addis Ababa Agreement is a corpse; they fail to understand that the Agreement is a relic of the past that cannot help them any more and in which the SPLA/SPLM has no interest.

After the attacks on Bor, Pibor, Fashalla and the revolt at Ayod and our heroic resisance we withdrew from these garrisons into the bush. We regrouped and formed the SPLA/SPLM, an organization still in its infancy as we now celebrate its second anniversary, but which has already shaken and will continue to shake the Sudan to its sectarian and reactionary foundations. I take this opportunity to pay tribute to those heroes who fell in the battles of Bor, Pibor, Ayod and Fashalla; they are the first martyrs of the SPLA. Their sacrifices will remain in the annals of the revolutionary history of our great country.

We did not organize the SPLA to fight for restoration of the Addis Ababa Agreement or for the reunification of Southern Sudan, or for more and better concessions for South Sudan. No, we organized the SPLA for much higher and national objectives, including of course regional interests for the South and for all other neglected and backward regions. The *national* and *higher objectives* of the SPLA/SPLM are borne out by the short history of the SPLA/SPLM which reveals its national and democratic content. I would like to share with you the difficulties we faced and the sacrifices we had to make in the formation and development of the SPLA/SPLM.

The birth of the SPLA/SPLM was not easy. From June to November 1983 we engaged in an extensive and intensive debate concerning the direction of the newly formed Movement. Ardent separatists, reactionaries and opportunists gave us a very hard time. People like Akuot Atem, Gai Tut, Gabriel Gany, Abdellah Chuol and others stood for the forces of reaction. They wanted a Movement similar to Anyanya I, a Movement connected with international reaction and calling for a separate and independent Southern Sudan. It took us six months of bitter struggle to resolve the correct direction of the Movement. The principles proclaimed in our revolutionary Manifesto prevailed. The forces of reaction and separatism were defeated. After resolving the problem of separatists, we had to confront the problem of the scattered forces of Anyanya II. We had to regroup them, win their confidence, politicize them and incorporate them into the SPLA. This was a very complex process. As an illustration, one Anyanya II unit of 250, that reached SPLA headquarters, consisted of 3 major generals, 6 brigadiers, 26 full colonels, 65 lieutenant colonels, 30 majors, 45 captains, 30 first lieutenants, 27 lieutenants and only 18 NCOs and men. Transforming such a unit into an organic unit of SPLA was indeed quite baffling, a situation for which there are hardly any textbook references. But with patience, cool approach and persistent political work we were able to incorporate all of Anyanya II into the SPLA; and the Anyanya II became an important component of the SPLA that made very significant contributions to SPLA successes. It was Anyanya II/SPLA units that closed down Chevron Oil in Bentiu. It was Anyanya II who had initially paralysed Bahr el Ghazal before units of Jamus arrived there in February 1983 to destroy the railway bridge on the Lol River at Wadweil. And indeed, the initial basis of the SPLA was formed from elements of Anyanya II. More than sixty per cent of our first five battalions (Battalions 104, 105, Jamus, Tiger and Tumsah) were formed from former Anyanya II members, while the remaining forty per cent were students and defectors from Sudan's organized forces of the army, police, prisons, and wild life. The transformation from Anyanya II to SPLA was neither easy nor peaceful. Before confronting Nimeiri's army a lot of blood had to be shed in order to preserve the principle of a United New Sudan.

Ironically, at the same time that the SPLA was defending the principle of Sudanese unity against separatists like Akuot Atem, Gai Tut, and Abdellah Chuol, Nimeiri and Swar al Dahab were conniving with these same separatists to undermine our efforts by giving them food, uniforms, medicines and ammunitions to fight the SPLA. Nimeiri and Swar al Dahab even gave meaningless ranks and titles such as brigadier, colonel, etc., to these reactionaries and separatists. An unholy alliance developed between the Nimeiri/Swar al Dahab May I regime and these bandits and separatists. But we stood our ground, the separatists were rooted out by forces of unity and progress. I take this opportunity to pay tribute to those who laid down their lives in this noble struggle against these Nimeiri/Swar al Dahab supported bandits, reactionaries and separatists; with their blood we shall cement real Sudanese unity.

The concrete proof of our belief in and commitment to the Sudanese unity lies in the blood shed with these separatists and bandits in order to preserve the unity of the Sudan. It was only after putting our house in order, in War Zone No. 1, that we started confronting Nimeiri's forces in the battlefield. Beginning on 17 November 1983, with the battle of Malual, we proceeded to Nasir on 12 December. In these two battles the SPLA shot down four helicopters, destroyed three steamers and inflicted heavy casualties on the enemy. We shut down the Jonglei Canal, captured nine CCI workers and three Chevron workers and shut down oil drilling in Bentiu. All these operations were timed to coincide with Nimeiri's visit to Paris in order to achieve maximum shock and embarrassment for the dictator. And indeed, for the first time, Nimeiri was hit by forces he could neither control, contain nor influence. The regime could not believe what was happening and it started to lie shamelessly that they were attacked by Cubans, Ethiopians, Libyans and Russians; and that they had killed 480 of these alleged foreigners. Of course these were all lies; the regime could not wish away reality. It was only the SPLA that hit them. I take this opportunity, to congratulate the commander of battalion 104/105, Lt. Col. William Nyuon Bany, and his officers, NCOs and men, and to pay tribute to the heroes of Battalion 104/105, who paid their ultimate sacrifice at Malual and Nasir; history will never forget them, posterity will ever be grateful. These heroes initiated a revolutionary process that was going to overthrow Nimeirism. These heroes initiated battles that shut down the Jonglei Canal; that shut down Chevron Oil; that exposed the vulnerability of the dictator and that heralded the collapse and demise of Nimeirism. After this the regime had only one way to go – downhill to the graveyard of history. To us in the bush this was the beginning of the March/April popular uprising. The regime had nothing to deceive the people with. The Chevron projects were closed, Jonglei was halted and Nimeiri could no longer plead to the masses to be patient on the grounds that prosperity was just around the corner. The SPLA effectively deprived Nimeiri of oil and water, resources that otherwise would have enabled him to remain in power much longer than 6 April 1985. This is a great contribution by, and compliment to, the men of Battalion 104/105 and to the Anyanya II of Bentiu and Bahr el Ghazal which for Bentiu have now been reorganized into "Oil Battalion". I congratulate all for your great achievements.

The rest of the events are history and well known to you and the generals. After Malual and Nasir the SPLA remained on the offensive. It continued to grow and gain confidence, while Nimeiri's forces stayed on the defensive and lost morale. Following the victories of Battalion 104/105, a new Battalion SPLA Jamus or Buffalo Battalion, under the command of the D/C-in-C, Lt. Col. Kerubino K. Bol, went to destroy CCI headquarters at Jonglei Canal mouth, to demolish the bridge on the Lol River, to bombard Aweil, to bombard Malakal, to capture APCs at Nakdier, to capture Dengjok and to wipe out the separatist forces of Gai Tut. I take the opportunity to congratulate Jamus Battalion and to pay tribute to the heroes who laid down their lives. To them posterity will always be grateful.

After these magnificent victories by 104/105 and Jamus Battalions two new animal Battalions were born: Tiger and Tumsah or crocodile, under command of Major Salva Kiir and Major Arok Thon Arok. Tiger and Tumsah proceeded to their objectives. They captured Fashalla and Pibor, and shot down two helicopters and two F–5 jet fighters and inflicted heavy casualties on the enemy. The shooting of the F–5s showed the maturity and sophistication of the SPLA. The two battalions went to Bentiu where they combined with the newly reconstituted Oil Battalion of Any-anya II under command of Paul Matip, Bol Nyawan and Khalifa Toc. The three battalions now continue to prevent the reactionary regime from mining the oil for use against the Sudanese people. I congratulate the commanders of these battalions, Major Salva Kiir, Arok Thon and Paul Dor and Captain Paul Matip and all their officers and men for these great achievements, and I take the opportunity to pay tribute to the fallen heroes of these Battalions. Posterity will always remember them as having shut down Chevron, frustrated Nimeiri's tricks and conspiracies in Bentiu, and hastened the fall of the dictator.

After Tiger and Tumsah, we trained and graduated the Locust or Jarad Division. Like the other battalions they inflicted mortal damage on Nimeiri's regime except that this time the damage was much more extensive. Jarad went in five directions. Jarad's Southern command, consisting of Zindia, Cobra and Raad, under overall command of Major Arok Thon Arok and unit command of Majors Bona Baang, Benjamin Nyankot, Gatwec Dual, Peter Panom Thanypiny and Benjamin Makor, scored victories that shocked and shook Nimeiri's forces in Southern Upper Nile and Equatoria. They wiped out two paratroop companies in Gemme-iza, destroyed an enemy company in Lokiri near Torit, wiped out an enemy battalion in Owinyikibul, captured Mangalla and Tarekeka and sent waves of fear into Juba. At the present Major Arok's forces have Southern Upper Nile and parts of Equatoria under complete siege. A second contingent of Jarad, under general command of the C-in-C and operational command of the Deputy C-in-C, Jarad's Central Command, consisting of Bilpam, Lion, Elephant and Hippo, and under unit command of Majr Daniel Deng Alony, Major Kuol Manyang, Captain Alfred Akuoc, Captain Francis Jago, Captain Deng Alor Kuol, Captain/Engineer Chol Deng Alaak, Captain James Jok Moun and Captain John Lem besieged and completely destroyed Jekou, wiping out more than one battalion under command of Col. Balaa on 3 March 1985, the same day that Nimeiri and Swar al Dahab announced their first ceasefire. Jarad's Northern Command of Hadid Battalion, under command of Lt. Col. Francis Ngor went northward to capture Dago, Padigli and Maban and sent shock waves to Damazine and Renk. A fourth Jarad column, Jarad's Eastern Command of Agrab Battalion, under command of Major

Ngachogak Ngachalok, swiftly and with minimum casualties captured a very difficult objective at Buma, dislodging three heavily entrenched enemy companies and capturing heavy weapons including many anti-aircraft guns, machine guns and ammunitions and food stores. Remnants of the enemy at Buma tried to escape to Kapeota, 200 miles away, but most of them were intercepted by the heroic Taposa and Buya people who have pledged their support to SPLA. Jarad's fifth column, of Rhino Battalion, under command of Lt. Col. (PSC) Martin Makur Aleiyou and political commissar Captain Pagan Amum, employed correct tactics and with minimum force completely paralysed the transport system in Bahr el Ghazal and also captured Yirol, Aluak-Luak, Tonj and now have put Wau and Rumbek under complete siege. Overall, Jarad as the name implies devoured everything in War Zone No. 1 and contributed greatly to the weakening and fall of Nimeiri's first republic. I take this opportunity to congratulate all officers, NCOs and men of Jarad and the brave people of Taposa and Buya for their great achievements and pay tribute to their fallen heroes, with the blood of these heroes we are cementing the unshakable foundations of a brave and proud new Sudan. Finally, I must mention an unconventional Jarad Battalion, Radio SPLA. I congratulate Atem Yaak Atem and his staff for effectively combating the enemy's obnoxious lies and propaganda and for correctly informing the Sudanese people and educating them in the realities of the new Sudan we aim to build.

I take the opportunity to congratulate each and every soldier of the SPLA, wherever you are today, whether in camouflage or engaged in battles with the enemy, whether you are doing political or military work, I congratulate you all collectively and individually. You have achieved and will achieve a great deal. You are making history, you are reshaping the old Sudan of exploitation, repression and blatant sectarian injustice into a new Sudan we want, a *democratic Sudan*, a Sudan of *equality, freedom* and *progress*, a Sudan that will take its rightful place among the nations of our planet and contribute its due share to the progress of humankind. I congratulate you, the SPLA soldier, for barefooted as you are, half-naked without pay or salary, hungry most of the time, always faced with all sorts of difficulties and dangers, from deadly mosquito bites to which you do not have chloroquine to the heat of battle with the enemy, you are making history. In that wretched condition, you are the subject of intensive discussions in the capitals of the world. You, the SPLA soldier, must realize and appreciate your greatness and your role in Sudan history. Coming to the SPLA from diverse backgrounds as students, workers, peasants, cattlemen or revolutionary intellectuals, you are invincible as SPLA/SPLM; you are invincible in your organizational unity; you were invincible in your unity of purpose. In armed struggle and in your unity in wretchedness the Sudan belongs to you, and you will vindicate Fanon that the future belongs to the wretched of the Earth.

The SPLA has fused together Sudan's revolutionary social forces in an effective politico-military combat form. For the first time in Sudan's history workers, peasants, students, revolutionary intellectuals and progressive nationalists find themselves in the SPLA/SPLM attending the same training programme and find themselves in the same trenches of combat. People from different nationalities and from different regions – North, South, East, West and Centre are coming together and being cemented together by ties of struggle, ties of sweat, ties of blood and ties of common concerns and tears. We are not brought together as in the old Sudan by ties of opportunism, of "trim trim" or of whisky- and beer-drinking parties. Our unity, achieved in the course of bitter struggle, will surely withstand all attempts by international and local reaction to perpetuate oppression and exploitation in our country. The SPLA/SPLM is the only Movement in our history that started in the South and that, because of the correctness of its aims, objectives and methods of struggle, has assumed a *national character* and now provides an *independent new force* capable of galvanizing all *revolutionary, progressive, democratic* and *patriotic forces* into a *united political alternative* capable of tackling and correctly solving the *fundamental problems* such as the *national question*, destruction of the present *exploitative* and *repressive* socio-economic and socio-political structure in our country and the building of new structures consistent with the particularity of the new Sudan so that we shall never again be hungry amidst vast agricultural and mineral riches; so that people are never again divided on racial, religious or any other sectarian lines and so that this great country shall never again be an appendage to any other country. This is why the SPLA/SPLM was formed. As I said, we did not organize the SPLA/SPLM to fight for restoration of the Addis Ababa Agreement, or for the unification of Southern Sudan, or for more and better concessions for the South. No, we organized the SPLA/SPLM for *higher* and *national objectives* – which of course include regional interests for the South and all other neglected and backward areas. You, the SPLA soldiers, with your compatriots in the streets of Khartoum, have gone more than halfway in achieving these objectives and in a relatively short time. It is only twenty-three months from 16 May 1983 when Nimeiri and Swar al Dahab attacked us in Bor and only sixteen months, three weeks and four days from 17 November 1983 when SPLA launched its first military operation at Malual to the day Nimeiri left *never to return*. In this short span of time the SPLA/SPLM has grown into a formidable vanguard of the Sudanese Revolution; this has been made possible by the steadfast determination of the SPLA soldier, his high morale, his high discipline under adverse conditions and his conviction of the correctness and justice of his cause. You, the SPLA soldier, and the soldier of the popular uprising in the streets of our cities, must persist in the struggle, you cannot stop halfway, you must proceed to destroy May II, and so on until a truly *democratic government* is established in Khartoum. This is the message and order to all SPLA forces and soldiers of the popular uprising on this great occasion the *second anniversary* of the founding of our historic Movement, SPLA/SPLM.

I have dwelt a great deal on the difficult birth and development of the SPLA/SPLM. I felt it necessary to share with you the successes, difficulties and problems of the SPLA/SPLM, because I sincerely believe that this *movement* is yours. It belongs to you, you the Sudanese masses. In the urban areas, in our capital and other cities, the SPLA/SPLM belongs to all those who work in the factories and earn so little; it belongs to those who work in textiles, glass, utilities, transport, construction, public service, and so forth, to those who shine shoes, to those who wash carts, to you all, the SPLA/SPLM is yours. The SPLA/SPLM belongs to those forgotten citizens who crowd under very difficult conditions sometimes ten or twenty to a room in Haj Yousif, in Hila Karton, in Dora al Shab, in Kalakala, in Um Bada, in Markhiat, in Fitihab, in Konyo-konyo, in Atalabara and in all the slums of our cities – to you all, the SPLA/SPLM is your Movement, you identify with it and work in it to enable it to realize the noble *ideals* and *objectives* of genuine Sudanese *unity, peace, democracy, equality, economic* and *social justice* for all. In the countryside, the Movement belongs to you, the masses – to peasants, the cattlemen, the nomads, to you all who have always been neglected, to those in Kapoeta whom no government has even ever counted in a census, to those in the far North who have been callously displaced from your ancestral homes, to you the Hadendawa and the Ingassena who never know of schools in your villages, to you the Nuba and Baggara in the Centre, to you the Fur, Zeghawa and Masalit in the West, to you all, the SPLA is yours. To all the masses of the Sudanese people, I welcome you to the SPLA/SPLM, a Movement that truly has no traces of opportunism and no political scheming, a Movement that solely represents your interests and nothing else.

The TMC Acting in Self-Defence

Having welcomed you all into the SPLA/SPLM and shared with you the difficulties that we faced and face in the bush, I would like to assure you that we would not stay one day longer here in the bush if we believed that the present military junta represented genuine change or even the potential for real change. *If we believed that the junta provided real conditions for real change, we would immediately go to Khartoum and participate in shaping that change*, not wait in the bushes for negotiations because no meaningful peace can be achieved without the direct participation of the SPLA/SPLM. It is with this background – of shared confidence with you, the masses, that I would now like to address some of the issues I enumerated earlier, including the military junta, the problem of war, negotiations and prospects for peace, drought, famine and other pressing national and regional issues.

First, on the military junta: have our views of the military junta changed after the junta's fifty days in office? The answer is a categorical no. On this I refer you to our address to you on 9 April, 1985, which was made three days after Nimeiri was exchanged for his Minister of Defence. On 9 April, we took the surgical instrument of analysis and stripped the junta naked of all its new clothing and pretences, and what did we see? We saw that the junta constituted the second republic of Nimeiri, May II and no more, and the junta is confirming this every day. In that statement of 9 April, we asked several pertinent questions about this military junta and how it came to power. These questions remain valid and relevant and I repeat them to you and to the junta. Why did the junta decide to take power when the people had already succeeded in overthrowing Nimeiri's regime? Why cannot the transition from Nimeiri to the people be direct without the military as was the case in the October 1964 Revolution? What is it that the military can do and which the people cannot do during the so-called interim period? What has motivated the generals to take power from the people at this stage? Why is it that it is Nimeiri's closest associates who now claim to be on the side of the people? Why have these generals been on the side of Nimeiri for the last sixteen years? Why was it that it was the masses who stormed Kober prison to release political prisoners? Why did the regime not do it, or might it be that some of these generals were a party to the arrest of those who opposed Nimeiri? Why did it have to take a lot of pressure from the people to convince the generals to disband the infamous State Security Organization? Has the State Security Organization been really disbanded or has its name simply been changed to National Security Organization? Why did the shooting of innocent citizens continue even after the military takeover? What role has international and local reaction played in this mock transfer of power from Nimeiri to Nimeiri's Minister of Defence? Why did Nimeiri send Swar al Dahab a message of support from Egypt wishing his Defence Minister good luck and success in his new job and expressing understanding and sympathy for the takeover? Has there been really a change, or is this Nimeiri's regime without Nimeiri? These are questions we asked you on 9 April, 1985. No doubt you must by now have formed your answers to these questions since the junta has had time enough to expose its real colours, and no doubt you must be asking new questions because this is supposed to be your revolution – you worked, sweated and bled for it. No doubt you must still be smelling Nimeiri everywhere. No matter what clothes and perfumes the junta puts on, the odious and obnoxious smell of Nimeiri always comes through very strongly. The generals have been beating the drums of innocence and salvation ever since they came to power, but the sound of music which comes out always spells *deceit* and *treachery* with capital letters – the people hear it loud and clear. The generals said and continue to say that they took over power to avoid bloodshed. Who was going to shed blood? Now let Swar al Dahab and his generals answer that question. We call on the junta to explain to the Sudanese people who was going to cause bloodshed. Who were the military preventing from shooting the people down? Well, we all know that it is the military that has guns in Khartoum. The only other force that has guns of consequence in the country is the SPLA; surely, even if we wanted, we could not possibly have caused bloodshed in Khartoum. But then, why would they do that? What could possibly force them to shoot at the people when according to them they had at that material moment switched to the side of the people? The truth is that if these generals were really on the side of the people, they should have simply announced an end to military rule as was done by the generals in October 1964, ordered their troops to the barracks and allowed the people to take over the formal instruments of power. But as it is, the generals stepped in to salvage what they could of the May regime. The generals have adopted a strategy similar to the maximum concept in operations research, that is, they are trying to save the maximum possible minimum of the May regime, in other words, minimize the damage to the May regime under popular pressure that calls for the total dismantling of the whole of the May regime. So, the truth of the matter about the fear of bloodshed is that if the people had taken over, they would have thrown the generals in jail, along with their master, Nimeiri, and they surely would have been made to account for the crimes of the May regime. So it was the generals' blood that was at stake, and like good soldiers they acted in self-defence by taking over the people's power so that that power is not used against them. Since then they have continued to deceive the people that they plan to hand over power to the people after twelve months. That is a transparent lie; it is a very bad joke. If the generals hand over power to the people, to whom shall they hand over the crimes they committed during May I regime, and the one they committed when they stole the people's victory and those that they are now committing and will continue to commit, or are the generals rather telling us that they plan to hand over power to a civilian government that will forgive them? It is abundantly clear that the junta will neither hand over power to the people nor hold elections; they will merely wait with uncertainty and bewilderment, hoping against hope to salvage what they can of the May regime until they are buried by the impending avalanche. So much for the junta. Our views have not changed about it, on the contrary we expect the junta to become much more repressive than May I regime when their illusions hit them in the face and their chief concern becomes survival.

Negotiations with whom? and about what?
As you all know, the junta has made a lot of noise about negotiations. The relevant questions are, of course, negotiations about
what and with whom? Let us leave for a while the question of
negotiations about what and talk about negotiations with whom.
Who is there in Khartoum to talk with? What is the real situation
in Khartoum? The reality of the situation in Khartoum is that
there is really no government with which to negotiate even if one
wishes to negotiate. There has been a lot of talk about the generals
negotiating with the SPLA/SPLM, but who are these generals and
what is their constitutional mandate? The generals are rebels like
the SPLA. We rebelled against Nimeirism in 1983 as a conscious
decision while the generals, under popular pressure by the masses,
rebelled against both Nimeiri and the masses when they usurped
the people's victory on 6 April, 1985. So, under what constitution
do these two rebels negotiate? The generals cancelled Nimeiri's
constitution, retained some of Nimeiri's decrees such as *Sharia*
and took it upon themselves to become the legislative body for
the country. What assurances do the masses have that one or all
of these generals, like Nimeiri, will not decree their dreams and
fancies into law?

Under the circumstances, the Trade Unions Alliance proposed
a most sensible course of action, namely, that the country should
adopt the 1956 constitution (amended 1964). Although the 1964
consitution cannot solve most of our present national problems,
it must be appreciated that any country must be governed by some
form of constitution, and we fully support the position of the
Trade Unions Alliance in that in the absence of a constitution it
is expedient to resort back to our original Independence constitution. Similarly, from a logical standpoint, since the 1964 amend-
ment was the result of the October 1964 popular uprising it should
therefore befit the spirit if not the letter of the March/April 1985
popular uprising. But the generals rejected the wise suggestion of
the Trade Unions Alliance. Like Nimeiri, they prefer and feel
comfortable working without a constitution, but by dictatorial
decrees. Well, the SPLA/SPLM being the advance guard of the
Sudanese National Democratic movement cannot and will not
negotiate with a bunch of fifteen generals that have no law governing them.

Besides having no constitution, the generals have only forty-
five weeks left to hand over power to the people according to

their own promise. They have already exhausted seven weeks of their fifty-two weeks, and very soon they will be left with the one week that we gave them, and by that time they will have done nothing substantive, nothing whatsoever, not even holding the elections which they have promised. The truth is that Nimeiri's May II regime, in the form of Swar al Dahab's military council, is an unncessary, expensive luxury which the country can ill afford in the very difficult post-Nimeiri period our country has to go through. Indeed, Nimeiri must get credit for the notoriety that his lifeless body in the form of Swar al Dahab continues to fight and beset the Sudanese people, while his head wickedly smiles at all of us from Egypt. The unpreparedness and bankruptcy of the present military council is dramatically illustrated by the fact that *four of the fifteen generals have secretly approached me through third parties, advising me not to accept negotiations at present* on the grounds that they will soon change things in Khartoum and that they will be the right generals to negotiate what they called permanent peace with the SPLA/SPLM. Like Nimeiri's offer to make me his First Vice-President, I feel obliged to tell you that I have rejected this new treachery. I am sincerely and profoundly disturbed and outraged when our country is so cheaply and irresponsibly put up for sale in "Suk-al-Shames", that is, in English, an open market where all sorts of goods are sold and bought by vendors of questionable integrity. So much for the question as to who to negotiate with; the generals are clearly not worth their salt; some of them are aspirant or actual thieves, while others are honest and innocent patriots who are genuinely concerned and disturbed about the future of the country, but hopelessly bewildered by their new and unexpected responsibilities. Generally, the generals are disorganized, suspicious of each other and totally unfit and unequipped as a group to negotiate seriously with anybody. For the last fifty days they have failed to show an iota of goodwill in their negotiation with the Trade Unions Alliance to reach an acceptable constitutional working relationship; how much less goodwill will they have if they negotiate with the SPLA/-SPLM. So, dear citizens, the truth of the matter is that the SPLA/-SPLM has not refused to negotiate as the junta would want you to believe, but rather there is just nobody to negotiate with; there is virtually no government in Khartoum. Those who call themselves the government in Khartoum want first to negotiate and indeed have been negotiating in Tripoli, Addis Ababa and

the other capitals, but not with the SPLA. The junta has shamelessly lied to you that they had sent a messenger to Col./Dr. John
Garang and that he was expected in Khartoum. This is a blatant
lie. I challenge the junta to tell the Sudanese people who the
messenger was and to explain how the odious lie was fabricated
that Col./Dr. John Garang was at one point coming to Khartoum.
No, for the last fifty days the junta has not made any direct contact
with the SPLA/SPLM. Their plan has been first to isolate the
SPLA diplomatically and then come to negotiate with a weakened
SPLA. But the other side of the coin is that this action had
exposed the junta's insincerity and lack of seriousness.

The other relevant question is negotiations about what? When
the junta or any other clique regimes in Khartoum talk about
negotiations, they mean negotiations to solve what they call the
"Southern problem". And if this is the context of negotiations,
then it is absurd to say the SPLA/SPLM is refusing negotiations.
We have repeatedly reiterated that the SPLA/SPLM is not a
regional movement; it is a national movement and as such *negotiations for concessions for the South or any other of our regions
are not within the terms of reference of the SPLA/SPLM.* Yes, the
SPLA/SPLM will solve problems peculiar to the South as it will
solve problems peculiar to other regions in our capacity as a
national movement. When preposterous questions such as what
concessions does the SPLA want for the South are still being
asked, then there is a fundamental problem of perception. The
junta has already negotiated with Southerners. They have formed
a Southern military junta and civilian cabinet in Juba, and the
SPLA/SPLM may find areas and ways of cooperation with these
Southern governments in Juba, Wau, Malakal and in the provinces, just as UMMA, DUP, and other political parties may have
an interest in them for both regional and national objectives. So,
for the SPLA/SPLM the issue of negotiations for concessions for
the South with the present or any other government in Khartoum
is a relic of the past. The SPLA/SPLM will participate directly in
the shaping of a new Sudan with other democratic and patriotic
forces in the country. It is not a matter of a group of fifteen
generals seizing power in Khartoum, forming a military council
and their civilian cabinet and then calling on the SPLA to come
in to take some reserved posts. No, we shall not take from anybody, we shall make the new Sudan together with other democratic forces in the country. Nimeiri did precisely what the junta

is trying to do in offering the SPLA/SPLM jobs in his government, except that he was more generous than his Minister of Defence; Nimeiri offered the SPLA/SPLM the First-Vice-Presidency, reunification of the South under the SPLA and six ministerial posts in the central government. We answered Nimeiri that we wanted 10,000 ministerial posts, one for every SPLA soldier, but before he could respond, Swar al Dahab took over. The subject matter of negotiations is misplaced, and the SPLA is wrongly accused of refusing negotiations. The truth is that *negotiations in the context of the so-called "Southern problem" are against the national interest and a recipe for disaster.* Suppose we solve the problem of the South, we will soon have to solve the problem of the Jebels (that is, the Nuba Mountains) because the Nuba can also take arms; after that the problem of the Beja; and so forth. It is a national, not a Southern, problem that we must address.

Because the junta has a very shallow conception of the fundamental problems that face our country, it is incapable of formulating correct solutions to these problems. Let us examine for example the junta's formulation for their solution to the war. Their basic assumption, like Nimeiri's, is that it is foreigners that are responsible for the war and this is why they have sent messengers and messages to foreign capitals (not the SPLA, as they lied to you). They did this in their naive belief that the keys of war and peace in our country are locked up in those foreign capitals. Accordingly, the junta's plan for a solution to the war and for peace is predicated on the following false assumptions:

1 That SPLA would be weakened or even collapse if foreign countries allegedly supporting the SPLA withdrew that alleged support.
2 That an agreement with a neighbouring country is necessary for a joint solution to problems they allege to be similar to what they call the "Southern problem" in that country.
3 That once the above rapprochement with these foreign countries is achieved then the junta would launch a big military offensive against the SPLA.
4 That these three steps would force the SPLA into negotiations with the junta, and on weak ground and terms.
5 That after SPLA has accepted an agreement similar to the Addis Ababa Agreement, the junta would appeal for and get massive relief and rehabilitation assistance from the international

community similar to that of 1972; and that this would give the junta breathing space to entrench itself, and

6   With peace, relief and rehabilitation achieved in the South, Chevron, Total and other companies would resume their work in the South, the Sudan would join the club of oil-producing countries under the junta, living conditions for the masses would improve, there would be no demonstrations in the streets and the junta's survival and entrenchment would be guaranteed. The Trade Unions Alliance and the political parties would pressure for elections according to the promised schedule, but the junta would reach into its bag of explanations to postpone elections and continue the May II regime. With oil, water and other development projects under way, the junta would feel confident, while the Alliance of Trade Unions and the political parties would find it difficult to move the people to the streets in efforts to force the junta into holding elections.

In a nutshell, these six points are the junta's programme to resolve the war and bring about peace.

I say, no, a big no to the junta. The fundamental problems of our country (and war is the main one at present) are not that simple. A bad peace, based on lies, deception and insincerity, like the one we had in 1972, is in reality worse than war as events have shown. The problem of war in our country has, above all, an internal basis. War in the Sudan, as we pointed out earlier, is the result of the fundamental contradictions of our society. It was not caused by foreign countries as the junta alleges and none of these countries can solve it, notwithstanding the fact that any neighbouring countries naturally have mutual interests in each others' problems. The solutions to our fundamental national problems are to be gleaned inside not outside the Sudan. To seek solutions to fundamental national problems from outside could turn our country into an abysmal chaos and it is best to avoid that. After the many visits to foreign capitals (in an apparent wild-goose chase), some of the generals in a fit of naive euphoria are reported to have celebrated their success in the alleged diplomatic isolation of the SPLA over bottles of whisky, mind you, not over *sharia*'s cups of tea, and they are reported to have been toasting and shouting a meaningless "We have got them", that is, meaning they had cornered the SPLA. Some of these generals are naive simpletons and the scum of our society. So, to summarize the

question of negotiations, SPLA/SPLM has not refused to negotiate. After all, eventually the guns will become silent as a result
of some form of negotiation or dialogue.

Even in the event that one side is defeated, somebody must
negotiate the terms of surrender. So, in our case, the truth of the
matter is that the subject of negotiation does not arise at the
present: there is nothing to negotiate about and even worse there
is nobody to negotiate with.

On Drought and Famine

Let us discuss the problem of drought and famine, particularly as
regards the South. What motivated the junta to declare the South,
and not the West or East, as disaster areas? The truth is, now
that the dust of false euphoria has settled down following the
March/6 April popular uprising the generals are disturbed and
bewildered by the dawn of reality because they do not know how
to handle reality; reality is not in their terms of reference. Having
been Nimeiri's disciples for sixteen years (the time it takes a
student starting primary school to go through to university), the
generals have completed and graduated from Nimeiri's faculty of
lies and with distinction. At the dead-end road of unfounded
euphoria, the junta, like a drowning man, is catching on to any
floating object. This is the context in which to correctly and concretely understand the junta's declaration of the South as a disaster
area. It is an SOS message that the junta's garrison towns are
faced with the disaster of falling under SPLA's protracted siege.
Of course, our people in the South are facing many hardships
and they certainly need relief. They have been living under war
conditions for nearly two years; that is bound to effect economic
and social life. Even without war the countryside has always suffered from hunger and famine during the months of June and
July, just before harvest.

Equally important is the fact that the war has seriously affected
availability of vaccines and drugs for cattle among cattle owners
and this could result in serious animal and disease epidemics. But
the junta's declaration of the South as a disaster area is totally
unrelated to all this and the people know it. The junta's aim is to
save their besieged garrisons. Many garrisons in Upper Nile and
Bahr el Ghazal have not received supplies for the last six months.
You will recall that Cobra Battalion destroyed two large river
Nile steamers by name of *Mariekh* and *Juba* last November. This

effectively stopped River Nile transport, the main transport artery to the South. The railway line to Wau was destroyed by Jamus Battalion in February 1984. Road transport in most of the three regions is completely paralysed. The only transport to the South by now is by air and that is also hazardous as the regime knows that we have the capability to bring down any plane in their arsenal. To date we have shot down eight helicopters, two Buffalos, one Hercules and two F–5 jet fighters. Only ten days ago a Buffalo aircraft heading for Wau narrowly escaped being hit by one of our missiles. Sooner or later we shall bring down some more military planes. The Sudanese Air Force has lost twenty-six officers through SPLA action and is completely demoralized. The SPLA controls the whole of the Southern Sudanese countryside, while the enemy is holed up in its garrison towns feeding on vultures, marabou birds and other exotic food. SPLA military strategy calls for the occupation of the countryside, the stopping of all transport in War Zone No. 1, and the strangulation of the cities so that enemy garrisons are forced to surrender or withdraw. This strategy is working, and it is a matter of military not humanitarian concern. The people in the cities must come to the countryside and they are doing just that, a fact which we announce daily as we read the names of government officials, soldiers and students who defect to the SPLA on this Radio. In the countryside, the SPLA has been conscious of the problem of food, and Radio SPLA has been persistently urging SPLA units and the people to grow more food this year. So, the junta is right on this score. Its garrison towns in the South are famine-stricken and are real disaster areas, and this is good; our military strategy is working. The enemy, of course, knows that this is our strategy, but like their artificial policies they think they can turn public opinion against us in the South, but the people know their real motives. We also know that the junta is massing troops in Juba, Malakal, Wau and Bentiu for a major offensive against the SPLA, and these humanitarian pretensions, such as the declaration of the South as a disaster area, are designed to prepare public opinion for the junta breaking its own ceasefire. It is also to find reasons to convince soldiers as to why they should fight, because they do not understand the reasons for the war when SPLA says it is fighting for national unity and the junta says the same. So, the soldiers are being told that the roads must be opened to take food to starving people in the South and that SPLA is sitting in the way.

We are surely sitting in the way, and we advise the soldiers not to come, for we shall be fighting and dying unnecessarily, while the generals who are responsible for the war enjoy their air-conditioned offices and homes in Khartoum.

The problem of drought and famine is indeed acute all over our country. The Western part of our country is in fact the hardest hit, especially Northern Kordofan and Northern Darfur. In Kordofan alone it is estimated that half a million people have been forced to leave their homes and according to a UNICEF estimate one in six children faces starvation. Last December Nimeiri closed the camp for displaced people in Um Ruwaba, evicting 8,000 residents, and trucked back tens of thousands who had trekked 200 miles to the capital to look for food. Now, near el Obeid, 47,000 people are encamped, living on a ration of one litre of water per day and one malwa of dura per month. Recently the Americans shipped in 60,000 sacks of dura but the new military governor of Swar al Dahab's regime confiscated it and declared it as a strategic reserve – you certainly know what the Governor-Major General of Kordofan means by strategic reserve and what he will do with it.

Despite all these hardships our people face in the West, both May I and May II have not declared these regions as disaster areas. Actually the former Governor of Darfur, Ibrahim Derej, had warned the government of the imminent drought and famine in Western Sudan as early as October 1983. *Although these areas are worse off than the South, the governments of May I and May II did not declare them as disaster areas* simply because there are no garrisons under siege there. In fact the government is even sort of embarrassed about the drought and famine in the West – very queer psychology indeed. So the West is not a disaster area because there are no what the regime calls "outlaws" in the West, whereas the South is a disaster area because there are what the regime calls "outlaws" there and there are garrisons under siege there. You can see how the generals are plunging the country into chaos. In their vain efforts to use the humanitarian weapon of famine relief against the SPLA, they are unwittingly telling the worst-hit areas of the West and East that your problems get solved when you take up arms, that is when you become an "outlaw". And armed struggle is not a monopoly of the South. The West or any other region can take up arms; even the capital, Khartoum, can take up arms. They just took up arms in our cities through popular uprising to bring Swar al Dahab into power! In Khartoum itself there is no dura and the little that is available is too expensive for those who brought Swar al Dahab to power. Quite recently in Kosti after Nimeiri was overthrown there were very serious food riots. Hungry people broke into a dura store and made off with 10,000 sacks before the police dispersed them with tear gas. The situation is grave everywhere.

The fact is that sixteen years of May I have turned the Sudan into a disaster area and May II will soon make an unprecedented calamity out of it. I take this opportunity to appeal to the world community to extend relief to the Sudanese people through the SPLA/SPLM. The SPLM is better qualified than the generals in Khartoum to receive and distribute relief in areas under our control, which is the whole of the Southern Sudanese countryside where more than ninety per cent of the people live. I here announce the formation of the Sudan Relief and Rehabilitation Agency (SRRA), a non-political organization, to solicit for donations of food, medicines, veterinary vaccines and drugs, and other material for relief and to find ways and means to transport and distribute this in Southern Sudan and other drought affected areas in other parts of the country which may in future come under SPLA control. We know that there are guerilla movements that receive relief assistance from some international and humanitarian organizations directly, and the fact that we are not a government in the conventional sense should not, we hope, inhibit donors, since there is a precedent. Any relief assistance to Southern Sudan (War Zone No. 1) must be channelled through the SRRA. The SRRA would be much more capable of distributing relief assistance than the Governor of Kordofan, for example, who declares relief as strategic reserve. We are much more concerned as we live daily among the people in the villages, not in different living conditions than they.

I have talked about the problems of war, negotiations, peace, drought, famine and relief in an honest, objective and critical way and exposed the callous attempts by the May II regime to use these issues for its own clique benefit. It is easy to analyze and criticize, but much more difficult to provide workable solutions. So, the junta has refused to hand over the stolen power back to the people and it holds deadly weapons. We believe that the junta will not hold elections. We believe it will become much more repressive than May I regime as a matter of clique self-defence and especially when problems begin to overwhelm it and it feels a sense of insecurity. It will soon launch an offensive against the SPLA despite its peace and humanitarian pronouncements in order to establish some credibility. We believe the junta is an expensive luxury the country cannot afford, and so on and so forth. But given all these, where do we go from here? Before I come to specifics it is necessary to summarize and underline essential points. For nearly sixteen years the Sudan has been ruled by a dictatorial regime which thrived on coalitions of convenience, intrigues, treachery and murder. By the end of the day, May I regime degenerated into a one-man-no-system rule and the whole country was turned into a disaster area. It is now the duty of all the Sudanese people to pick up the pieces, and from these pieces, from the ashes of the old Sudan build a new brave and proud Sudan worth its real potential. There is no denying that Nimeiri was the chief villain in the drama that was running on Sudan's political stage for nearly two decades. However, it is important to underline the fact that *he is not the lone cause of all Sudan's ailments*. Some of the chronic economic and political diseases, which he certainly aggravated by his arrogance and high-handedness, were inherited from past regimes and arose from the fundamental contradictions in our society and the international arena. It is indeed because of the realization and objective appreciation of those contradictions that the SPLM has made it clear from its inception, in its Manifesto issued in July 1983, that the problems of the Sudan are not in the far-flung regions, such as the so-called "Southern problem", but rather are right there in the centre; they are essentially national in character. It is necessary to reiterate and underline the fact that the SPLM is a broadly-based organization that transcends one region, and which has succeeded in attracting to its ranks a large number of Sudanese and is not there to defend the rights of one region, but rather of all regions. As such it is a Movement which is committed to the *unity, territorial and political integrity* of the Sudan. If the SPLA/SPLM has emerged in a specific region it has done so because of geographical, historical and political considerations like all other internal parties and movements. In this sense the SPLA/SPLM considers all regionally based and biased political movements as ones inspired by a sense of inferiority complex. Why should people crawl into regional shells instead of basking in the national sunshine of our great country? By the same token, the SPLA/SPLM considers that Khartoum-based political groups that deny the *national character* to movements that emerge in the regions are suffering from sectarian chauvinism and religious bigotry.

Call for Dialogue and Democratic Consensus

With this broad framework in mind, I would like to underline that the SPLA/SPLM is committed to an open-minded dialogue on the fundamental problems of the Sudan, for without settling those problems satisfactorily, there can be no stability, unity or development. It is time for the Sudanese to come to grips with the root causes of their political malady, rather than flying reality in the face or dwelling on the symptoms of the ailments. Such a dialogue must be undertaken by all democratic and patriotic forces in the country so that a *national democratic consensus* is reached on the fundamental issues. Such a national democratic consensus cannot be brought about by a bunch of generals, or interim political establishments; it can be brought about only through *dialogue* among the national democratic and patriotic forces in the country, and the SPLA/SPLM is *willing and ready to enter into a broad discussion that will study fundamental issues of the Sudan*, such as the system of government, conditions for national unity, economic and social development, Sudan's foreign policy, including its African and Arab commitments, and so forth. We reiterate and underline that the SPLM, a Movement for all the Sudan, believes that the only way for the creation of a strong, stable and united new Sudan is through a *national democratic consensus* on the fundamental problems that face our country. For neither the manoeuvres of despotic rulers like Swar al Dahab, nor sectarian and traditional political parties of years past, nor paying lip service to the ideals of socialism (such as the SSU), regionalism (such as Nimeiri's fake autonomy for the South), non-alignment, and so forth would help the Sudan to come out of its present economic and political quagmire. If only one things stands out clearly, the lessons of the last thirty years after our nominal independence have taught us that such hypocrisies were nothing but a recipe for disaster. But still the question remains: How do we bring about a *national democratic consensus*?

In order to bring about a *national democratic consensus*, given the refusal of the military junta to hand over power to the people, the SPLA/SPLM presents the following programme for the intensification of the struggle, in order to bring about peace quickly:

1   Today, the 27 May 1985, I here ring the bell for round two of the popular uprising in the streets of our cities and SPLA's revolutionary armed struggle in the bushes and sands of our great country. Last time we won in round one against the May I regime. There is nothing to prevent us from winning in round two against the May II regime which is much weaker than May I. The struggle must continue and SPLA/SPLM will give all necessary assistance including alliance or unity with those national democratic forces that are ready to continue and intensify the struggle beginning from today.

2   As of today, 27 May 1985, I put all SPLA forces on maximum alert and declare general mobilization in War Zone No. 1. All SPLA leaves are cancelled with immediate effect and all SPLA soldiers on leave are to report to the nearest SPLA unit. This is to intensify the struggle and in view of the fact that the generals, despite their peace-mongering, are actually massing troops now in Juba, Wau, Malakal and Bentiu with the intention of launching a major offensive against the SPLA as the only way, as they say, to achieve some credibility.

3   During this limited phase, when the enemy intends to make a show of force by moving in large convoys, battalion commanders are advised to shift to the tactics of classical guerilla warfare in order to paralyze and annihilate the enemy while moving, while harrassing a stationary enemy.

4   All SPLA battalion commanders are to organize commando units to apprehend opportunists and collaborators with the enemy in War Zone No. 1 and escort them to SPLA GHQs.

5   I repeat my appeal of 22 March and 9 April to the Sudanese Army in War Zone No. 1 to disobey orders, stay in your barracks and start talking with the SPLA, mainly at the junior officer and NCO level, and where appropriate with senior officers who are patriotic. I am confident that it is you, the junior officers and NCOs in the army, police, prisons and wildlife wardens, those who are doing the actual fighting, who can bring about a genuine peace in coordination with other genuine democratic forces, such as in the professions, trades and students unions. We are already

talking with these officers and exchanging gifts in War Zone No. 1. The aim of these contacts and talks between the SPLA and Sudanese Army in the field is to form joint committees that will lead to the formation of a provisional administration from below, so as to save the nation from the impending chaos to which the generals are bent on steering the country. We sincerely believe in national unity and so do you in the Sudanese Army. You have fought for national unity; so have we, as I explained yesterday. So we do not have any fundamental difference. Let us then agree to throw out the generals, stop killing each other and save the nation from below. You do not have to run and seize the radio station in Omdurman to throw out the generals. Let us set up joint commands here in the South and that will surely lead to the fall of the generals in Khartoum.

6 I order all SPLA units not to attack garrisons commanded by members of the Free Officers Movement since these officers are formally under the symbolic command of the SPLA Commander-in-Chief. However, since SPLA unit commanders cannot possibly know who is a free officer, it is the responsibility of the free officers to make contact with SPLA unit commanders in the field to identify themselves and coordinate cooperation and action.

7 Immediate steps must be taken to unify the general command of the SPLA and the Free Officers Movement so as to achieve unity of objectives, plans and execution.

8 SPLM/SPLA shall immediately open and keep open channels of communication with the Trade Unions Alliance and other national democratic forces, not with the aim of negotiating with Swar al Dahab's Nimeiri's second republic, but rather to create conditions for the convergence of all national democratic forces from all parts and work places of the country with the aim of forcing the military council to resign and a national democratic government instituted on a provisional or interim basis.

9 The experience of the March/April popular uprising shows that the generals were encouraged to usurp more and more powers until eventually they took all the power because of lack of vigilance verging on opportunism on the part of some trade union leaders. Surely sixteen years of Nimeirism affected leadership of the trades and professional unions. In order for round two against May II to be effective and not to be aborted or stolen again, I

75

call on the rank and file of the trades and professional unions to put your house in order as we did ours at the beginning of SPLA/SPLM in 1983. The rank and file must root out all elements in their leadership that were connected with Nimeirism and those who might have captured the leadership because of electoral rigging by Nimeirism. The unions must purge their leadership of undesirable elements and elect a new patriotic leadership that will be able to contribute effectively during the coming round two of the popular uprising against May II.

10   Finally, we believe that the May II regime is much weaker than May I, and we have the ability to bring it down in less than one week of demonstrations with a few blows by SPLA here and there. So let us all be in touch, plan, act and bring down the generals. This is the only course of action that can bring about peace and prosperity to the country quickly. The continuation of the generals in power can only prolong your suffering.

Chapter Three:

The Search for Dialogue Among Equals

The search for national dialogue began long before the fall of Nimeiri. The SPLA/SPLM has called, from its inception in 1983, for honest and frank discussion by all the Sudanese political forces on all the problems of the nation and how to tackle them. Nimeiri and his government failed to respond to this challenge and eventually forfeited their right to a say in the future of the country by years of using and abusing the Sudanese people and all the Sudanese political groups.

With the fall of Nimeiri it was assumed that the SPLM would engage in dialogue with his successors, but Nimeiri is one man, and his absence does not mean the end of the system that allowed him to emerge and to dictate his hollow messages to the nation. Instead, the Northern elite, in the shape of the Transitional Military Council and its many emissaries, offered to "negotiate" with the SPLM for the spoils of the people's victory of 6 April, and thus fell short of the SPLM's challenge to build a new Sudan. What they sought were "negotiations" between two adversaries involving give and take; per contra the SPLM called for an open "dialogue" among all Sudanese political forces, without exception, to resolve once and for all Sudan's political crisis. Because of their failure to see Sudan's problem in this light the new rulers have reached the end of their political life before they even started.

But the democratic and peace-loving forces of the country have not kept silent, the National Alliance for National Salvation, a loose confederation of professional trade unions, academic groups and political parties has succeeded in forming itself into a viable political force committed to dialogue with the SPLM. Though there have been problems and though the National Alliance was made up of a mixed bag of individuals, some more committed to higher national objectives than others, their deliberations with the SPLM have enabled further progress to be made towards a national constitutional conference. That conference has long been a declared objective of the SPLM and deemed the only real way to come to grips with the problems of Sudan, problems which are deep rooted and go back to the pre-Nimeiri years. Those problems still distort the vision of Sudan's Northern elite including those who aspire to be rulers.

Through its consistent stand, first against Nimeiri the man, then against the "Nimeiri system" and its unflagging adherence to concrete and identifiable objectives of unity, peace, democracy and equitable development, more and more individuals and groups from different social classes and different regions of the country began responding to the SPLM challenge for real change. They realized that Sudan has now an alternative future to that offered by the myopic rulers of the past. The SPLM's stand, reinforced by military victories, has become strong with time. Its leadership refuses to allow the country to be deprived once more of its rightful inheritance of strength and independence, or be subjugated by internal or external forces.

Ironically, the SPLM, the only Sudanese political group that has consistently called for bona fide *dialogue* on well articulated national issues is still accused by many Northerners of intractability and shadiness of objectives. Those accusations do not only come from sensationalist media muggers, but also from outdated politicians with a proclivity to shoot at their feet. Furthermore accusations come from a sector of Northern Society who suffer from a self-deception, bordering on delusional insanity reflected in such claims that the war in the South is a foreign-inspired conspiracy, as if the history of the last thirty years is not enough guide. Equally, despite the all-encompassing impact of war on the Sudan those same people still view it as Sudan's "running sore", i.e. the South, completely paramnesic to the national haemorrhage. The SPLM, however, is confident that despite the ferocity of war countries never bleed to death; if accommodation does not come through dialogue it will certainly come through exhaustion.

If it has taken so long for the dialogue to commence the reason is not difficult to find. To begin with, it was the hesitancy of Khartoum because of lack of goodwill on the part of some, and a crisis of perception on the part of others, that little progress was registered in the first months of the transitional government. Later on, in spite of the start of serious discussions and agreement on the objective conditions for holding national debate, the media and some political circles in Khartoum persisted in calumniating the SPLM and deliberately misrepresenting its ideas, actions and objectives wherever and whenever they could find an audience.

We recall that the speech of 26 and 27 May 1985 by the SPLM leader stated the "objective conditions" necessary for the commencement of a meaningful dialogue. In that speech a crucial distinction was made between "negotiation", which involves two adversary parties, and "dialogue", which involves all those groups and individuals concerned for the future of Sudan. That speech went to the root of the problem and underlined that for any dialogue to take place there must first be viable interlocutors in Khartoum. The reality of the situation in Khartoum, in the period immediately following the 6 April events, there did not exist a government with a constitutional mandate; those who took over power were "rebels, and rebels cannot negotiate with rebels." What the SPLM was seeking was a political force capable of engaging in a serious dialogue and with an ability to deliver. Those in the National Alliance who viewed the SPLM's stance towards the TMC and its council of ministers in May 1985 as unnecessarily intransigent must have had other thoughts a few months later when they themselves disowned that inept government because of the deviousness of the Prime Minister on issues like Sharia' and openly expressed suspicion as to the motives of some members of the toothless TMC.

The political forces with whom the SPLM sought to engage in dialogue represented both the modern political sector (professional and workers trade unions) as well as traditional (in the historical sense) political parties, as was the case later at Koka Dam and the Peace agreement with the DUP. There is no denying that the traditional parties are facts of life in the Sudan; some of them have taken up arms against Nimeiri in the early 1970s, e.g. Sadiq el Mahdi, Sharif al Hindi and Philip Abbas Ghabboush. To the same degree those parties have had their share in the past in aggravating if not creating the North/South polarization. Also, over the sixteen years of Nimeiri's rule every political group and party and countless prominent individuals have, at one time or another, been used and abused by the tyrant. In doing so, Nimeiri has exploited their intrinsic divisiveness in order to divide and misrule. So if those forces are to ensure a permanent peace in Sudan they would have to change their bad old habits and face squarely the dilemma of the Sudan, rather than "the problem of the South." But Sudan's problems are not only those of political unity and cultural diversity; there are also economic inequities if not deprivations due to a self-centred approach to politics. This self-interestedness cannot be put down on the traditional parties because when you strip those parties to the bone they are not one man called el Mahdi or one man called al Mirghani, it is equally their elitist supporters who make and break governments. There is a consensus in opinion in Sudan as in many developing countries that development in the post-colonial period has been biased towards the urban areas, and mainly benefiting the elites.

Immediately following the events of 6 April, while the radio lambasted the malpractices of the Nimeiri regime (i.e. corruption, patronage, bloating the public service and giving unwarranted high salaries and unearned increments to certain officials) the same system of privilege was being perpetuated if not enhanced by the new rulers. The public service was further inflated, senior government officers (including ministers) continued to enjoy the same privileges which were inveighed against when practised by Nimeiri, and the army establishment, badly in need of reform, carried on as before. In fact, some of the senior officers were promoted, including some members of the TMC who claimed to be arch-enemies of Nimeiri's policy of patronage. This was a bleak reminder of the reality of Sudan's unproductive economy and the mire of destitution in which the disfranchised vegetate. On the other hand while Nimeiri's presidential shoplifters were tried and condemned, the fat cats in the business world who benefited from their thievery and pilfered the country for a decade (including the "holy" den of thieves clustered around the so-called "Islamic banks") remained at large, some using their illicit gains to support the mushrooming political parties. Social equality and economic justice would require, on our part, a close look not only into the history of political misrule and the geography of poverty but also the physiology of wealth, relative as it is, if we are at all to be taken seriously by other people.

Evidently, the Sudan witnessed important changes following the 6 April events, for example the restoration of the rights of the people resulting in the emergence of forty political parties and ninety trade unions, for the first time in sixteen years. Some of those parties reflected certain political realities which could not be ignored, the essence of democracy, in the end, is that the ordinary citizens decide the direction of a nation by casting their vote at the ballot box, but the democratic process does not stop there. The SPLM, in all its declarations, called for the creation of a new democratic Sudan, a democracy achieved through consensus on fundamentals among all political forces in the country.

Regrettably, not only was the role of the SPLA/SPLM in fighting Nimeiri underrated, also its new vision of Sudan has been misunderstood, often deliberately. Critics of the SPLM in Khartoum because of their short memory failed to see how far this Movement has gone compared to the Southern-based movements of the past. The message from the South in the Khartoum Round Table in March 1965 was loudly expressed by the President of the Sudan African National Union (SANU), Mr. Aggrey Jaden. In his opening statement Jaden had this to say: "The Sudan falls sharply into two distinct areas, both in geographical area, ethnic group and cultural system. The Northern Sudan is occupied by a hybrid Arab race who are united by their common language, common cultural and political inspiration. The people of Southern Sudan, on the other hand, belong to the African ethnic group of East Africa. They do not only differ from the hybrid Arab race in origin, arrangement and basic systems, but in all conceivable purposes. There is nothing in common between the various sections of the community, no body of shared beliefs, no identity of interests, no local signs of unity and above all, the Sudan has failed to compose a simple community."

This is the type of polarization which the SPLM managed to demolish. By failing to grasp this historic opportunity afforded to them by the SPLM, Northerners are giving credence to the distorted vision of the Jadens of the world. In effect, more important than the fact that the SPLA/SPLM played a major role in the armed struggle against Nimeiri is the fact that a Southern-based party has emerged as a national party, with an incalculable impact on the country. The fight of the SPLM/SPLA against the separatist elements in the South should have been enough proof of its commitment to Sudanese unity. The SPLM provided the Sudanese people, for the first time in their recent political history, with a framework for reshaping all Sudan, moulding democracy, equality, freedom and progress, all essential ingredients for stability and genuine democracy.

The term "democratic" might mean different things to different people. For years after the May Revolution when the Communist Party was at the forefront, the Nimeiri regime talked in terms of a National *Democratic* Front and that, in reality, meant a front which included the organized professionals, workers and peasants as well as leftist parties to the exclusion of all other historical political formations. But it is one thing to denounce the traditional political parties as an impediment to unity, because of their divisive nature; it is something else to recognize them as a fact of life that can only be changed by time, not repression. All that has now become history and even the Communist Party, after the fall of Nimeiri, was among the first to call for democracy in its liberal sense, the sense of pluralism. In the end if any political movement wants to reshape the country in its own image then this should be free for all to try: the Muslim Brothers might like to do it; the Communists might like to do it; the pan-Arabists might like to do it. But, above all, for any democracy to operate there should be agreement on fundamentals, particularly there should be no constitutionally entrenched positions or subjective exclusions otherwise democracy is but a chimaera.

The Sudanese uprising in April 1985 was a movement of all the people, those who took to the streets were not only the trade unionists and professional workers but also housewives, children, farmers and street boys, known as Shamassa. They embraced not only the bourgeoisie and "proletariat" but also the Sudanese "sub-proletariat". Sudan's "sub-proletariat" is made up of the naked of the South and the Nuba mountains; the nomads in the West and East; the traditional subsistence farmers all over the country who are not organized in trade unions that articulate their interests and who are, in the end, the ones who suffer the most. The uprising in the cities comprised many of these elements despite their different sectarian, religious and ethnic allegiances. All of them were driven to revolt by a feeling of betrayal and reaction to the high-handed and arrogant way in which their so-called "President" was treating them. In his last speech before leaving

Sudan, Nimeiri told the people of Sudan that he was there to stay, that he intended to continue his economic policies, that he did not care if the value of the Sudanese pound plummeted to zero. Nimeiri treated a proud people like dirt and they fought back for their dignity.

The analysis of why and how the military junta came to power in April 1985 needs to be carefully considered. At the time, some thought, for understandable reasons, that the movement was instigated by Nimeiri, but Nimeiri was not the type of ruler who would give up power at will. For years he played people off, one against another, and got away with it, and probably he believed that he would get away with it again this last time. In effect, it was the pressure from the Army's lower ranks that forced the generals, not to align themselves with the masses, as they have claimed, but to bow down to the will of the masses. The army which coerced the generals was an army stripped of many of its powers. The people are vigilant and the pressures to which the army has been subjected by the civilian forces since Nimeiri fell were putting them well on their guard and ensured enough checks and balances on the army's power, at least for now. But the sad thing about those pressures is that they were, mainly, related to sectional gains (gains of the professional elite) rather than addressing global national issues: problems of famine, national unity and genuine political stability.

In a sense, the generals acted in self-defence in April 1985. In fact, General Nimeiri would not have been able to remain in power had he held the simple title of Mr. Nimeiri; he remained in power because he was Field Marshal Nimeiri. At the same time, it would be a mistake to think that the SPLM/SPLA under-estimated the extent to which the army was essential to maintaining a semblance of unity and stability in a deeply troubled country. That is why the SPLA continued to appeal to the rank and file and patriotic officers to join in the struggle against oppression and injustice. The SPLM also, on several occasions, hailed the patriotic role of twenty-two senior army officers who stood up against Nimeiri and his corruption in his latter years, not all the generals were of the same mettle.

All those issues were addressed in John Garang's speech of May 1985. In that speech he made plain that the SPLM does not consider war to be an end in itself and that whoever wants to engage in dialogue in Khartoum should start off by going to the root causes of the problem, and ask themselves why are those people fighting in the bush. This is the only way to move forward. Until Sudan's political forces have identified and discussed the real problems of the nation, problems to do with national unity, cultural diversity, development patterns etc., there shall be no peace, attempts to solve the problems of Sudan, either by arranging coalitions with forces outside the country in order to isolate the SPLM/SPLA or by offering political handouts, reveal a lack of seriousness and betray ignorance of the real nature of the problem.

In the following pages are the text of letters exchanged between Khartoum authorities and political forces and the SPLM leader which reveal the gnawing gap between two visions. The first letter came from the Sudanese Minister of Defence and remained unanswered, if anything because the Movement did not recognize the TMC. Other communications, however, reveal what we call a crisis of perception. For example, the letter from the Prime Minister dealt with the so-called problem of the South and surprisingly offered nothing new for the solution of that problem; only Nimeiri's remedy, as if all the declarations of the SPLM about the national objectives of the Movement meant nothing. The SPLM responded to the Prime Minister's letters only because he was the man chosen by the National Alliance for the post. No sooner had Dr. Gizouli lost the support of his political constituency than the Alliance took the matter in its own hands and engaged with the Movement in direct dialogues. But in that Khartoum atmosphere of acrimony and hostility the Alliance emissaries to the SPLM soon became the town's "bêtes noires"; theirs was an arduous mission and a fraught position.

Letter from General Osman Abdullah, Minister of Defence and member of the Transitional Military Council, to John Garang in May 1985, shortly after the fall of Nimeiri

I write to you for the first time knowing that you will appreciate the nationalistic motivation of this letter.

Our country, my friend, has suffered divisions for many years and many lives have been lost as a consequence of the war. The revolution that has deposed the dictator has still not been able to enjoy peace because our wound in the South is still bleeding.

I have been following your broadcasts on the radio, awaiting news of your return to your country to participate in establishing the new direction of the Sudan, after the years of destruction that have afflicted our country from end to end.

I am well aware, my friend, that you are not fighting as a rebel or secessionist but you are striving with honour for the achievement of national unity and to improve the lot of the Sudanese, Northerners and Southerners.

Accordingly, I invite you to meet us in any place, at any time, to discuss and decide upon what is best for the security and stability of our country and I am very hopeful that what unites us is greater than what divides us and that together we can remove all obstacles standing in the way of victory.

Letter from Dr. El-Gizouli Dafaalla, Prime Minister of Sudan, to John Garang, 1 June 1985

Dear John

History never repeats itself and decisive moments are rare and hard to come by in the history of nations. Our country is now passing through such a period. This wonderful, peaceful people have revolted in a popular uprising against their hateful, degenerate oppressors and their army sided with them at the crucial moment thus avoiding bloodshed. So the Sudanese whose craving for freedom, democracy and dignity is insatiable did it again in twenty years to the bemusement of the world.

You did your bit in paving the way for the revolution by the means available to you and the nation appreciated that. Now Nimeiri and his defunct regime are no longer breathing over our necks, the Sudanese in the climate of freedom and democracy are entering into a serious dialogue about the future of our motherland and its complex problems with a genuine desire to settle them in a peaceful civilized manner. Your place is with us and it is an honour that must not be missed. Nobody has a ready panacea for all our ailments. Nobody is satisfied with all we have achieved so far but revolution is a continuous process. Together we succeed, fragmentation is the surest way to failure. The political field is now teeming with the future scenarios and your contribution can easily find a place in this mosaic.

I know that the whole Sudan is your concern but there is a chronic bleeding sore in the South since 1955. The government of the popular revolution is giving the solution of the Southern problem top priority. The following points are not offered as a final solution to the problem but as food for thought:

1   The national charter agreed upon by the Trade Union Federation, the political parties and the army stated that the Southern problem should be solved within an autonomous regional framework in a united Sudan.

2   Commitment of all sides to Addis Ababa as a base for running the affairs of the South for the time being.

3   The recognition of the cultural and ethnic characteristics of the South.

4   Acknowledging that the South is mostly underdeveloped, genuine efforts should be exerted to bring it to the level of parity.

5   Religion truly perceived is never a divisive force. There are Muslims and Christians in both the North and the South. Some Sudanese are neither. Though the Southern problem has not started with the so-called Islamic laws, I appreciate their impact on it. Should other facets of the problem be agreed upon I would not have thought that these laws would be a stumbling block and ways and means can be found as these laws and others are under discussion now.

The South is now suffering from serious famine and people are dying of starvation every day. Sufficient help has been provided by the international community but it cannot find its way to the starving in the South because of the security situation. I call upon you as a true patriot to extend this uneasy lull in the fighting to a real truce so that humanitarian help can reach the needy. I give you my solemn pledge that no military advantage will be taken and nothing but food and medicines will be carried on the means of transport.

Though our beloved land is the natural host of deliberations concerning its problems, a delegation can meet you anywhere to establish a meaningful dialogue. It will be a tragedy if the favourable circumstances now available are choked by previous suspicions and fixed stands.

Yours sincerely

Dr. El-Gizouli Dafaalla
Prime Minister

Response of John Garang to Dr. El-Gizouli, 1 September 1985

Dear Dr. El-Gizouli

1   Greetings in the name of the Sudanese people and in the name of the Glorious March-April popular uprising. This is an official reply to your letter dated 1 June 1985, and which I received on 25 June 1985. The letter had to be discussed in various committees of the Movement, a necessary democratic process that culminated in final resolutions by our highest organ, the SPLM/SPLA Politico-Military High Command. I am communicating these resolutions to you for perusal by all the political forces in the country, including the Sudanese Army, the Council of Ministers, the Trade Unions Alliance, political parties of all hue, and students unions.

2   However, before going to these resolutions, I would like to discuss, correct and underline certain points that have either been distorted, misinterpreted, or simply not taken seriously in Khartoum, matters which, I believe, are fundamental to a correct and serious appreciation of the resolutions.

3   I begin by assuring you and your colleagues that, contrary to the propaganda by the Transitional Military Council (TMC), the SPLM/SPLA has always taken the interest and initiative in calling for dialogue (not negotiations) among all political forces in the Sudan. But, perhaps, Khartoum did not listen, or chose not to listen. I here enclose all our three official statements on the problem of war, dialogue and peace for your close reading, hoping that you and your colleagues will find them informative and helpful in your deliberations. They are dated March 22, April 9, and May 26–27, 1985, respectively.

4   As shown by these documents, we are on record for calling for dialogue and peace, even before Nimeiri's fall. In the public statement made over Radio SPLA on March 22 by the SPLA C-in-C, we called for direct talks between the SPLA and the Sudanese Army in the South: while, at the national level, we called for convening a *National Congress* to be attended by all political forces in the country to discuss the formation of a *New Sudan*. Clearly, the stand of the SPLM/SPLA is unambiguous. We called for national dialogue under the form of a National Congress, or conference as the TMC now calls it, 14 days before

Nimeiri's fall. Yet there is a great deal of talk in Khartoum about the SPLA not interested in peace, being warmongers, refusing "olive branches", and all that.

5   When Nimeiri did fall on April 6, and his Generals took over, we called on them to transfer power to the people immediately. This stand was necessary both on principle and to respect your own Charter (of the Political Alliance) that those who were associated with the May Regime should be excluded from any Interim Government. Nimeiri's Minister of Defence and many others in the present Government in Khartoum undeniably had a lot to do with the quasi-defunct May Regime. On these bases we urged you to continue the struggle to effect the immediate transfer of power. The one week we gave the Generals was actually more than necessary. How long did it take General Aboud to transfer power to the people? Those who sweated in the streets of our cities and in our bushes in the south are steeled enough by the struggle not to be taken in by the TMC's short-legged stories of how they sided with the people at the decisive moment.

6   While we are calling on the Generals to hand over power to the people, we continued at the same time to call for dialogue with the unions and political parties. I said:
   I call on General Swar al Dahab to immediately transfer power to the people . . . I call on the workers, professional and students unions to continue the strikes and demonstrations until the Generals hand over power to the people, and we are prepared to talk with you. (Page 14–15, speech delivered on Radio SPLA by the C-in-C on April 9, 1985, here enclosed).

7   When the Trade Unions Alliance and political parties capitulated to the Transitional Military Council, we still continued to call for dialogue among all political forces in the country. On 26–27 May 1985, in our third public broadcast, I said:
   I would like to underline that the SPLA/SPLM is committed to an open-minded dialogue on the fundamental problems of the Sudan, for without solving those problems satisfactorily, there shall be no stability, unity or development . . . such dialogue must be undertaken by all democratic and patriotic forces in the country, so that a National Democratic Consensus us reached on the fundamental issues . . . The SPLM/SPLA is willing and ready to enter into such broad discussions that will

study the fundamental issues of the Sudan, such as national unity, economic and social development, Sudanese foreign policy, including its Arab and African commitments, and so forth. (Page 37–38, Statement Delivered by the C-in-C on Radio SPLA on May 26–27, 1985, here enclosed).

8   Contrary to the TMC's claims, it is abundantly clear from all the above that for two months, between March 22 and May 26–27–1985, the SPLM/SPLA consistently and persistently called for national dialogue. The indisputable truth is that despite all the talk about talks by the TMC, the first contact between the new Regime and the SPLA was through your letter of June 1, 1985 and Brigadier (PSC) Osman Abdhalla's letter dated May 27, 1985, both of which I received in the third week of June. But what was the TMC doing during this period, between April 6 and June, 1985? It is interesting, but sad.

9   I want to underline the very unfortunate fact that, while the SPLA was calling for dialogue and a National Congress, the TMC was very preoccupied with totally different plans and programmes of how to destroy the SPLA, not talk with it. The TMC adopted a strategy to talk a lot about dialogue and peace, while their real intention was to gain time to plan and prepare for a major military offensive designed to achieve military victory over the SPLA, after which, as the junta assumed, they could become heroes and thereby create conditions to entrench themselves in power. Evidence to support this charge is overwhelming. We actually warned the people of an impending TMC military offensive against the SPLA as early as three days after the coup, when we were reliably informed from Khartoum about the true intentions of the TMC. We said then:

The Junta's High Command made it clear in the fourth public statement that it intends to open the road and river transport . . . The intentions of the Junta are clear. The new rulers want to use force to open up these routes. All indications are that the new Junta is preparing to launch an offensive against the SPLA in their mistaken belief that this will divert the Sudanese masses. (Page 11, Statement of April 9, 1985, enclosed).

Mr. Prime Minister, how could the Junta open the roads and rivers without contacts with the SPLA, except through the use of force? Otherwise, and this is even worse, the TMC took the SPLA for granted.

10 The Free Officers Movement warned us of the Mangalla operation as early as mid-April. The TMC code-named this offensive "Sabur Ziada," or "Greater Patience" because the strategy called for a great deal of smoke-screen talk about dialogue and peace to prepare public opinion against the SPLA, while the TMC gained time to "patiently" plan and prepare the offensive. So, while you in the Council of Ministers, Trade Unions Alliance and political parties might have been genuinely calling for peace through dialogue, the TMC was preparing for peace through war. On the other hand, the SPLM/SPLA was preoccupied with preparations to destroy the offensive. This, Mr. Prime Minister, is the truth. The TMC did indeed launch the Mangalla offensive on July 8, 1985, when more than 10,000 troops attacked our positions in the Gemmeiza area. Given the material, personnel and other conditions of the Sudanese Army, it would take about two months to mass 10,000 troops in Mangalla. We were prepared and we destroyed the TMC's Mangalla "Sabur Ziada" offensive. And now, perhaps without your knowledge, but most certainly without the knowledge of most patriots in the Trade Unions and Political Alliance, the TMC, after the fiasco at Mangalla, is already preparing another offensive. This time the Sudanese people will be shocked to see the country invaded by foreign troops to guard major installations in Khartoum, while the TMC deploys most of its troops in the South.

11 Besides the military offensive, the TMC also launched a concerted media and diplomatic offensive against the SPLM/SPLA in attempts to isolate us internally and abroad. The TMC invented the incredible stories that Col./Dr. John Garang was at one point on his way to Khartoum and, at other times, that negotiations with the SPLA were at a "delicate stage." All these, of course, were fabricated to justify the Mangalla offensive. When Dr. John did not come to Khartoum (a guaranteed outcome, since no contacts had been made then with the SPLA whatsoever), when no talks took place (since the TMC did not envisage any) and public opinion had been drummed up against the SPLA, the Mangalla offensive would be justified as necessary: presumably the SPLA would be defeated and the junta would be heroes. The TMC code-named their presumed victory as "Nuzal Shambat," alluding

to air dropping of "Shambat paratroopers" between Bor and borders of neighbouring countries in order to cut off the would-be retreating SPLA. Nuzal Shambat was supposed to end in the capture of Radio SPLA.

12   On the diplomatic front, as you all know, the TMC went globetrotting (some to Tripoli, others to Addis Ababa, Nairobi, Aden, Kampala, Dar es Salaam, etc). The TMC, although well trained in footdrill, started their peace initiatives on the wrong foot by assuming that the key or keys to peace in the Sudan were locked up in these foreign capitals. This is a tragic error and an indication of the TMC's lack of faith in the Sudanese people. Whereas friendly and neighbouring countries can help, such efforts are of little value if there are no objective conditions for peace within the Sudanese body politic. But I point out this globe-trotting to underline the unpreparedness and the qualitative unsuitability of the TMC to enter serious dialogue then, and, most likely, now still.

13   The other political forces in Khartoum, besides the TMC, have been very slow in transforming their outlook(s) towards the SPLM/SPLA. I underline here the failure in Khartoum to recognize and accept the SPLM/SPLA for what it is, a national force and a national Movement. Instead, the political forces in Khartoum continue to view the SPLM/SPLA from the point of view of what they would like it to be, that is, in terms of the old North/South perceptions. It is often forgotten that the Sudan is not just North and South. The Sudan is also West, East and Centre, no matter what definitions you wish to attach to these labels. If a National Congress (Conference) were held today, there would be patriots from Western and Eastern Sudan sitting on the side of the SPLM/SPLA. Would it not be absurd for such a conference to have the "Problem of Southern Sudan" as its main agenda?

14   No, all patriots must appreciate the reality that we are a new breed of Sudanese who will not accept being fossilized into sub-citizens in the "Regions". This appreciation is necessary to peace. It boggles the mind why the political forces in Khartoum ascribe to themselves a national role and responsibility to decide on the fate of the nation as a whole (North, South, West, East and Centre) and deny this to the SPLM/SPLA, relegating it to a

"Southern Movement" that must negotiate with them for what they can "give" to the South. This attitude, of taking others for granted, is an ultimate basic cause of instability.

15   The TMC's claim to legitimacy as the Government in Khartoum, is their dubious claim that they "sided with the people on April 6, 1985", something the SPLM/SPLA did long ago in 1983 when the TMC still sided with Nimeiri. The political parties and Trade Unions were represented on the Council of Ministers for no other reason than the leading roles they played in the struggle against Nimeiri. Despite unanimity of views in Khartoum about SPLA's role in the struggle against Nimeiri, the SPLM/SPLA was never consulted in the formation of the TMC and its Council of Ministers. Membership of these structures does not concern us as such, they are Khartoum's structures, and, for now, Khartoum has the prerogative and responsibility for their formation, terms of reference and composition. I only point these out to underline the inconsistencies, the magnitude of a *crisis in perception in Khartoum*, and how others are taken for granted. Peace in the Sudan will require much more than paying lip-service to the necessity of national dialogue and transparently deceptive schemes of how to accomodate the so-called "minorities" within the economic, political and socio-cultural boundaries of the "Old Sudan". *Nobody is anybody's minority* and nobody is anybody's majority. We are all Sudanese, full stop. Above all, peace in the Sudan will require unflinching objectivity and corresponding actions that are consonant with that reality.

16   I hope that the preceding preamble provides the necessary background for you, your colleagues, the Trade Unions Alliance, the political parties and the Sudanese people in general to appreciate and discuss the resolutions of the SPLM/SPLA, which I now communicate to you. Please distribute them as widely as necessary for discussion and feedback.

17   *RESOLUTIONS OF SPLM/SPLA POLITICO-MILITARY HIGH COMMAND ON NATIONAL DIALOGUE AND PEACE IN THE SUDAN*

a   The High Command reaffirms and assures the Sudanese people that the SPLM/SPLA fights to bring about real and permanent peace and to maintain the unity and territorial integrity of the Sudan.

b   The High Command recognizes the necessity for and will continue to seek national dialogue among all political forces in the
Sudan for the formation of a "New Sudan" as was affirmed in all
our statements over Radio SPLA on 22 March, 9 April and 26–27
May 1985.

c   In the present situation, the SPLM/SPLA will come into dialogue with the other political forces, as represented by the Trade
Unions Alliance, other Unions that may be outside that Alliance,
the political parties, the Sudanese Army, and the Government of
the day in Khartoum.

d   It is the responsibility of the Government of the day in Khartoum (since it has the de facto legislative and executive powers
there) to ensure the necessary favourable conditions for national
dialogue, so that such a Government does not become an
unnecessary (armed) fetter to the national dialogue and peace.

e   Since the Transitional Military Council has taken upon itself
the responsibility for legislation in Khartoum, it must also take
the responsibility of ensuring the necessary favourable conditions
for national dialogue. Generally, the Government of the day in
Khartoum must be seen by all to be genuinely interested in and
"doing" not just talking peace. Specially, in the present situation,
in order for the SPLM/SPLA to come into national dialogue, the
TMC, as the Government of the day in Khartoum, must first do
the following:

1   Commit itself publicly to an agenda to discuss the "Problem
    of the Sudan", not the so-called "Problem of Southern
    Sudan." This concretely means convening a National Congress
    (Conference) to discuss, first, the fundamental national issues
    (such as the system of Government in Khartoum, etc), and
    then the problem of Regional Governments (federations or
    regional autonomies), second, as reflections of the structure
    of power at the centre, in Khartoum.

2   Lift the state of emergency. It is incongruous and absurd for
    the TMC to declare a cease-fire, as it has done, and maintain
    the state of emergency at the same time.

3   Commit itself publicly to dissolve the TMC and the Council
    of Ministers, all to be replaced by a new Interim Government
    of National Unity, representing all the political forces, includ-
    ing the two warring armies (SPLA and the Sudanese Army),
    and that as shall be agreed upon at said National Congress.
    (The SPLM/SPLA was not a party to the formation of the

TMC and the Council of Ministers. The two structures must, therefore, be dissolved and replaced by new structures agreed to by all involved.)

4 Cancel Nimeiri's *Sharia* Laws. It is pointless for the SPLM/SPLA to participate in a conference of national dialogue within the context of *Sharia* Laws. It is an objective indication of lack of seriousness to gloss things over by talking about exempting the South or any other region from (any) national laws: and it is meaningless to talk about "modifying" the *Sharia* Laws. Nobody will be amused by such phraseological niceties, and finally

5 Cancel two personal agreements made by Field Marshal Jaffar Nimeiri with Egypt, that is, the Defence Pact and the Economic and Political Integration Treaty: and also cancel the other personal agreement made recently by Brigadier (PSC) Osman Abdhalla with Libya, also a defence arrangement. Without any prejudice to good-neighbourly relations with these two sister countries, such agreements, which commit the whole Sudanese people and which impinge on statehood (or sovereignty), can only be made by the whole Sudanese people in plebiscite, never by individuals.

18 I end, Mr. Prime Minister, by wishing you the best of regards and health. Please convey our greetings to all the political forces in the country and assure them that the struggle continues. It is our hope that the necessary mutations have matured within the Sudanese body politic to enable most of us to find it necessary and have the will to shed our various parochialisms, which are obstacles to peace, and to combine forces to create a New Sudan that truly belongs to all of us, no matter our (accidental) region, "tribe", race, or religion. We look forward to hearing from all of you.

Yours sincerely:

J.G.

Letter from Dr. El-Gizouli Dafaalla to John Garang, 10 November 1985

Dear John,
I wish to thank you for your letter of September 1, 1985 which I

only received on October 11, 1985, the eve of my departure on a foreign tour from which I have just returned.

I have discussed the contents of your letter with my colleagues at the Council of Ministers at great length and, in the light of the said deliberations, I am sending you this response.

First: It is indeed gratifying and reassuring to note that SPLM/SPLA stands for dialogue and for peaceful settlement of all major outstanding national problems and for the creation of a just and democratic society within a united Sudan. The political forces which have struggled to bring down the dictatorial May regime have always rcognized the effective role played by the SPLM/SPLA which helped get rid of that corrupt and oppressive rule. From this angle, it is perhaps a paradox that, in spite of the fact that the common enemy of the Sudanese People has been defeated and that seven months have elapsed since then, we are still struggling to stand united on a joint platform to rebuild a united democratic Sudan to befit our patriotic aspirations.

Second: My reaction to your reference that certain points may have been distorted, misunderstood or not taken seriously in Khartoum is that we also felt here inside the Sudan that there are certain facts about April 6 revolution and other political realities which have been misunderstood or not correctly conceived by the SPLM/SPLA. This, we feel is mainly due to the SPLM/SPLA's physical distance from the internal political scene, our mutual inability to establish proper channels of communication for constructive dialogue and, perhaps, the distortions reflected by local elements in Sudan or misinformed reporters and commentators in the international mass media.

This failure in communication has not helped maintain the positive image of the SPLM/SPLA in the minds of members of the general Sudanese public. In particular, I would like to emphasize the following:

SPLM/SPLA attitude towards the TMC as a representative of Nimeiri's Generals who "took over" power and who may not be serious about transferring it to the People in a democratic process. Also SPLM/SPLA contention that it was not consulted in the formation of the TMC and the Council of Ministers.

SPLM/SPLA call on the workers, professionals and students Unions to continue the strikes until "the Generals" hand over power to the People and the view that the Trade Unions Alliance and political parties have "capitulated" to TMC.

SPLM/SPLA continued denunciation of the TMC and its accusation of planning a major military offensive to achieve "military victory" over SPLA so that "they become heroes and entrench themselves in power."

SPLM/SPLA accusation of the TMC launching a concerted media and diplomatic offensive against SPLM/SPLA to isolate them internally and abroad.

I feel that the above are extremely significant points which have to be clarified for the sake of proper mutual understanding and struggle for peace, democracy and unity. In this connection, let me outline the following:

1   Both the TMC and the Council of Ministers were given their mandate as governing constitutional bodies by the forces that brought about the revolutionary change and, as such, enjoy the support of the National Alliance including the Armed Forces.

To describe the Armed Force's decision to align themselves with the People on April 6 as a "take over" of power by the "Generals" is a misconception of a clear political reality. It follows from this that it is also untrue to state that the National Alliance Forces have "capitulated" to the TMC.

The political forces that made the popular revolution have freely accepted the establishment of the TMC as a political necessity in the wake of the Popular Revolution. You may recall that when you made your statement of April 9, 1985 denouncing what you described as a "take over" by the Generals and gave seven day's notice for them to transfer power to the People, the National Alliance forces of which I was then President, broadcast a statement on April 10, 1985 recognizing the role of SPLM/SPLA in bringing to an end the dictatorial regime and calling upon the Movement to join hands with the revolutionary forces. In that same statement we expressed our concern about your statement of April 9 and called upon you to join the political forces in the formation of the government and participation in the interim period.

The TMC and the Council of Ministers have worked and continued to work closely together within the framework provided by the approved Interim Constitution. (A copy of the Interim Constitution is attached).

I have no hesitation in assuring you that both Councils are committed to dialogue, peaceful settlement of national issues and surrender of power to an elected government at the end of the interim period that is ordained to end by April 1986.

As for contention that the SPLM/SPLA was not consulted in the formation of the TMC and the Council of Ministers, I should reiterate that we had no doubt then that you would arrive in Khartoum soon after April 6. Instead, SPLM/SPLA reacted by the referred statement of April 9 and the mentioned National Alliance forces statement of April 10 received no response from SPLM/SPLA.

2   Your letter referred to several military operations within what you described as the TMC plan to achieve military victory over SPLA and entrench themselves in power. Firstly, as I have emphasized above, there is no truth in accusing the TMC of trying to entrench itself in power. This will be contrary to the National Charter which defines the political contract accepted by the people, the political forces and the Armed Forces. Secondly, the TMC, the Council of Ministers and all the political and popular forces in the Sudan have and continue to reject any military solution to any of our problems because such a solution is neither desirable nor attainable. In such battles or wars there is no victor or vanquished and, in all cases, only loss of Sudanese lives and resources and destruction of all prospects for democracy and national unity. Finally, the question of military operations has to be taken in its proper perspective. If we talk about battles and incidents planned by the TMC or the Sudanese Armed Forces we will have to take that in the context of battles and incidents planned and executed by the SPLA and publicly acknowledged by SPLM/SPLA in various parts of the country including Kordofan, Darfur and all parts of the South. I should not dwell unduly on this point but it is perhaps essential to bear in mind that there may be arguments and counter-arguments on both sides. Whilst you have highlighted certain operations, the Armed Forces can, I am sure, be prepared to enumerate operations and incidents by the SPLA where they could not and cannot want to be seen to stand aloof nor would ordinary citizens expect them not to react. They naturally consider it the proper duty of the army to protect them and their property against any aggression.

3   The contention that the TMC has launched a concerted media

and diplomatic offensive against SPLM/SPLA does not seem to be well founded. What is reflected in the mass media is the normal news of the progress, or the lack of it, towards a peaceful settlement and, to this extent, the media has carried both the positive and negative aspects of the military and political news. Your interpretation of this may be matched by the interpretation of those who listen to Radio SPLM.

As for the diplomatic front, you would agree that the defunct May regime has done serious damage to the country's external relations internationally, regionally and, especially, with neighbouring countries such as Ethiopia and Libya. This has made it imperative, within the principles of April 6 Revolution and the National Charter, to move swiftly to repair such damage and to restore normal relations with friendly countries. The TMC, before the formation of the Government, which took some time, had to move in this direction in several African and Arab countries. The Government continued the same policy after its formation in the spirit of normalization of diplomatic relations.

Third: The fact that the Sudan faces tremendous constitutional, political, economic and social difficulties can hardly be over-emphasized. Within that context, the South may be considered the epitome which brings these problems into focus. It was with this in mind that the Council of Ministers announced its Preliminary Political Declaration on August 25, 1985 which emphasized the need to address ourselves to these problems from a national viewpoint in a National Congress with particular emphasis on the South. Since all the political forces have agreed that the proposed Congress should address itself to such national issues from this perspective we are in no disagreement on the principle of convening a National Congress.

With this understanding, the issues described in the Preliminary Political Declaration form the basic Agenda for the proposed congress in addition to whatever other proposals the parties concerned may wish to make. As I mentioned in my first letter to you "Nobody has a ready panacea for all our ailments. Nobody is satisfied with all we have achieved so far but revolution is a continuous process. Together we succeed, fragmentation is the surest way to failure. The political field is now teeming with the future scenarios and your contribution can easily find a place in this mosaic." All this is as true now as it was on June 1, perhaps even more so.

Such a national congress should deal with and, hopefully, reach consensus on how to resolve all the country's major problems. It is hoped that such consensus will be included in a National Charter to which all parties will commit themselves to abide by, and to include in the country's Permanent Constitution. This will consequently exclude regional or partial solutions and will reflect the agreement of all parties concerned and accommodate all interests.

Fourthly: This having been said, it is clear that the proposed congress will address itself to all our major problems: in particular, the constitutional issues relating to the form of government, the source and type of laws which will be applied to ensure justice, economic and social equality; economic planning for development of all parts of the country, equitable distribution of national wealth, determination of the shares of individual regions in local natural resources. . . . etc.

In this context, it is quite legitimate to expect the TMC and the Council of Ministers to fulfill their respective responsibilities to ensure that all favourable conditions, including adequate security measures, are made for a useful and constructive national dialogue.

Once such arrangements are satisfactorily ensured, and once it is agreed that *all* major national issues will be dealt with and, hopefully, adequately resolved and agreed upon, it will not be logical for any party at all to attempt to impose any preconditions prior to the convening of the Congress.

As such, some of the points enumerated in paragraph 17 (e) of your letter would not seem to be justified at this present stage. We are determined to lift the state of emergency prior to the date of the Congress, provided the conditions for its imposition are no longer there. The Congress should also be in a position to discuss the structures of government during the remainder of the transitional period. The *Sharia* Laws will be within the Agenda for the Congress. The same could apply to the Defence Pact and Economic and Political Integration Treaty with Egypt as well as the Agreement with Libya within the context of Sudan's relations and mutual interests with the two countries. Whatever is agreed upon and included in the proposed charter should bind all parties.

Fifthly: Summing up, having endeavoured to make some clarifications which I trust will clear the clouds which have prevailed due to lack of channels of communication and which resulted in distortions and misunderstandings causing unnecessary loss of Sudanese lives and waste of national resources. I would like to reiterate my feelings of satisfaction on the many positive aspects of your letter emphasizing *SPLM/SPLA commitment to permanent peace and maintenance of the unity and territorial integrity of our nation and SPLM/SPLA recognition of the need for dialogue among all political forces in the Sudan.* On my part, I would like to reciprocate by assuring you that this is also the unequivocal wish of all political and popular forces including the TMC and the Council of Ministers. *We are all firmly committed to peace and dialogue to resolve our national problems within a free, democratic and united Sudan.* Let us pool our resources and put our hands together and work to convene the National Congress at the earliest possible opportunity in order to realize the acute yearning of the Sudanese people for Democracy and Unity.

I will be pleased to hear your reaction especially in connection with any proposals you may have on the necessary arrangements and possible dates for convening the proposed National Congress.

Finally, I wish to conclude this message by thanking you for your letter and reciprocating my wishes of best regards for you and your colleagues in the SPLM/SPLA.

Let us all pray that all this will not be in vain. My personal conviction is that it will not.

Yours Sincerely,
Dr. El-Gizouli Dafalla,
Prime Minister

Letter from the General Secretary of the Trade Unions Alliance to John Garang, 2 May 1985

Dear Brother,
I would like, on behalf of the Trade Unions Alliance, to express our deep appreciation of the role played by the Sudan People's Liberation Movement in the struggle against the infamous May regime and in the propagation of revolutionary ideas which the Trade Unions Alliance shares fully with you. We believe that the

struggle ahead of us is going to be much more difficult than the struggle against Nimeiri's dictatorship, hence our call to you as a comrade-in-arms to join hands with us in the struggle to establish a truly democratic and free society.

We further believe that the unity of all national democratic forces in our country is of paramount importance at this stage of the country's development as you yourself have indicated on several occasions.

I have the honour to introduce to you Dr. Faroug Mohamed Ibrahim who is fully authorized and empowered to make preliminary contacts with you on behalf of the Trade Unions Alliance.

Dr. Ibrahim enjoys the full confidence of the Alliance and I hope it will be possible for him to discuss with you the modalities as well as the venue for further contacts and deliberations with you or your representatives with a view to finding a genuine, comprehensive and democratic solution to the problems of our country.

Dr. Ibrahim will also explain to you our viewpoint as to the recent developments in the political situation in our country.

With the opportunity given to our representative to meet you, we sincerely hope to come to a common understanding as to the ways and means of attaining our immediate and common goal of National Unity as well as realizing our strategic objectives for a harmonious and equitable development for the different regions of our beloved country.

In the hope of receiving a prompt and positive response to our request, I would like to express to you the assurances of my highest consideration and regards.

Awad-Al-Karim Mohammad Ahmad
Secretary General of the Trade Unions Alliance

Letter from John Garang to Dr. Khalid Yagi, President of the Council of the National Alliance for National Salvation, 9 October 1985

Mr President
Greetings in the name of the struggle of the Sudanese people.

We appreciate your patriotic concern over the future of our nation and our joint efforts for finding suitable solutions to the fundamental problems which face it, as shown by your message which has been recently delivered to our office by your representative Dr Taisier Mohamed Ali. Your message and its contents have met from us the attention it deserves; positive response. As you in the Alliance have expressed concern over how we can approach our national problems we in the SPLA/SPLM welcome this development. Because of the importance we attach to this approach I decided that I should come to meet your representative personally.

During the meetings we had with your representative we were able to exchange views on the current political situation in our country in general and in reference to the suggestions in your message. Our discussions were cordial and mutually useful.

It is our considered opinion that the SPLA/SPLM politico-military leadership welcomes the exploration and opening up of channels of contacts between you in the Alliance and the SPLA/SPLM. We are convinced that such contacts would be in the interest of our people. For this reason we propose that a joint meeting between representatives of the SPLA/SPLM be held during the first week of December 1985. However, as you may be aware of the nature of our responsibilities, that date is subject to alteration as may be dictated by unforeseen circumstances. In such an event we shall notify you in good time.

Finally, please accept the sincere regards of the SPLA/SPLM politico-military leadership in the course of our joint struggle for the creation of a new Sudan.

Col. Dr. John Garang de Mabior
Commander-in-chief of the SPLA/SPLM, and Chairman of the SPLM Executive Committee

Letter from Dr. Yagi, President of the Council of the National Alliance for National Salvation, to John Garang, 26 October 1985

Dear Mr. Chairman,
Thank you for your letter of the 9th October which we received with great interest and which was thoroughly discussed in the Council of the National Alliance.

Your letter, and the goodwill it generated, gained further

impetus from the cease fire declared by the SPLA/SPLM on October 19th. Both the letter and the cease fire, created a new situation in which additional groups perceived with greater urgency the need to seize the opportunity and speed up our intended dialogue.

We are keen that such a dialogue remains representative of the broad spectrum of all political currents included in the Alliance. In view of above mentioned developments, such a task, we trust you recognize, is not an easy one, as it is difficult to compress all diverse stances in any one delegation. We therefore would like to propose that a delegation from the SPLA/SPLM visit Khartoum and to which we are prepared to extend all satisfactory guarantees. Such a step, we genuinely believe would better serve the purpose of launching our joint initiative for a national dialogue on a scale that would give the SPLA/SPLM a most accurate, realistic and truly representative appreciation of the alliance and the post-uprising political situation at home.

In addition, Mr. Chairman, we remain committed to spare no effort to consolidate and enhance the cease fire which we hope both parties would maintain and extend.

Moreover, we hope that during the proposed visit by representatives of SPLA/SPLM, we would be able to lay down the necessary foundation of the National Conference which you referred to in your letter to Dr. Gizouli on September 1st and of which we have received a copy only recently after the return of our emissary. Copies of this particular letter were made available to all political forces in the Alliance.

Once again, Mr. Chairman, allow me to express our hope that it would be possible to have in Khartoum, among their brethren and compatriots, representatives of the SPLA/SPLM.

Best regards,
Yours truly,
Dr. Khalid Yagi,
President, Council of the National Alliance for National Salvation

Letter from Dr. Garang to Dr. Yagi, 23 December 1985

Dear Compatriots in the National Alliance for National Salvation:

1 Greetings in the name of the struggle of the Sudanese people.

No doubt you in the National Alliance and we in the SPLM/SPLA have the future of our beloved Sudan at heart. In our various ways, using various forms of struggle we succeeded in bringing down dictator Nimeiri. We are all proud, satisfied and we applaud the Sudanese masses for accomplishing this great feat. We are convinced beyond any shade of doubt that the Sudanese people have even greater victories ahead.

2   The solidarity between the SPLM/SPLA and the National Alliance stems from the irrefutable fact that the two organisations were in the same trenches against Nimeiri. Our solidarity with you is therefore based on concrete realities of struggle, of having fought together against a common enemy. The necessity to fight together to destroy the whole edifice of Nimeirism and to build a new Sudan, a new Sudan of real democracy, progress, equality and justice for all irrespective of tribe, race, religion or any other form of localism that still remains is even more necessary in the months and years ahead.

3   To fight together and succeed, it is absolutely necessary that there must be full confidence between the National Alliance and the SPLM/SPLA and that communications between the National Alliance and the SPLM/SPLA must not allow room for distortion or deception and therefore misunderstanding and embarrassment. Any message(s) from the National Alliance to the SPLM and vice versa must be conveyed in documented form so that it reaches the recipient in the intended form. Verbal messages, especially of very important matters, can allow room for distortion, deception, trickery, etc., and this cannot be in the interests of the National Alliance, the SPLM/SPLA or the Sudanese people, and must therefore be avoided.

4   I now specifically refer to our letter of November 4th, 1965, addressed to the National Alliance through its Council's President, Dr. Yagi and entrusted to Dr. Taisier for delivery. A copy of this letter is here attached. Instead of this letter being discussed and replied by the National Alliance, a story was created in Khartoum that the SPLM/SPLA had accepted to come to Khartoum and to the Wadi Medani meeting. The local press made a great deal of fuss about SPLM/SPLA's alleged coming to Khartoum. The National Alliance even drew up a programme to receive an SPLM/SPLA delegation in Khartoum. All this was and is still very

unfortunate. There developed a failure of communication between the Alliance and the SPLM/SPLA. We in the SPLM/SPLA, when we were hearing in the press about our coming to Khartoum, were asking ourselves "Why is the National Alliance making such fabrications?" And most of you in the Alliance who were not or are still not aware of our November 4th letter must have felt disappointed. The simple and true explanation is that there was a breakdown in communication between the SPLM/SPLA and the National Alliance. Whether this was done in good or in bad faith it should not have happened. It is very difficult, if not impossible, to cheat history!

5   Our letter of November 4th (true copy, enclosed) is very, very unambiguous about our coming to Khartoum. The five points as the letter states in its opening are *"directives"* from the SPLM/SPLA Politico-Military High Command to our coordination office in Addis Ababa to be communicated *"verbatim"*, as stated at the end of the letter, to you in the National Alliance as a reply to your letter of October 26 . . . Our letter is unambiguous and it was written after full consultation with all members of the High Command, which is our highest political and military authority. The SPLM/SPLA is therefore not responsible for the misinformation that an SPLM/SPLA delegation was coming to Khartoum or Medani and for your subsequent embarrassment. The responsibility lies fully on Dr. Taisier, the bearer of the letter, and Dr. Yagi to whom the letter was addressed. They owe the National Alliance an explanation as to why the letter was not delivered. I am aware that there is a story that there was some protracted discussion between Dr. Taisier and members of our Addis Ababa office who "agreed" that the SPLM/SPLA was sending a delegation. This story cannot be believed by any serious minded person, given the contents of our letter and the fact that the Addis office, like any other SPLM/SPLA office abroad, do not have powers to decide issues like the sending of a delegation to Khartoum! In the absence of any official letter from SPLM/SPLA GHQ of November 4th, the story may make sense to some people, but given the reality of the presence of the letter and the fact that it was hidden from the Alliance, our Addis office stands resolved of any responsibility for the incident.

6   In order to clear the air of this unfortunate incident, and as we have information that our November 4th letter is still not

public knowledge to most members of the National Alliance and in order to conduct political dialogue on an objective and trustworthy basis in the future it is necessary that:

a   Our November 4th letter be read in full meetings of the National Alliance, which we know you hold weekly, so that the Alliance is fully informed and so that public responsibility and accountability of the failure in communication is traced to its source within the Alliance so that it does not repeat itself in the future as our contacts are bound to continue.

b   The National Alliance replies to our letter of November 4th as this is still the last official correspondance between the SPLM/SPLA and the National Alliance.

7   Dear compatriots, I end by assuring you that the doors of cooperation and dialogue between the SPLM/SPLA and the National Alliance for National Salvation still remain open. However, this last incident in which the National Alliance was kept in the dark about our 4th of November letter must first be cleared, so that confidence and credibility are restored and so that it does not repeat itself in our future dealings. Until we are satisfied by the National Alliance that the air is cleared of this incident the SPLM/SPLA will not receive any delegation from National Alliance as this would serve no purpose when the air is polluted with possibilities of distortion, deceptions, trickeries and lack of trust. We are all revolutionaries, both in the SPLM/SPLA and in the National Alliance. Let us take each other seriously so that we save our nation. Thank you, and greetings and regards to all in the National Alliance. We assure you that the struggle continues.

Col. Dr. John Garang de Mabior,
Chairman and Commander-in-Chief, SPLM/SPLA Politico-Military High Command

Letter from John Garang to Samuel Aru Bol, Deputy Prime Minister and President of SSPA, 19 October 1985

Dear Brother,
1   I received your letter of August, 1985 together with the copy of the SSPA document addressed to the TMC, signed by Brother Lual Lual Akuey, and concerning SSPA position on the current

political issues in the country. We read with interest all the views expressed in those two letters, and we concur with many of them. However, I could not immediately reply as I was at the front.

2   The struggle by regional political groupings and/or parties for the rights of Sudan's backward areas is a subject of the Struggle of the masses of the Sudanese people for democracy, human dignity, progress, equal opportunity and justice. The SPLM/SPLA has undertaken to spearhead this noble goal using all means, both political and military. The contributions(s) to this effort by the SSPA, SSK(SAC), GUN, Sudan National Party, Darfur Development Front, Armed Force for Western Sudan and other regional structures is acknowledged and appreciated by the SPLM/SPLA. Indeed, during both war and "peace", the incidence of suffering falls very heavily and unbearably on the backward areas, which are represented by these regional political groupings. The SPLM/SPLA, therefore, has every reason to cooperate with regional political groupings so as, at the minimum, to seek and find ways and means to ameliorate the human suffering in those areas affected by war and natural disasters.

3   I have been briefed on meetings held in Addis Ababa by our side and an SSPA two-man delegation. I also learned that your side specifically wanted to talk with me. Unfortunately, I was in Nasir area at both times, and we were also satisfied that your delegation had been met at the appropriate level. On our side both meetings were headed by Major Alfred Lado Gore, Secretary of our Ideology Committee and membership of Captains Deng Alor Kuol and Marko Maciec. I am informed that the discussions went well and were fruitful to both sides.

4   However should you feel that there is need to have further discussions between the SSP and the SPLM/SPLA, at a higher or similar level, I assure you here that we are willing and ready. In point of fact, many changes have occurred since August, including our letter to the Prime Minister Dr. El-Gizouli Dafaalla. I therefore take this opportunity to formally invite an SSPA delegation either to Addis Ababa or our GHQs in Southern Sudan. If there is need I can be available at such a meeting.

5   Again, I acknowledge and thank you for your correspondence and initiative. Please pass our greetings and regard to all members of the SSPA, and assure them that the struggle continues, whether it rains spears or fire.

In the struggle,

Col./Dr. John Garang de Mabior, Chairman, PEC, SPLM & Commander-in-Chief, SPLA.

Letter from the General Secretariat of the Congress of Trade Unions and Political Parties to John Garang

Greetings
The forces that are behind the great April revolution and which acknowledge the role that your movement played in the demise of the oppressive and repressive regime strongly believe that there are no substitutes to national dialogue as a way of removing the obstacles hindering the progress of this nation.

Accordingly, the forces of the popular uprising represented in this congress are preparing for a National Conference in which all the parties that have endorsed the National Charter on 12–11–1985 shall meet in order to approve a programme of action.

Given the high regard with which we respect your Movement we should like to invite you to participate in this National Conference which raises the banner of "A Unified and Democratic Sudan". We sincerely hope that you will play a prominent role in this conference and wish to point out that this conference is not a substitution for the Constitutional Conference which the Prime Minister has called for. We hope that the National Conference will prepare the ground for the latter.

We wish to establish the following time-table:
1 The proclamation for the Conference, 3–9–85
2 Report on the preparation for the Conference, 5–11–85.

We welcome you amongst the ranks of the leaders of the Sudanese National Alliance assembled in the glorious city of Wad Medani; unity of ranks is needed more than ever before.

Joint Communiqué by SPLA/SPLM and SSPA, 8 February 1986

After lengthy, elaborate, frank and constructive discussions conducted on 2.2.86 and 4.2.86 by the SPLA/SPLM and the SSPA on the current outstanding national problems of the Sudan, the two high-level delegates of the above-mentioned organisations agree to make the following communiqué:

1 The SPLA/SPLM and the SSPA recognize that the root causes of Sudan's chronic social and political instability are essentially national. As such, they should be tackled nationally, which, in the view of both the SPLA/SPLM and SSPA, necessarily envisages the forging of a *NATIONAL DEMOCRATIC CONSENSUS* by all the country's *NATIONAL DEMOCRATIC AND PATRIOTIC FORCES.*

2 Both the SPLA/SPLM and the SSPA acknowledge that the overthrow of the May regime through the combined thrust of SPLA military exploits in the bush and the relentless mass political action in the streets of our cities, marked a significant leap forward in the struggle of the Sudanese masses for a NEW SUDAN; it was also a starting point for the realization of the NATIONAL DEMOCRATIC CONSENSUS. The two sides further believe that this revolutionary gain should be protected consolidated and developed so that the country does not revert back to the dictatorship and chaos of the Nimeiri era.

3 Both the SPLA/SPLM and the SSPA believe that, in order to achieve the *NATIONAL DEMOCRATIC CONSENSUS* and thereby bring about *DURABLE PEACE, SOCIAL JUSTICE, NATIONAL UNITY* and *PROGRESS*, a process of *DIALOGUE* among the *NATIONAL DEMOCRATIC* and *PATRIOTIC FORCES* should quickly and vigorously be undertaken and a *NATIONAL DEMOCRATIC PROGRAMME* arrived at.

4 Within the context of such a programme the SPLA/SPLM and the SSPA hereby affirm the need for convening a National conference to solve the problems of our country, such as the Nationality and Religious Questions, the laying down of a *CONSTITUTIONAL FRAMEWORK FOR A NEW SYSTEM OF GOVERNMENT*, as well as resolving once and for all, the serious imbalance inherent in the unequal socio-economic development levels of the relatively developed areas of the Sudan on the one hand, the relatively backward areas on the other.

5 In order to create a conducive atmosphere for convening such a conference, SPLA/SPLM and SSPA deem it necessary that:

i   The September 1983 Laws and the State Security Act 1973, be immediately repealed;

ii   The state of emergency be lifted;

iii   Military and/or political agreements between former Dictator Nimeiry and Egypt be abrogated;

vi   Military Protocols concluded between Sudan and Libya be cancelled.

v   There should be a commitment to solve the PROBLEMS of Sudan and not the so-called Problem of Southern Sudan;

vi   Both the TMC and the CM should make prior commitment to dissolve themselves after such a conference in order to pave the way for the formation of a broad-based national government.

6   The venue and time for such a conference shall be agreed upon by all the political forces concerned, but without prejudice to the right of the forces concerned to select a venue of their own choice. However, both the SPLA/SPLM and the SSPA strongly believe that the selected venue should as much as possible offer an atmosphere absolutely conducive to the attainment of the conference's desired objectives.

7   Profoundly dedicated to the goal of actively partaking of any endeavours to improving the lot of Sudan's backward RURAL AREAS, both the SPLA/SPLM and SSPA view the emergence of *REGIONAL POLITICAL GROUPS* as a natural revolt against the appalling conditions in which the masses live in those areas. It is further considered that the appearance of *SUDAN RURAL SOLIDARITY* (SRS) in the Sudanese political arena is a manifestation of the sharp contradictions between the RURAL and the URBAN Sudan, and that SRS could be one of the possible ways of convergence into a *NATIONAL DEMOCRATIC CONSENSUS*.

8   Both the SPLA/SPLM and the SSPA recognize the unacceptable situation in which many people find themselves today in the Sudan as a result of disasters. Consequently, the efforts being made by the SUDAN RELIEF AND REHABILITATION ASSOCIATION (SRRA) in soliciting relief aid to people affected by famine and other disasters are commendable, and that, from a purely humanitarian standpoint, both the SPLA/SPLM and the SSPA deem it necessary for actual and prospective donor organizations to consider channelling relief aid to needy areas in the

Sudan through SRRA; SRRA being strictly a non-political relief association.

Signed:

1 Major Deng Alor Kuol for SPLA/SPLM

2 Lawrence Lual Lual for SSPA

Chapter Four:

Peace Around the Corner

It has taken Khartoum nine months to come to terms with the realities of the situation: if there was to be dialogue it would have to address the Sudanese political crisis in its entirety, rather than the problem of the South. To this end the National Alliance; over the head of its inept government, decided to bear the brunt. Following the exchanges between the Alliance and the Movement, both parties agreed on a framework and an agenda for national dialogue. The two parties met in Koka Dam, Ethiopia, in March 1984 and committed themselves not only to a dialogue between themselves but also to broadening the debate to include others. This debate was meant to be a prelude to the convocation of a national constitutional conference which was to seek a comprehensive solution to national problems that "were rendered complex during the *past three decades*."

Alongside the Alliance the Movement has also held separate discussions with the Southern Sudanese Politicians Association (SSPA), an amalgam of traditional Southern politicians, many of whom lived through the ordeals of the last decades. In its turn the SSPA committed itself to work for the convening of a national constitutional conference. It is noteworthy that the joint declaration between the SPLM and SSPA has underlined as preconditions to the constitutional conference the following:

1   abolition of the so-called Islamic laws imposed by Nimeiri in September 1983
2   the lifting of the state of emergency
3   the abolition of military pacts with Egypt and Libya concluded both by Nimeiri (in the case of the former) and the TMC (in the case of the latter)
4   a commitment by all parties to resolve the problems of Sudan (and *not* the so-called problem of the South)
5   the dissolution of the government in place to be replaced by a broad-based national government.

The first preparatory meeting between the SPLM/SPLA and the National Alliance took place in Koka Dam, Ethiopia on 20 March 1986. That meeting was attended by all political forces in the Sudan excepting two parties: the Democratic Unionist Party (DUP), the Khatmiya-based political organization, and the Muslim Brothers.

Addressing that meeting the SPLM leader underlined the commitment of the Movement to national unity, democracy and social and economic liberation. The meeting was neither acrimonious nor unaccommodating; in less than a week the minds of the parties were at one, and all committed themselves to an open national dialogue on the basic problems of Sudan and not the so-called Southern problem. It was also agreed that a national constitutional conference be convened in Khartoum in the first week of June 1986 and that a joint follow-up mechanism be established. As for the preconditions for the preparation of the conference it was agreed by both parties that the September laws be repealed, the state of emergency lifted, military pacts with Egypt and Libya abolished and steps be taken by the two sides to effect a cease-fire. It was also agreed that in the interim period, the Sudan constitution of 1956, as amended in 1964, with incorporation of "regional government" and all such matter *on which a consensus opinion of all political forces* shall be reached, be adopted. Following the implementation of all those conditions, a broad government of national unity, in which the SPLM shall participate, would be formed to replace the government in place. The signatories to this understanding were not only the representatives of the professional and workers' trade unions but also major political formations in the Sudan including the Umma Party, the Communist Party, the Baathists and pan-Arabists, all Southern Sudanese parties, newly formed progressive fronts as well as the alliance of Rural Fores, which comprised all regionally based political organizations.

At all events the Koka Dam meeting and declaration in March 1985 were a breakthrough in the search for a consensus of opinion among the democratic and peace-loving forces of the Sudan on the problems of the nation and how to tackle them. That declaration paved the way for the holding of a Constitutional Conference in Sudan in the last week of June 1986. The SPLM showed no reluctance to come to Khartoum once the conditions for coming, including the abolition of the 1983 *Sharia* laws and freezing of military pacts with Egypt and Libya, were met. The removal of the Transitional Military Council and government, in time, became a moot question. If those conditions were not met, it was not because of the SPLM. None the less the question persisted in Khartoum "Why is the SPLM fighting? The question was suspect, for were the SPLM guided by the same crooked thinking and distorted logic of its Khartoum critics it should have concluded that, either the signatories to the Koka Dam agreement were not serious or that they were afraid to face the reality of a genuine debate and, therefore, failed to implement the Koka Dam prerequisites for peace. It is no secret that the question of ceasefire was openly raised at the Koka Dam meeting and it was agreed that the matter should only be discussed after the stage was set for the realization of the other prerequisites which meant the abolition of the September Laws and military pacts and the lifting of the state of emergency. Up to that point the continuation of war should have been of surprise to nobody. Of late these prerequisites were reduced to the abrogation of the September laws and the military pacts; the lifting of the state of emergency, it was mutually agreed, was to be tied up to the ceasefire.

This is the context in which we should read Dr. John Garang's speech opening the Koka Dam Conference and his references to Rumbek. The Rumbek incident, which involved the bombing of that town by Libyan TU22 bombers, proved the SPLM's point about the inherent danger in military pacts, involving a foreign power in local conflicts. Rumbek was the same town which government forces evacuated ("for the safety of civilians"). The Rumbek incident also proved the SPLM's respect for the safety of the ordinary Sudanese soldier who was fighting not because of political commitment but because he was trapped in the profession of being a soldier who fights on orders or for his honour. At the time, John Garang appealed to the garrison of Rumbek to form a New Army Joint command with the SPLA even though every-one knew the garrison was about to fall. The SPLA did not request the garrison soldiers to surrender their arms, out of respect for their military honour. It was obvious that the Rumbek soldiers had more in common with the SPLA "enemy", who are fighting for a new Sudan, than with the generals in Khartoum or the government which ridiculed their valiant effort to defend the garri-son by dismissing the town as being, to paraphrase the words of Dr. Gizouli Dafaalla, of no importance to his government.

The ball was, thus, in Khartoum's court where all those political formations were based. By any standard those who followed closely the history of the three years that followed Nimeiri's fall and understood well the history of the last thirty years could not but conclude that the Koka Dam declaration was a breakthrough. The SPLM, once Sudan's objective realties were accepted for what they are by Northern politicians did not need an authoris-ation from anybody to sign that declaration. John Garang, who was presumed not to be a free agent, was the first in the Movement to hail that agreement which was freely arrived at by the Sudanese themselves.

Six months elapsed after the Koka Dam declarations and no progress was registered. In the first place there was the reluctance of the transitional government and the TMC to take a bold decision on the two issues of the abolition of the September laws and the abrogation of the military pacts. Their inaction was incomprehensible, given the position taken on both issues by the political constituency that elevated them to authority. The political parties who assumed power after the transitional government would have been only too pleased, if that decision was taken by the TMC and its government, if only to be saved from the "embarrassment" of abrogating those laws, they were now left to face the music.

A new government soon thereafter ascended to power in Khar-toum after partial elections. No sooner had the results of the elections become known than the Prime Minister elect, Sadiq el Mahdi, contacted the SPLM through personal emissaries. His message comprised four questions:

1   whether the SPLM was ready to join his government?

2   if not what sort of government did they want to see in Khartoum?

3   what were the views of the Movement on the conditions necessary for the convocation of the national constitutional conference?

4   whether his meeting with John Garang was feasible?

The SPLM welcomed el Mahdi's initiative and told his emissaries that, had the Khartoum kingmakers taken a similar initiative before the TMC was firmly established, things would have been different in Sudan. The Movement, however, declined to participate in a government that resulted from a partial election; its constant position was that elections should follow, not precede, the Constitutional Conference. This view was equally voiced in Khartoum, before the elections, by Southern parties and the Alliance of the Rural Forces.

Khartoum, for its own reasons, wanted to proceed with the elections. The political landscape was overflowing with political animals of all sorts, the worthy and the unworthy, and worthiness in politics, like beauty, is in the eye of the beholder. Those elections, Khartoum thought, were needed to separate the wheat from the chaff. So the decision to hold elections in the North and dubious elections in parts of the South was dictated by reasons peculiar to the Northern-based parties, particularly those who have thought, or known, that they would carry the day because of their preparedness and the very nature of the choices offered to the people.

Another argument for holding parliamentary elections was the necessity of getting rid of the generals. Some of those generals were disinterested in continuing in power and were counting the days; the ill-conditioned among them, however, were already talking of an extended transitional period and the formation of a national government. The Movement was not insensitive to this argument; its answer was that both the SPLM and the Alliance (which included all Sudan's political parties with two exceptions) should proceed with the implementation of the Koka Dam conditions, form a widely based national government and convoke the Constitutional Conference which will put into mould the new constitution on the basis of which elections shall ensue. The aspiring generals would have been sobered by such a consensus.

For all those reasons the SPLM not only declined participation in the new government but also emphasized, for reasons of consistency, that it would have no say in the way it should be formed. However, the Movement reiterated its commitment to the Koka Dam declaration and impressed on el Mahdi's emissaries that the only road to peace was through the implementation of the conditions agreed upon in that declaration. And while there was nothing sacrosanct about Koka Dam the wobbly attitude of Khartoum regarding the two preconditions, whose fulfilment would have opened the way for dialogue and peace, did plunge the Movement in doubt, not only about the new government's commitment to the declaration, but also the sincerity of some Northern politicians. The sceptics have behind them a record of thirty years of betrayal. *"De novo*, here they come again," they must have said to themselves.

In effect, the language of officialdom in Khartoum has soon changed, Khartoum no longer talked of the abolition of the September laws but of substituting them with new laws that reflect "true Islam." But who is to determine what "true Islam" is? Nimeiri has claimed it and the Muslim Brothers still do. The record of both during the 1983–1984 bureaucratized barbarism did no honour to either and certainly did a lot of damage to Islam. For this reason the SPLM maintained that no man is good enough to impose on the Sudanese people his own vision of laws or life; the whole issue of religion and politics occupied a high place in the agenda of the Constitutional Conference and it was for nobody to prejudge that issue. The Sudan has been living without those laws for a quarter of a century, with many imams at the political helm and it could have continued to do so for a few more months, pending the national consensus on the question of religion and politics. All Khartoum Muslim leaders, the genuine and the counterfeit, have vowed an oath of allegiance, one time or another, to the "ungodly" laws with which the Sudan was governed during that quarter of a century and they had no reason to presume, therefore, that if they continued with those laws, they would he held up to execration.

But the question was not wholly holy; Khartoum politicians were being harassed by the fundamentalists in a way that might have eroded the power base of some of them, so their wavering should only be understood in the light of this extortion and blackmail. Their action was guided by the sheer arithmetic of parliamentary power. Faced with this situation some of them tried to jump both ways; this was hardly the way to face up to the realities

117

of the Sudanese situation. The choice was between keeping a government in, or dislodging it from power on the one part, and keeping the country intact, on the other.

Below is John Garang's statment to set the stage for the Koka Dam Conference as well as the final declaration of Koka Dam.

Statement by John Garang de Mabior at the Opening Session of the Preliminary Dialogue between SPLM/SPLA and the National Alliance for National Salvation, held at Koka Dam, 20 March 1986

People's Power

I greet you in the name of Sudan's able mass movement, symbolized today in this hall by the National Alliance, a mass movement that has proved to Africa and to the world in 1964 and 1985, that dictatorships, no matter how well armed, are not invincible. Sooner or later, when human tolerance reaches its boundaries, these people smash tanks with their bare fists and take the ancient regime. Specifically, I greet you in the name of the great October 1964 and our glorious March–April uprising which has brought us here now.

Finally, I greet you in the name of the United New Sudan, a democratic new Sudan of peace, progress, equality and justice for all. No matter our skin colour, no matter our ethnic group, family background, region, race, sex, beliefs or religions, there is a new Sudan that I am confident will and must soon be brought into being by our popular mass movement like October, like the March – April uprising and by revolutionary armed struggle like the SPLM/SPLA. But most certainly, and more quickly, a new Sudan that will and must be realized by a correct simultaneous application of these two forms of struggle, that is, the convergence of the mass movement and of the armed struggle.

I hail the efforts of the SPLA soldier and the peasant in the bushes and countryside of our great country and the worker, soldier, student and revolutionary intellectual in the cities and towns. I hail them for their invaluable sacrifices in their struggle against all faces of Nimeirism, oppression and exploitation and urge them on to quickly establish true peace and a happy and prosperous new Sudan. I also take this opportunity to reiterate my congratulations to each and every one of you and the Sudanese masses for bringing down that monster of a dictator called Nimeiri; although we continue to fight with the Nimeiri corpse, having cut off his head, we remain confident. We have achieved a great deal and we will indeed soon bring down the whole dirty edifice that is called Nimeirism, in all its forms. The March – April uprising has restored to the masses some of their fundamental and democratic human rights, and as a result there is a flowering and mushrooming of political parties, trade unions and associations, reaching two hundred as brother Yagi just said, for the first time in sixteen years of Nimeirism. This is a victory of the March – April uprising. The masses through various political, trade and professional organizations, are able to hold rallies and air their views, in a new breath of freedom. I don't have to remind you of this; you are free now in Khartoum. The people have regained their dignity, their ability to fight and bring down unpopular governments, be they military or civilian or quasi both. Even this great historic opportunity for this preliminary dialogue in which more than fifty Sudanese members of the SPLM/SPLA and the National Alliance sit to discuss their fundamental national problem and to prepare for a more genuine national or constitutional conference. This, in itself, is a great achievement of the March – April uprising. If we had not chased Nimeiri away, we would not be meeting today. I urge that we use this opportunity well, very well, for the sake of our forsaken country instead of using it as a platform for parading apparently transparent deceptions, lies and new schemes for maintaining the old Sudan, because this will not take us anywhere. I urge you to use this opportunity as a concrete and frank basis for initiating the development of a conducive atmosphere and conditions for creating a truly new Sudan. Finally, before I end my greetings and salutations and congratulations, I must take this opportunity to thank the Workers' Party, Government and Peoples of Ethiopia for according us the opportunity to hold this meeting in the capital of Addis Ababa, a historic city that gave birth to the OAU and also gave birth to that child of ours that is called the Addis Ababa Agreement that died in its infancy.

We proved the TMC wrong
This meeting today is a concrete realization of the beginning of real dialogue among all political forces in the Sudan and which

SPLM/SPLA and various political forces initiated and called for, a long time before the fall of Nimeiri. Despite the TMC's obstructions, by every means military and otherwise, you, the SPLA and the National Alliance for National Salvation have continuously and persistently struggled to bring it to fruition, as we are sitting here today.

I thank the Secretariat of the Alliance that has been doing this fine job: those of Taisir have been doing shuttle diplomacy; they have been the Kissingers of the Sudan. Excuse me if I am informal because, while I have to thank you also for allowing me to speak in this conference because technically I am not a member of this conference. So if I may be informal as I go along, this is because I will not be here. I will leave you so I will need to talk. Talking is good, it can produce more talks and more talks can produce peace. So the very idea that we are here is a good beginning. I congratulate each and every member of the SPLM and of the National Alliance for Salvation for proving the TMC wrong by conducting this preliminary dialogue. The success in convening this preliminary dialogue clearly indicates the total commitment of SPLM/SPLA and the National Alliance to the peaceful resolution of our problems. It will go down in the modern history of the Sudan as one of the contributions of the March – April popular uprising to which the SPLM/SPLA is, we believe, an inseparable part, to search for establishing a new Sudan. It is also another indication and assurance that persistence in the struggle of the Sudanese masses for their future will lead to final victory, under long-term minimum costs. The costs at the moment may appear to be large, but the costs in the long run may be minimized.

In this connection of proving the TMC wrong, by holding this conference, I wish to explain why the conference was late by three days as it was supposed to be held last Monday. Well on your side, some members had not and still have not arrived. But on our side the delay was caused by something more serious. It was caused by TMC itself. The TMC, as was to be expected, wanted to take advantage of this conference for military advantage. While I was to be here and talking in the conference, the military operations would be stepped up in the Sudan. As you yourselves heard over the media, the TMC vowed that they were determined to recover Rumbek and Yirol within a week; that is while I was engaged in the conference. They rushed to some neighbouring countries saying that Arabism and Islam were threatened by the

SPLA. *Mind you, it is not Sudan that is threatened – Arabism and Islam are threatened.* They said they were going to move two batallions from Juba, via Maridei to Yambio, to Tombura and to Wau. They said they were going to move two other battalions by railway from Khartoum; they are now on the way with others through Tali and others by air from Khartoum. But the Transitional Military Council makes these plans in air-conditioned offices and air-conditioned houses. They do not know what is happening in the trenches. This is true. They do not know what is really happening on the ground, in the trenches. Some of these troops in Juba, who were supposed to be taken to recapture Rumbek and Yirol, rebelled and they seized the Trans Arabian Airline to take them to Khartoum instead of Rumbek. You heard this yourselves on the BBC. These were soldiers who were beleaguered, besieged in Bor for four months. They were relieved; they went to Juba expecting to go to Khartoum. There was a new situation. Rumbek and Yirol had been captured by SPLA; the TMC wants to take them over, so they were diverted instead of being relieved to go to Khartoum. They were diverted to go to Rumbek. They said, "No, Brother, it is not logical that we leave from Bor to Rumbek," and they did it. They took the airliner and they went to Khartoum. Some others have been deceived by the Military Council and they are on their way to Rumbek and Yirol. Under these circumstances, I as Commander-in-Chief of the SPLA had to shift my troops for the new challenge and ship my ammunition from front to front. You know we have in Bahr El Ghazal, captured more than fifty trucks, Magirous and Austins. So tactical mobility and strategic mobility is not a problem for us. We can move troops from front to front within Bahr El Ghazal. And this is precisely what we did. It is not a secret. That is, you are patriots, I have to tell you this. This is precisely what I was doing. I was moving troops, reshuffling ammunition, because of this new threat to us by the TMC, of course. On their side, of course, they would say brother, why did they capture Rumbek? This is the situation of war. I had to move anti-aircraft guns to Rumbek and Yirol from other fronts. I had to create new situations for the TMC. I had to capture the Bucketwheel – this is the excavator of the Jongli Canal. Dr. Amin (an engineer in the Jongli Canal who participated in the meeting as a member of the Alliance delegation) says the excavator is in a good state. There is minimum damage but we invite the CCI, the Sudan Government

121

and the Egyptian government to check it. They can repair it and they can grease it and we protect it. We are not against the Canal; *when peace comes we in the Sudan and in Egypt will need the water*. Twenty-eight billion cubic metres of water get lost every year in those swamps. And if we do the necessary scientific things it will be to our benefit both in the Sudan and Egypt. The excavator is a very expensive machine; we would not want to destroy it. So you are welcome to grease it. We will protect you a hundred per cent.

Let us agree on Fundamentals

This is why I was late. I was preoccupied by the war situation and I have to explain this honestly and frankly to you. As this dialogue is a prelude to the proposed National Constitutional Conference that is to discuss the fundamental problems of our country, and reach a consensus, a democratic consensus on them. And this success is to breed more success on the way to real peace and prosperity. It is necessary at the onset to agree on fundamental propositions. I may be cheating you on time but I will not be here. You will be here for the rest of the days. It is necessary to agree on certain fundamental propositions, some of which have been stated on more than one occasion by the SPLM and by the Alliance itself. Such propositions, simple propositions, are:

1   That it is the Sudanese people alone who can bring real and lasting peace to the country. And that the forces of peace must identify themselves because we are not all homogeneous. There are forces of peace and there are forces of war. The forces of peace must identify themselves so that they bring about peace. We believe that, the National Alliance being one, there are genuine forces for peace and for a new Sudan. In this connection the National Alliance is a genuine representative of the aspirations, genuine aspirations, of the Sudanese people: *you are of course heterogeneous just as we are heterogeneous, we are a movement*. I appeal to the National Alliance that whether there are elections, or there are no elections, whether there are partial or complete elections, that the National Alliance must not commit suicide by dissolving itself. You must remain as a National Alliance. There are those who may not wish to remain in the National Alliance for whatever reason; they can quit, while the National Alliance remains. And it would even remain stronger as it would have

purged itself of various persons. This is my advice to you. You take it or leave it. But we strongly recommend that you remain as an Alliance, as a force. If you are going to dissolve yourselves after the elections, partial or otherwise, then you only come to Addis Ababa for excursions; those talks we have initiated shall have come to a dead end. Because with whom shall we go to talk after this if you come to an end after the elections?

2   Another simple proposition similar to our first proposition is that the solution to the Sudanese problems are for us, we, the Sudanese. I have seen every time SPLA hits somewhere, people run outside to look for solutions, not inside the Sudan. It is for security reasons that we could not hold this meeting in Khartoum. But I assure you we would have loved to hold this meeting in Khartoum.

3   Another simple proposition is that the solutions to the fundamental problems of our country are not beyond attainment, we only need to be frank and serious. And I assure you that we, in the SPLA, shall be sharp in our frankness, as sharp as sharpness itself. Because there is nothing that we fear, we talk, we speak our minds because that is what it means to be free. If you refuse to say that this is a spade when it is a spade, then I present to you that you are not free. And this is our position in the SPLA and SPLM and this . . . should be the position of all human beings, not only in the Sudan. In the whole world people should be free, so that when they see a snake, they say it is a snake. When they see a spade, they say it is a spade.

4   The fourth simple proposition is that the necessary objective conditions exist for stopping the Sudan from disintegrating into fragments, inviting new recolonization and deepening crisis. Those internal conditions exist; similar external conditions exist in combination with the internal conditions also to tear the Sudan into pieces something that has already been referred to by some people as the Lebanonization of the Sudan, a situation no true Sudanese patriot would wish to see. But these two possibilities are there. We can be frank, honest and solve our problems or we can disintegrate.

These simple and obvious propositions are necessary in order to correctly perceive the Sudanese realities and thereby be able to transform it and avert an impending disaster. This dialogue which we are holding, this preliminary dialogue, is meant to bring nearer the views of SPLM/SPLA and the political forces represented by the National Alliance for National Salvation on the fundamental problems of the country, and on the ways and means to resolve them. One of the ways to bring closer the views of the two sides mentioned above is to know the views of each other and to have a correct outlook towards one another *and not to take each other for granted*. The SPLA/SPLM must present its views very frankly, because nobody is breathing down our necks. Nimeiri is not present, we are alone.

What the SPLM/SPLA stand for
I have the honour on behalf of the SPLA/SPLM to present roughly some of the views that our delegation will remain to explore with you.

1 I say that SPLA/SPLM is committed to the liberation of the whole Sudan and to the unity of its people and its territorial integrity. We have said this many times. When we say liberation some things ring in the minds of certain people; they ask, liberation from what? You people in the SPLM drop the 'L' and let it be SPM. Let it just be Sudan People's Movement or what is your liberation? From what? We have explained this many times, that liberation is composite. In our villages, people have to walk over twenty miles to bring water in tins carried on the head. This is a reality that in our countryside, if we reduce this distance to zero, and the zero may not be possible, but if we reduce it to some few yards, we call this liberation. We look at liberation in a broader context.

2 SPLA/SPLM is committed to the establishment of a democratic new Sudan. *We are democrats*, we, contrary to what people say that the SPLM/SPLA wants to impose a one-party system on the Sudan. No! *We believe in the democratic process as you do in the National Alliance.* We want to assure you of this, that democracy which embodies equality, freedom, economic and social justice and respect for human rights, not as slogans but as concrete realities that have concrete content which we should promote, cherish and protect. We are committed. SPLM/SPLA is committed to solving the nationality and religious questions, to the satisfaction of all the Sudanese citizens and with a democratic and secular context and in accordance with the objective reality of

our country. The nationality question is something that must be discussed. We are an Arab country, we are an African country. Are we a hybrid? Are we Afro-Arab, are we what? You discuss it. Discuss it in this conference. You can discuss it in this conference, you can discuss it in the next conference, but it must be solved. SPLM/SPLA stands for genuine autonomous or federal governments, for various regions of the Sudan – a form of regionalism or federalism that will enable the masses not the regional elites to exercise real power for economic and social development and promotion of their cultures. SPLM/SPLA is committed to a radical restructuring of the power of the central government in a manner that will once and for all end the monopoly of power by a few in Khartoum. They say there is a Southern problem; the problem in itself is in Khartoum, meaning that the government has been taken by the people of Khartoum alone. And this is a problem, and we must address it very frankly. When in one of the papers Dr. Gizouli said that we just find ourselves six people from one region, from the Gezira, this is a coincidence. Anyway, it is not a coincidence. We want to say it is not a coincidence and we must discuss it. Why do you find yourselves six from the Gezira in a cabinet of twelve? Oh! Where are those of the Nuba mountains, where are those of the South, where are those of Ingassena and where are those of the Beja? Why don't they find themselves also accidentally six? These practices must be addressed very, very concretely and very frankly because nobody is going to hoodwink anybody else.

SPLA/SPLM firmly stands for putting an end to these circumstances and policies that have led to the uneven development; we can transform the situation, and it has been done in many countries. Those areas of our country that are backward relative to other areas can be transformed. We are after all the Sudan, and the Sudan is backward as a whole for that matter. We all are undeveloped. One of the poorest countries in the world, one of the richest also potentially. There must be ways and means to redistribute the fruits of development. SPLM/SPLA is committed to put to an end to racism. Various regimes in Khartoum have found racism a useful thing to institutionalize. They say you are a Nuba, you are a Westerner, you are a Southerner you are an Arab and you are so and so. Is this how to create a new Sudan? These things must not be there because we must all be Sudanese. SPLM is dedicated to the eradication of tribalism, sectionalism

125

and provincialism. We, in addition to racism, go down to the family level. This is from such and such a family, even in the same tribe or nationality within the same village. This person is from such and such a family, and when it comes to appointments or when two people apply for a job and one has a slightly higher qualification while the other person comes from the same village as the decision maker, that person has better chances over the other. This thing must, of course, come to an end in a new Sudan. These are our commitments. SPLA is committed to a rapid transformation of our country from its present state of helplessness, backwardness, underdevelopment, bankruptcy, dependency and retrogression so that we become an industrial and agro-industrial society where we shall not again be the dwarf of the Arab world. We are the smallest child of the Arab countries and the sick child of Africa. We want to be a Sudan, a strong one, and to do this, we must develop, we must end our backwardness, we must transform our society.

These are a few of the views of the SPLM/SPLA which our members will discuss with you. The above views in their concrete implementation constitute what we call the new Sudan. So that the new Sudan does not become a slogan. We said we wanted to form a new Sudan, and we must put concrete contents into a new Sudan. We have been consistently and persistently calling for a new Sudan since July 1983, when we published our manifesto. But to bring about such a new Sudan the edict is that a cancer called Nimeirism must be torn down in its entirety and that is not easy to do as brother Dr. Yagi said before, that even the symbols of May have not yet gone and I am still wearing the May Regime uniform. We discussed it once, we said that, well, the insignia on the head gear is just a bird and the caption under it says victory to us. So since we do not have the means in the bush for making new gear, let us continue wearing this and with the confidence and conviction that victory is not to Nimeiri but to us. I believe that these are the ideals for which you in the National Alliance drew the national charter on the eve of 6 April 1985. It is for these ideals that you organized and conducted the Medani Conference, the resolutions of which we were very satisfied with. It is for them that you made a declaration for the defence of democracy in the Sudan. And it is for them that you have come to consult with the SPLM/SPLA. We believe that we have similar ideals.

In Search for Sudanism

But, brothers, these are very grave issues. Having briefly identified our views, I believe it is necessary to have a higher look at the Sudanese reality and exchange preliminary ideas as to how to transform it. The reality of the Sudanese society is that modern Sudan is a product of historical development before, during, and after the alternate colonial rule of the Turks, the British and the Egyptians. In this we are not alone. Like other nations, nations and states are products of history. At present our immediate task is to form a new Sudan. We call this the process of national formation. At the same time, this new Sudan that we are trying to form must be liberated from external dependency and internal exploitation. We call this the process of national liberation. The two processes are central to SPLM/SPLA thinking, national formation and national liberation, must go on concurrently because of the nature of our wearily historical epoch. And to be meaningful revolutions must consummate in true democracy that brings peace and prosperity to the masses of our people.

When we call for national formation, we are being very concrete. I will illustrate these by concrete or real examples. It is not a secret that the Sudan is composed of many nationalities that are sometimes wrongly referred to as tribes. Use whatever word you want to use; there are Arab tribes; there are Nuer tribes. The Nuer itself is not one tribe. There are Dinka tribes, Zande tribes, Toposa tribes, the Nuba, Fur, Beja and so on. To fuse these nationalities or tribes into a nation is our immediate task and challenge. But how do we do it? Some immediately would say that we must all be Arab, to be one Sudan. Others would say that we must all be Africans to be one Sudan.

I present to this historic conference that our major problem is that the Sudan has been looking and is still looking for its soul, for its true identity. Failing to find it (because they do not look inside the Sudan, they look outide), some take refuge in Arabism, and failing in this, they find refuge in Islam as a uniting factor. Others get frustrated as they fail to discover how they can become Arabs when their creator thought otherwise. And they take refuge in separation. In all of these, there is a lot of mystification and distortion to suit the various sectarian interests. For example, say, if a person from Dongola gets up today and says all the Sudanese must be Dongalaween (people from Dongola) or a Latuka gets up and says all Sudanese must be Latuko people will say that this

127

person is mad, take him to the psychiatrist. But when our fellow countrymen of Arab origin get up and say all Sudanese must be Arabs, maybe it is taken for granted; there is not sharpness of our identity. This must be said frankly.

In the process of national formation in the Sudan, we need to throw away all these sectarianisms and look deep inside our country and the experience of others. There are many countries, nations and people that have been formed. See the English who went to America and formed thirteen colonies. They were the same Englishmen, who all spoke English, and all were Christians. But they had to fight England – Britain – in order to get their independence. They are now the United States of America, one of the two greatest nations in the world. They don't claim to be English, although they speak English. They are Christians. The same thing with the Spaniards. They went and colonized Latin America. They formed colonies. They formed civilizations. So it is with the Portuguese who have their civilization in Brazil but the Brazilians do not call themselves Portuguese. They are Brazilians and they are proud of it. The Argentinians speak Spanish and are Christians, but they are Argentinians not Spaniards and are proud of being Argentinians.

I present to you that we can do this in the Sudan. I present that we can form a unique Sudanese civilization that does not have to take refuge anywhere. But, of course, these things will die hard. We take examples of pronouncements of Sudanese political parties, organizations, personalities, etc., etc. On 1 June 1985, Dr. Gizouli (I wonder whether he is a member of the National Alliance) wrote a letter to me in which he enumerated five points. In the introduction he says, "I know that the whole Sudan is your concern but there is a chronic bleeding sore in the South since 1985. It is a small problem affecting part of the body."

This is a crucial point because we believe that it is the Sudan not the finger, that is at stake. Dr. Gizouli went on to say that the government of the popular revolution was giving the solution to the Southern problem top priority: "the following points are not offered as a final solution to the problem but as food for thought." Well, let us think about them:

1   The national charter agreed upon by the Trade Unions Federation, the political parties and the army stated that, "the Southern

problem should be solved within an autonomous regional frame-work in a United Sudan''.

2   Commitment of all sides to Addis Ababa as a base for running the affairs of the South for the time being.

3   The recognition of the cultural and ethnic characteristics of the South.

4   Acknowledging that the South is mostly underdeveloped, genuine efforts should be extended to bring it to the level of parity.

These four points all deal with the South. Ah, where is the West, where is the East? Do they have to take up arms also, so that there is a bleeding sore there? So that we solve their problems after they have taken up arms? Brother Mahmoud present at the meeting is the Secretary General and Commander-in-Chief of SUNIA, which is a new organization in Darfur. So when we come to talk about the Southern problem, and solve it with El Gizouli, then, we will have to start again and solve that of SUNIA, that of the Nuba Mountains. After we get peace, we will divide the ministerial positions among ourselves. You Southerners, take six, seven or nine positions and be happy. Ah, the Nuba, Fur, Beja, etc., will say that the people who take up arms get six ministerial jobs, so we should do the same to be considered in the share-out of government positions. When they do that, we shall have to solve their problems. So all these four points, in our context, in the context we were talking about before, are irrelevant to us, not because we are unconcerned about the South. *We are very concerned about the South*. The South as a region has suffered a great deal. For 17 years the bleeding sore has been in the South. So our people in the South are suffering and they need peace. The people from other regions also suffer from the same.

5   the fifth point is about religion, which we brought up before. It says that ''Religion, truly perceived, is never a divisive force.''

There are Muslims and Christians in both the North and South, but some Sudanese are neither. ''Though the Southern problem has not started with the so-called Islamic laws, I appreciate their impact on it. Should other facets of the problem be agreed upon, I would not have thought that these laws would be a stumbling block and ways and means can be found as these laws and others are under discussion now.''

A very convoluted argument – if I may intepret it correctly, he wants to educate us first. Religion truly perceived is never a divisive force. So we have to truly perceive it first in order to find out that it is never a divisive force. It is going to take us a very long time to go down into the exercise of being educated as to how religion is not a dividing force. He is also asking that should other facets of the problem, that is, of Islamic laws, be agreed upon, what parts of *Sharia* we agree on and what parts we do not agree on. This is an absurdity; we don't agree with any of it, clear and simple. We cannot talk about which parts we agree with and which parts we do not.

But this was a widely publicized letter in which it was said it was the beginning of the dialogue (*Hewaar*), which unfortunately does not begin like this. It does not begin by you defining your problems and finding solutions and then you call SPLM/SPLA to come and bless your solutions. We are not priests. The dialogue begins by us sitting like this, and exchanging views. This is the meaning of a real dialogue. This is why we refuse the word "nego-tiations" because it has its own connotations. There are two sides which negotiate; they depart to consult with their other friends, after which they return to the negotiation table until they agree somewhere near the middle. We say we prefer dialogue, because in a dialogue we sit like this as equals and as Sudanese so that we frankly talk about our problems and so that we can frankly solve them. This is why we have refused negotiations and accepted dialogue. This is very often distorted into the view that SPLM/SPLA is refusing negotiations. That is absolutely true. But when some journalists say that SPLA is refusing dialogue, that is not true, otherwise we could not be sitting here today. We only made the distinction between the two.

We replied to Dr. El-Gizouli's letter very clearly on what he called "the problem of Southern Sudan". Is this a condition? If we want to create a new Sudan, then this is almost redundancy. But because the process of change and adaptation takes time, and we are conscious of this, this is why we are still wearing the symbols of May (*Ramouz Mayo*). It takes time, and idea changes also take time to occur. How to govern the state whether through federation, regionalism or whatever, will be discussed later as you can see in our delegations that we have people who are not Southern Sudanese. Where do we take them if we came to discuss the problems of Southern Sudan? Maybe that is the reason they do not want Dr. Mansour Khalid in the meeting. I do not say that is the reason; I say maybe it is, so I leave room for the other reasons which I believe are there in terms of the people who are suggesting them. We will discuss it. The other reason may be that we do not want him because he is one of those who established the May Regime, as somebody protested before. Up to now we have tolerated Nimeiri's very Minister of Defence. If he did not establish the May Regime, he protected it and these two are closely linked to one another. Without protection, the regime would have gone a very long time ago. We also said that the state of emergency must be lifted. This is really not a condition, because you cannot have a dialogue within the state of emergency. This was a very simple logic, not a condition.

We also said that they must commit themselves publicly to resign. When we come to a conference like this, next time the Constitutional Conference, and there is a good result for which I am optimistic, another interim government will be formed, then they should commit themselves publicly to resign. It is also redundant because if you come to the conference and you have an interim government, then it goes without saying that that government should go after the successful conclusion of the conference. But we know the tricks of the generals. We wanted them to tell the Sudanese people publicly and aloud that after the National Constitutional Conference, they are going to quit. We want them to say they are part and parcel of the National Constitutional Conference. This is why we included it; otherwise it is not a condition. Therefore all these three are not conditions if the people are serious about and committed to the formation of a new Sudan. The fourth point, concerning the cancellation of the September 1983 laws – these laws are neither Islamic nor Constitutional. Nimeiri decreed them and we all have been condemning them to the extent of people working outside. Dr. Mansour is here as an example. People walked out of the Sudan in protest at this. Nimeiri is actually here because El *Sharia* which he decreed for his own protection is still not abandoned. We know that this man (Nimeiri) was a Communist in 1969; according to him, he became an Imam in 1983. He has worked to prove his commitment to Islam but this is a divisive issue. We should concentrate on things that unite us, not on things that divide us more. Therefore I see no reason why we should concentrate on these issues.

The fifth point, a very important one, was the cancellation of two agreements – defence pacts. These agreements diminish our statehood, our sovereignty. These mutual defence pacts were made not for defence of the Sudan as such, *we could not have had any quarrel with that*, but for the defence of the May regime. Therefore, if the May regime has gone, they should go with the May regime. As I talk to you now, and as a result of one of these two defence pacts, on 13 and 14 and 15 of this month, March 1986, fifty bombs fell on us. These bombs were not thrown by Sudanese planes, not by Sudanese pilots, but by the implementation of one of these two defence agreements. Fifty bombs were thrown into Rumbek, Yirol, Akot and Mbolo. This is part of the reason I said before that I was late. The May II regime is seriously fighting us. They have closed El Obeid airport and they have converted it into a military airbase and we have counted the bombs. This is not a secret. Khartoum bombed Rumbek, Yirol, Akot and Mbolo at 8.30 a.m. (Sudan Local Time) on the 13, 14 and 15th. And yet the Swar Al Dhahab regime claims that they withdrew from Rumbek for the sake of avoiding bloodshed to the people! Why are they bombing the same people again, if this is not a contradiction? Our forces are not all in these places that they have bombed. So as long as you have defence pacts to protect a regime, and they are an expensive law, it gives that country the right to intervene even in your conference if it is not impressed by what you are saying. Exactly one of these defence treaties has now been involved. When you go back to Khartoum, you will find that this is happening. These are the points we gave to create a conducive atmosphere for talking, a friendly atmosphere, not conditions as some of my countrymen would like to call them. As I said earlier, we are going to be frank because I am going to leave you here to thrash this out and it is your historic responsibility.

On Islam and Arabism

This is Dr. El Gizouli's letter. I will give another example and this is from (*Mustagbal El Islam wa El Arouba fi El Sudan*) "the future of Islam and Arabism in the Sudan". I do not want our brothers from the Umma Party to be disappointed. These are not my own words; I am only giving examples.

Five ways to Islamize and Arabize the Southern Sudan: by brother Sadiq El Mahdi, pages 114–115: "The Southern Sudan will inevitably be Islamized and Arabized in the following ways:

1   Through differences among the Southern leaders, particularly those from the pastoral and agricultural tribes and through mutual relations.

2   Through Islamic scholars (*Fukah*), merchants who go to settle in the interior of the South and mix with Southerners in a friendly way."

We are a product of historical development. *Arabic* (though I am poor in it – I should learn it fast) *must be the national language in a new Sudan* and therefore we must learn it. We are as frank and as sharp in everything. Arabic cannot be said to be the language of the Arabs. No, it is the language of the Sudan. English is the language of Americans, but that country is America, not England. Spanish is the language of Argentina, Bolivia, Cuba and they are those countries, not Spain. Therefore I take Arabic on scientific grounds as the language of the Sudan and I must learn it. So, next time, I will address you in Arabic if Daniel Kodi, my Arabic teacher, does his job well and if I am a good student.

We give these examples without bitterness, we only state them as facts. There is no bitterness at all because we are serious. We are serious about the formation of a new Sudan, a new civilization that will contribute to the Arab world and to the African world and to the human civilization. Civilization is nobody's property. Cross-fertilization of civilization has happened historically and we are not going to separate whose civilization this and this is, it may be inseparable. But at this stage of our development we need to form a new Sudan in which we use our resources, our vast resources, our vast manpower – more than one million of them are abroad. They are running the economies of other societies. We are convinced that without these sectarianisms we can form a new Sudan.

Another example – and I am not taking a grudge against anybody, I am only stating facts. There was a lecture delivered by brother Sadiq El Mahdi in Saudi Arabia at the end of October 1985. He delivered a political talk in Minhal Hotel down Riyadh Old Airport Road. The summary of the talk is that:

1   It is a fact that Garang was oppressed (Garang means SPLA) under Nimeiri's regime. But after the fall of Nimeiri, he did not come back to the country for a peaceful solution of the Sudanese problems. In this case, he is considered an oppressor and the problem for which he is fighting is groundless.

2   Garang should be isolated inside and outside the Sudan. He should not at all be given any chance to represent the South, the Africans or the Christians.

3   We should confess that the past regime stood against the regional rights and there are some parts of the country which are under-developed such as the South.

4   People from the regions in which there are mineral resources could request the government for a certain percentage.

5   We were expecting Garang and his people to come back to the Sudan after the revolution (March–April) for an internal solution but he is still awaiting the blessing of Addis Ababa.

6   They want in the SPLA a Scientific Socialist Sudan of negroid non-Arab origin and this is impossible even by force.

In the first place, scientific socialism, or socialism itself, we don't understand. Capitalism itself, which I studied for nine years in America, up to now I do not know its meaning. I cannot define it, but even when you make it negroid scientific socialism it becomes more confusing. Negroid origin and non-Arab origin, we are a good mix of people; Arab blood runs in some of us. Let us make this cocktail into a viable country, Sudan. This is precisely what we stand for and will continue to stand for. As for Socialism, Communism and all of these isms, one cannot be a socialist or capitalist without one's presence. We have to be, to be Sudanese, to form a new Sudan. Therefore our starting point would be and is Sudanism not capitalism, socialism or whatever. Do we accept it or don't we accept it? If we do not accept it, then you can go and build your socialism in the sky or you go and build your capitalism in the sky, because there has to go a Sudan to begin with before we go to ideologies. Nimeiri was a socialist for sixteen years, let us not forget that. So we are here being wrongly accused. The issue of non-Arabs: we cannot say that the Sudan will be a non-Arab country because we have Arab blood in us.

7   Sadiq went on to say that Garang's ideas are very dangerous and that is why some Sudanese believe that a front should be made on the following basis:

(i)   Arabism against Africanism.

(ii)   North against the South.

(iii) Islam against Christianity.

(iv)   Garang does not represent the whole South. The Nuer and the Equatorians are against him.

Nimeiri, according to Sadiq, applied Islam wrongly, in a way that kept the people away from Islam. He kept Christians from their rights by whipping a priest for carrying a mass drum. Brother Sadiq should understand that that is not the reason for our fight. That Italian priest was inhumanely lashed but he was lashed after we had already started the fight and had already organized the SPLA. Even if you gave that priest a hundred lashes, it doesn't concern us. It concerns Nimeiri. We cannot be annoyed by the lashing of priests. Sadiq suggested the following to the government:

1 To strengthen the Armed Forces and enable them to defend and secure the Sudan (We should also help the government in this issue.)
2 Organization of a force which could be able to fight the guerilla fighters by guerilla means and transfer the war to the enemy.
3 To assist and enable the Southerners who are against Garang by necessary force in order to fight him.
4 To enable our forces which are in the enemy area to defend themselves.
5 Islam and Arabism will continue to be in the Sudan either through peace or by force.

We are inside Sudan

People's ideas change, including mine, Sadiq's and everybody's. When we criticize these views, we don't rule them out or say that they don't have a role to play. When we all come to form a new Sudan of course everybody will play his role and everybody will learn, including those of us in the SPLM/SPLA. We will have to study you in the National Alliance. You will study us in the SPLA/SPLM.

The last example which I would like to give is that even though people think that we are outside the Sudan we really are not. We are inside Sudan, inside the General Headquarters of the Army. This is how we get our information. How do we know that two battalions have left Khartoum? We are not an external force and this is a misconception that some people have. In your meeting of 9 March, a meeting between the political parties with the chairman of the Military Council, the TMC Political Affairs Committee and the Ministers of Interior, Foreign Affairs and so on, the topic was the security situation in the country, with the emphasis on the South as depicted by the capture of Rumbek.

Some of you might have been in the meeting or might have been briefed by your parties about this meeting on 9 March 1986. The Chairman Swar al Dahab enumerated the declaration of amnesty. That is the thing that the TMC has done well and we have not responded. They insulted us by declaring an amnesty. Amnesty to whom? We were all fighting Nimeiri. The Alliance was fighting Nimeiri and the SPLA was doing the same. If Swar al Dahab at the last moment sided with the people on 5 or 6 March 1984, he can technically also be said to have been fighting Nimeiri. Therefore, what right does he have to give us amnesty? Therefore, this issue of the amnesty is very provocative because we cannot be given amnesty. Brothers, we have not done anything wrong to be granted amnesty for. We were only fighting Nimeiri just as you were doing it, so if you give it to yourselves then it is a general amnesty including all of us here. In turn, the Alliance also should give themselves amnesty for organizing the strikes. Then we would accept it as our amnesty, all of us. But for SPLA/ SPLM to be singled out and the SPLA be given amnesty, this is going back again to SPLA being a Southern movement and they are rebels. The declaration of the unilateral ceasefire – there was no real ceasefire and we have explained this many times before. The Transitional Military Council never declared any ceasefire. On the contrary, they were fighting us in Mongalla for four months when they massed ten thousand (10,000) troops. Anyway, they invited us for dialogue, the invitation which I read to you before, that of 1 June 1985. It was the first contact between us and the Khartoum Government.

That was through Dr. Gizouli who I believe is a member of Alliance. Some of you have reservations about that (if I may add), I don't know whether the Prime Minister is representing the whole Alliance or whether he is from the medical association. He is from the Alliance. You should have given him a rank also when he was appointed Prime Minister so as to be a member of the TMC. This is because most of his pronouncements are to that effect. This was lacking; if he was made a brigadier, we would be able to put him together with the TMC, but now I talk with reservation and respect because I am and we are in solidarity with the National Alliance and here we find Gizouli confusing us over where he belongs, whether he is with you or with the TMC.

Anyway, some of the points discussed in the meeting referred to earlier were how to counter the SPLA activities. I will not read them to you because some of you are informed about them. I just want to bring it to your notice that we are informed of your meeting and the meeting was to discuss how to destroy the SPLA. A few days later after your meeting, the political parties, with the Military Council, the Military Council met alone. They made very serious resolutions. These resolutions are very necessary for this meeting to know.

The joint TMC and Council of Ministers Meeting resolved the following (this is after you left):

1 That the war in the South must be intensified to teach the SPLA a lesson it should never forget. So while we came to talk about peace, some people in Khartoum were talking about intensifying the war. If they intensify the war, we also have the capability, and the means, for intensifying the war on our side. Otherwise we would not have captured Rumbek and Yirol and there would not have been any problems at all. As a footnote to this war hysteria of the TMC, I would like to mention in person that in their meeting the Minister of Commerce and Trade dissented from this view. He said that it was enough, the South and the North must be two separate countries. The minister argued that the war will only bring disintegration and fragmentation and a great loss of lives and bitterness, so why should we wait for this great loss of lives and bitterness? It is better for us to separate now. He went on further to say that after dividing the country, the next problem will be how to divide the assets and debts between the two parts. These statements are in the minutes of the meeting. Brothers, as we have said many times before, we are not secessionists. And *if anybody wants to separate even in the North, we will fight him because the Sudan must be one.* It should not be allowed to disintegrate or fragment itself. We still maintain this opinion.

2 The second resolution was that it was reaffirmed that the question of arming the Northern tribesmen had become most urgent and of paramount importance now. The armed natives will fight along and side by side with the Sudan Army. These tribes will be encouraged to harass their Southern neighbouring tribes with a view to destabilizing and impoverishing them by destroying their properties and looting their belongings and animals with the

overall aim of eventually depopulating Northern Bahr El Ghazal and Bentiu areas and creating a buffer zone between the North and the South.

3 In order to intensify the war and keep it within the South, Maridi in Western Equatoria will be the operational headquarters for the execution of the war. For this reason, they are going to widen Maridi airport.

4 Since Egypt is taking a neutral stand the Joint Military Protocol signed between Sudan and Libya is to come into effect at once. El Obeid Airport shall be closed to civilian traffic. In return for this Sudan shall immediately stop and withhold support to the Hussein Habre Government and work instead for the overthrow of that government and to cool relations with Egypt.

5 To forestall and stop any possible help from Zaire to the Southern rebels (SPLA/SPLM), on the grounds of what the meeting called possible racial solidarity, Sudan, through their friends, will encourage and arm Zairian dissidents along the common border so that Zaire becomes preoccupied with its own problems.

6 The resolution is that since the new president of Uganda, Yoweri Museveni, was a schoolmate and a friend of Dr. John, General Okello will be given sanctuary in Southern Sudan. Their army regrouped, reorganized and re-equipped to conduct guerilla warfare against Museveni in Northern Uganda and West Nile and thereby forestall Museveni from helping Garang or force Museveni to cooperate with Sudan against both Garang and the Okellos. General Okello met Swar al Dahab on 12 March 1986.

Let us nucleate as a Nation
These are the resolutions which are important, which I thought are really important for this meeting to be aware of because they impinge on our meeting. I have just given you a sample of ideas about the real situation we are in today. This is why I read these things so that we are crystal clear about what we are, about the possible solutions and how to reach those solutions; so that nobody comes to us with small notes saying that if we give Southerners six ministerial positions, if we give them the vice-presidency or the vice-premiership, etc., they will come over to us. Nimeiri had given us those positions but we did not join him. *Unless we create a new Sudan, we are in for a lot of trouble.* And in order to appreciate these things, we must say things as they are whether we like it or not because this is our reality. This is

why I gave this example. There are many other examples; I have quoted brother Sadiq El Mahdi, brother Dr. Gizouli and they could still have a positive role to play in the building of a new Sudan.

But I pose a question, having explored the various views, is it possible to form a new Sudan? This is a central question for this conference. Whether the formation of a new Sudan is feasible and possible, we have to explore it. If it is possible and feasible what is the agenda of this new Sudan? And if it is not possible and not feasible, then we pack our bags and go away. This is why this preliminary dialogue was called for. I leave this to you to deliberate on and I wish you success. Because I will not attend the rest of the conference, I wish to leave you assured that I believe that the Sudanese have the will and courage to throw away all those sectarianisms and start building a new Sudan. I call on you, let the Sudan nucleate, let us have a nucleus not to run here and there to the Arab Community or the African Community or even stand in the middle. Let us nucleate as a nation with its own specific identity, not as a satellite of other nations, some of which are even more mediocre than the Sudan. We are and can be a great people. We can be a great civilization in our own right and we can do this. We are more than 20 million people in population or possibly we are more than 30 million because some people are not being enumerated, some people are not known. Somebody goes to a microphone in Khartoum and says Dear Countrymen, where are those countrymen? Some of them are in Kapoeta but he doesn't know them. There are people called the Koromo who are not known. There are people in Kurmuk area called the Watawit who are not known. When we went to Kurmuk area, Comrade Kerubino Kuanyin Bol was the Commander. We went and met the Ingassena people – come and join the SPLA. They said no, no, no. We accept that we are slaves, but God grant you all best wishes. They ran away from SPLA. We asked them to join us so that God grants us all the best. We have more than 20 million people, lots of natural resources, lots of oil, lots of agricultural land, lots of water and lots of educated people. More than one million graduates are outside the Sudan, not because they do not love the Sudan. Every Sudanese loves his country and if there were a correct system of government, they would come back into the Sudan and develop it. They have only been put off by the systems in Khartoum. I am confident of this as a person; as a conference, you are free to discuss it.

There are specific issues I would also like to address; issues which may preoccupy some of you may be more than building of a new Sudan. There are very urgent things – the issue of the ceasefire, for example. You will discuss it but I believe that you will get nowhere because you are a National Alliance, and we are in solidarity with you. We are not fighting you. We cannot cease-fire with you because we are not fighting in the first place. We are fighting with the TMC. Unless you are the representative of the TMC, it would be absurd of course to ask for a ceasefire. The details of a ceasefire, what is happening on the side of the SPLA/SPLM and on the side of the TMC, are more known to us than to you. You did not know until I told you that on the 13th, 14th and 15th, for instance, fifty bombs were thrown on us. Is this, brothers, an atmosphere in which to call for a ceasefire? In the resolutions I read to you before, that "the war must be intensi-fied in order to teach SPLA a lesson it will not forget", is this an atmosphere for a ceasefire? So brothers, a ceasefire would be out of the question until we reach a viable solution that would be lasting. It is not on our side, it is on the side of the TMC.

The other issue is that of the present elections. This is the programme of TMC. We said soon after the April uprising that May II came to power, maybe they are working on May III now. The process in our thinking has been a kind of reverse. We would have thought that a conference like this would have been first necessary. *A constitutional conference before anybody talks about going for elections.* Of course, last time we said that we understand why the National Alliance is in support of elections and we also support you. Since your argument is that this will be the only way to get rid of these generals, this is a concrete reality. They are armed, so how do you get rid of them? We in the SPLA are armed and so we can get rid of them through fighting with them. But one of your weapons could be the elections, a means to throw them out. But also we cannot bless it because we are not priests. We are not just going to bless something which Khartoum does or says. If the SPLA were to be involved in elections, we would have to be involved in the elections commission and we cannot do that till we agree to go to Khartoum. But when you hold partial elections and claim like General Tag El Din (of the TMC) that you will form a National Government, this is an absurdity.

They are a Transitional Military Council. Unless the people vote them in, they do not have the right to determine any form or forms of government after the elections. They have no say anymore. However, when you start to smell things like this, TMC talking about a government of national unity after the elections, there is something which is not in order. The TMC is therefore not serious about its previous commitment to resign soon after the elections. We are occupying the constituency of the Vice-Premier Sayed Samuel Aru Bol. This is nothing personal but it is a hard fact that the SPLA is sitting in his constituency Rumbek. Where is he going to contest? Therefore the elections are ridiculous as far as the SPLA/SPLM is concerned. A government that will come up will be partial and whatever constitutional authority that it will have will also be partial. *We will not be bound by its constitutionality.* We must make this clear now. We have to be frank and we believe in frankness. Things have been done upside down; instead of agreeing first in a constitutional conference, we did things in reverse and we must say in advance that the coming government will have traces of the May Regime.

The issue of the future relationship between the Alliance and the SPLM is very important, irrespective of the outcome whether you agree or disagree. I want the SPLM/SPLA and the National Alliance to keep their doors open to each other. First of all, I pleaded with you before to remain as an Alliance. Remaining as an Alliance and keeping the doors open for real dialogue not for propaganda dialogue and window dressing and archaic ideas about the South. Here is somebody from the Sunia Liberation Front; what are you going to do with him; are you going to hold a conference in order to solve the problems of Darfur? Therefore, a national conference is necessary.

In conclusion, I have taken too much of your time. But then, I will not be talking again tomorrow, you will be. So I have taken my time for today, for tomorrow and for the day after tomorrow. I would like to say that we are confident, I am confident. Do your work, it is your duty. If you engage in schemes to maintain the old Sudan, I want to assure this meeting this is unfeasible, it is unworkable. The old Sudan cannot be maintained in a new form. We must devise ways and means to arrive at a new form. We must devise ways and means to arrive at a new Sudan: a Sudan where we will all respect each other. No one should say, these are those who carry the buckets of waste products (human wastes) or this is from the South, this is a Fur and this is a Sudanese National. What are we, we are all nationals. Everybody must have his voice, the voice of the Fur, the voice of the Dinka, the voice of the Nuer? We want to make the voice of the Sudan. This is our concrete reality.

The Koka Dam Declaration, 24 March 1986 (A proposed programme for national action)

1   On the basis of experience of the past years making up the post-independence period, and mindful of the heroic achievement of our people in their continuous mass political and armed struggle against all forms of injustice, oppression and tyranny; a struggle which was expressed in the course of two decades through two two great revolutions,
And rejecting all forms of dictatorships and *absolutely committed to the democratic option*,
And out of the conviction that it is necessary to create a *New Sudan* in which the Sudanese individual enjoys absolute freedom from the shackles of injustice, ignorance and disease in addition to enjoying the benefits of real democratic life; a *New Sudan* that would be free from racism, tribalism, sectarianism and all causes of discrimination and disparity,
And genuinely endeavouring to stop the bloodshed resulting from the war in Sudan;
And fully aware that the process leading to formation of a *New Sudan* should begin by the convening of a National Constitutional Conference,
And in the firm belief that the propositions put forward and herein spelt out by the Sudan Peoples' Liberation Movement and the Sudan Peoples' Liberation Army (SPLM/SPLA) and the National Alliance for National Salvation as essential prerequisites for convening the said constitutional Conference do constitute a sound basis for the launching of such a process,

2   The delegation of the National Alliance for National Salvation and that of the SPLM/SPLA, both of whom shall herein after be together referred to as *"THE TWO SIDES"*, agree that essential

142

prerequisites which would foster an atmosphere conducive to the holding of the proposed National Constitutional Conference are:

a   A declaration by all political forces and the government of the day of their commitment to discuss the *Basic Problems of Sudan* and not the so-called problem of Southern Sudan and that shall be in accordance with the agenda agreed upon in this "Declaration".

b   The lifting of the State of Emergency.

c   Repeal of the "September 1983 Laws" and all other laws that are restrictive of freedoms.

d   Adoption of the 1956 Constitution as amended in 1964 with incorporation of "Regional Government" and all other such matters on which a consensus opinion of all the political forces shall be reached.

e   The abrogation of the military pacts concluded between Sudan and other countries and which impinge on Sudan's National Sovereignty.

f   A continuous endeavour by the two sides to take the necessary steps and measures to effect a ceasefire.

3   The SPLM/SPLA believes that a public commitment by all the political forces and the government of the day, that the said government shall dissolve itself and be replaced by a New Interim Government of National Unity representing all the political forces including the SPLA/SPLM and the Armed Forces as shall be agreed upon at the proposed conference, is an essential prerequisite for convening the proposed Constitutional Conference. Consequently the two sides have agreed to defer the matter for further discussions in the near future.

4   The two sides have agreed the proposed Constitutional Conference shall be held under the banner of peace, justice, equality and democracy. They have further agreed that the agenda for the conference should comprise the following:

4   (i) a   The Nationalities Question.
     b   The Religious Question.
     c   Basic Human Rights.
     d   The System of Rule.
     e   Development and Uneven Development.
     f   Natural Resources.
     g   The Regular Forces and Security Arrangements.

    h The Cultural Question, Education and the Mass Media.
    i Foreign Policy.

(ii) The two sides have agreed that the above agenda does not in any way purport to be exhaustive.

5 The two sides have provisionally agreed that the proposed Constitutional Conference *shall be held in Khartoum during the third week of June 1986*, to be preceded by preliminary meetings, and that the conference shall actually be held after the government of the day provides and declares the necessary security arrangements and the necessary conducive atmosphere.

6 Mindful of the need for regular consultations with one another, the two sides have agreed to set up a joint liaison committee comprising five members from each side.

The two sides have further agreed that Wednesday, May 7th, 1986 shall be the date for conducting the committee's first meeting which shall take place in Addis Ababa.

7 This "Declaration" is issued in both English and Arabic. The two sides have agreed that the English text of the same shall be the *"Original"* and in the event of any discrepancy it shall prevail over its Arabic equivalent.

8 Having issued this "Declaration" the two sides appeal to the Sudanese people as represented in their various political parties, Trade Unions and Associations to work earnestly for the realization of the objectives of this "Declaration".

LONG LIVE THE STRUGGLE OF THE SUDANESE MASSES.

For Sudan Peoples Liberation Movement and Sudan Peoples' Liberation Army. (SPLM/SPLA)
Lt. Col. Kerumbino Kuanyin Bol,
Deputy Commander in Chief of SPLA and Deputy Chairman of SPLM Provisional Executive Committee

For National Alliance for National Salvation.
Awad El Karim Mohamed,
Secretary General for The National Alliance for National Salvation.

Chapter Five:

The Return to Hostilities

The conference at Koka Dam was an important milestone in the history of the SPLM, as it was the first occasion on which the seriousness of the movement was conceded, albeit grudgingly, by politicians representing Northern parties. Equally it was the first occasion on which a practical programme for the cessation of hostilities, and guidelines for the political restructuring of Sudan, were discussed and approved. Nonetheless, the high hopes raised by these discussions were quickly dashed. The reasons for this are not hard to see, though extremely disappointing to the more enlightened campaigners for peace on both sides of the fence. Although many of the participants at Koka Dam had been aware of the significance of the occasion, others were not seemingly ready to face the implications of what they had discussed and agreed upon.

Amongst these must be counted Prime Minister Sadiq al Mahdi, who was accused by some (probably unfairly) of authorizing his representatives at Koka Dam to affix their signatures fraudulently to the final document, never intending to honour it. Others believe that Sadiq has later suffered a radical change of heart and a new-found confirmation of faith that caused him to renege on his commitment at Koka Dam. Less charitable are those who argue that Sadiq, after a hurriedly held parliamentary election, in which he came at the top, was bracing himself to become Prime Minister for the second time in his career, and all political questions, including those relating to the survival of the nation, only had significance in his view in relation to their capacity to further that end. One suspects, however, that the choice in Sadiq's mind was not one between the national interest and his own aspirations; those were one and the same thing to the Oxonian leader who is also the grandson of the Mahdi.

The SPLM, on the other hand, was not party to this personified vision of the Sudan, if anything they were set to dismantle it. Also the movement has also assiduously refused to participate in any elections before the holding of the National Constitutional Conference and, thus, did not become part of the new Parliament while the NIF did. Sadiq's pandering to the NIF and dithering after Koka Dam is better understood in this light; he was all in favour of the elections even though he had already been party to a conference where grave doubts were expressed by Garang about the validity of whatever mandate such an election might confer as long as the problems of the Old Sudan were not resolved at root. If the participants in that conference were serious about what the SPLM thinks they would have read attentively Garang's every word. This infatuation with immediate elections was not Sadiq's alone; revealingly all the urban-led parties of the North, irrespective of their political dye, were for immediate elections. Only the Alliance of Rural Forces, a conglomeration of all Sudanese rural political formations from the South, West and East, supported the SPLM's plea for the postponement of the elections pending the successful conclusion of the National Constitutional Conference. Clearly the battle lines were drawn between the beneficiaries of the *ancien régime* and those who stood to gain the least from that regime.

Similarly, the DUP, which had never been involved in the Koka-Dam talks, was equally absorbed in the preparations for the coming elections, and was yet to be convinced of the merits of talking to the SPLM, something that would only arrive in 1988. The DUP, by that time, did not only fail to grasp the significance of the Koka Dam Declaration, but it also acted as if the war raging in the South and the South-East of the country was but an event to be wished away. Since the political influence of the DUP in Khartoum, where the game was still largely played out, was second only to that of the Umma, their non-participation was a serious blow to the peace process initiated at Koka Dam. They too began to solicit the support of the NIF, and for that end, laid on thick their predisposition to Sharia without realizing that in the multi-religious Sudan, the politicization of religion was a dead-end ideology in practical political terms. This pseudo-religious politics, in the circumstances, was not only an irrelevancy since it would neither stopped the war nor feed the hungry, it was also a factor of division.

The Koka Dam Declaration, it may be recalled, had envisaged a Constitutional Conference, to be held *inside the Sudan in June 1986*, and in which the SPLM would have participated. Also the SPLM pledged to participate in a broadly-based government to oversee the work of that conference once the conditions conducive to that participation were met. In other words the country could have had another short transitional period, with a generally broad-based government that would set the ground for the emergence of a New Sudan; any other path was nonsensical as it was amply proven later. Those who have installed the post-Nimeiri transitional government in power had their reasons to be sceptical about transitional governments; for no good has come out of the one they established in 1985. However, they have themselves to blame for ever entertaining the thought that that government, with its dubious leadership, could have presided over Sudan's political rejuvenation. That thought is now accepted for what it really was, a bad historical joke; both the Chairman of the Transitional Military Council, General Swar al Dahab and the Prime Minister, Dr. Jizouli Dafa'a Alla, have subsequently shown their real colours as adherents of the NIF.

Regardless, the two main Northern parties (the Umma and the DUP) as well as the Alliance have persuaded themselves that immediate parliamentary elections and a "return to democracy" were the panacea for the country's ills. Another excuse offered by those groups was that the Transitional Military Council, if left in power, might be unwilling to surrender authority and, thus, the sooner civilian rule was restored the better; the latter view was maintained by the trade unions, and it was convenient for the politicians to concur. But whatever the excuse, that was a serious error of judgement; given the existence of hostilities, the military were bound to play a leading role in politics, either behind the scenes, as they did between 1986 and 1989, or openly as they later did in the form of the coup of 1989. In reality, no civilian government is safe in Sudan as long as the problems of the country are not resolved at the root and armed conflict brought to a halt.

The period of parliamentary government that occurred between 1986 and 1989 compounded, rather than helped the situation. The way parliament was formed proved to be an impediment to peace: a myriad of political parties had come out of the woodwork after the fall of Nimeiri, and elections were contested between them. Still, these parties were living in a world of their own and an old world for that. The parties were encumbered by all manner of preconceived ideas about the country's problems including the one that has been troubling the country since independence. Characteristically all deluded themselves that Sudan's problem was still one of the North versus the South and that it could still be resolved by a return to the Addis Ababa agreement, the seminal achievement of the May regime that they have relentlessly discredited.

The growing influence of the extreme NIF, which managed to hold the balance of power between two traditional political foes, the Umma and the DUP, did not help the situation. The NIF was put in a position to dictate policies to the new "democracy", which it did unstintingly. Obviously, under their benign guidance the military situation was inflamed, the religious and racial sides of the conflict emphasized, and the country brought to ruin, the NIF held both parties hostage on the issue of Sharia and, as a result, Nimeiri's madness was accepted by his heirs as inviolable law. All have persuaded themselves that Islam was no longer a matter of personal faith; it has become the mainspring of politics. In a multi-religious country like Sudan there was no surer recipe for disaster.

Consequently, the government of Sudan began to act as if its only function in life was to be God's policeman; for the first two years of his government Prime Minister Sadiq al Mahdi gave the impression the Sudan's abiding problem was Shari'a, particularly the penal aspects of it. The whole government and Parliament were wrapped up in what came to be known as the alternative Islamic laws i.e. laws that would replace Nimeiri's Islamic Code and be acceptable to both the NIF and the SPLM. The government was, in fact, stewing in its own juice because of the fickle and dishevelled manner in which its Oxonian leader had approached governance; one would have thought that there were other more urgent problems to occupy his mind and energy. As a result managerial politics also suffered. The Prime Minister between 1986 and 1988 has reshuffled his government several times and concocted various so-called national charters. He also put together diverse committees in order to help him achieve his "mission impossible".

One such committee was the one known as the committee of national concord that came out in November 1987 with a draft law to replace Nimeiri's Codes; the guiding principle to the committee's work was that "Muslims should have the right to pass laws that satisfy their Islamic aspirations". By and large the committee adopted laws that were akin and sometimes identical to Sudan's pre-September 1983 secular laws except for certain aspects of the penal law. The Prime Minister reported with satisfaction to the nation that ninety-five per cent of the penal law was agreed upon, only five items remained at issue. That statement alone revealed both Sadiq's predicament and his play-acting; the so-called ninety-five per cent of the law was copied from Sudan's old secular laws; the five items he referred to were the very items of "hudoud", Islamic punishments to which the SPLM and the Sudan Bar Association (predominantly Muslims), among others, were objecting. In reality, by accepting the secularization of all the laws (without calling it so) except for the "hudoud", the NIF and the government were virtually suggesting that the Islamic aspirations which Sudanese Muslims were constrained to satisfy were the amputation and cross imputation of each others limbs. This did no honour to the intellectual abilities of the imams of the day nor justice to Islam.

There was, accordingly, war on all sides; inside the army war was waged with fire power, and within the political circles it was fought with words including accusations of apostasy against the nay sayers. Attitudes hardened, and produced a breed of Sudanese who became committed, as never before, to the continuation of the war (now taking the form of an Islamic jihad) despite the fact that this war seemed increasingly futile. The paradox, however, was that those "warriors" wanted to carry out their "holy war" to the last soldier of the Sudanese army led, among others, by its Martins and Iseaha's from the South. Within the SPLM/SPLA too, fighters were more and more convinced that the movement has to intensify the war because it would not have received the patina of recognition it had received from Northern politicians were it not for the irreducible stamina of the SPLA, so any call for a cease-fire that lost sight of the other conditions agreed upon to bring about the cessation of hostilities, was considered suspect. This tenacity was demonstrated most visibly in Sadiq's meeting with John Garang for talks subsequent to Koka Dam, on 31 July 1986. Far from attempting to push the process already underway any further as wisdom dictated, Sadiq offered to restart the entire discussions under his own auspices.

Howbeit, a frank discussion took place between Sadiq and Garang, and it was with great dismay that the SPLM realized that all Sadiq's proposals were virtually aimed at pulling the rug out from under the feet of the movement and all those in the North who stood against the politicization of religion, so as to allow him, and it appeared, the NIF, to set their own agenda. To distance himself from the Koka Dam process Sadiq went to the extent of claiming that his representatives at that meeting were not mandated to sign anything, as they had not been invested with the proper party authority. The reaction of the SPLM to this disavowal was predictable outrage particularly in view of the fact that the Joint Liaison Committees of the SPLM/SPLA and the National Alliance for National Salvation (of which the Umma Party was a member) met only few days before the Sadiq-Garang encounter and reiterated their commitment to the letter and spirit of the Koka Dam Declaration.

The impression Sadiq left on some, in the course of that meeting with Garang, was not that of a recalcitrant war horse, rather of a self-absorbed politician who wanted the nation to spin around him and who was very much in a hurry to assume power. Sadiq wanted to renegotiate Koka Dam so that he might be the one to define the agenda and determine the action. No one would have grudged the Prime Minister that aspiration were it not for the unviability of his agenda; Sadiq wanted to carry on board the Umma, the DUP, the Professional Alliance, the NIF and the SPLM/SPLA, and he wanted them all to be blessed by Sharia, now christened "the alternative laws". Evidently the Prime Minister was not ready to rock his parliamentary boat; and stand his grounds on Koka Dam even if that cost him the premiership; that eventuality Sadiq was not ready to contemplate.

The SPLM/SPLA saw how events had conspired to block progress in the peace front and set about consolidating relations with like-minded Sudanese, capitalizing on what had been achieved at Koka Dam and seizing all opportunities to make its case known. In this connection a seminar was held at the Woodrow Wilson Centre in Washington in 1987 at which the viewpoints of a number of groups were aired, despite the refusal of government officials to attend. Similar meetings were subsequently held in Bergen, Norway under the auspices of the Centre for Development Studies and Harare, Zimbabwe, in the course of the meeting of the Policy Board of the high powered Inter-action Council. Pained by the events in Sudan – all those groups intervened in order to help the Sudanese help themselves. Those meetings represented an occasion for the SPLM to outline its views on peace and beyond, and these offered by the SPLM have hardly deviated from the Koka Dam principles, the only agreed upon agenda of peace with practical ideas as to how to turn around the country, and revamp its hopelessly divided body politic.

The period after Koka Dam saw feverish activities for peace by all those who stood to gain from peace: the rural popular organizations reflecting the sentiment of the vast majority of the Sudanese people; those continued to hold discussions with the SPLM with a view to activating the peace process. Amongst them were the Sudan African Parties who held several constructive dialogues with the movement, on a number of occasions in Nairobi, Addis Ababa and Kampala. Instead of viewing this as a strengthening of the peace process, which he, among others, has initiated and using this added strength in order to neutralize the Muslim extremists, the Prime Minister, instead, embarked on a divisive policy; first by driving a wedge between the SPLM and those parties; and secondly by intimidating all other Sudanese who had a good word for the SPLM to the extent that intimidation became the government's language of politics. The order of the day became the consolidation of the so-called internal front against the external forces; that is the SPLM/SPLA. It appeared as if the Prime Minister had invented his own geography that places the whole axis from Kurmurk to Yirol out of Sudan. However, it was not difficult for the Prime Minister, in Sudan's weird political landscape, to find few "insiders" belonging to those areas and whose only purpose in life was to make hay while the sun shone; that had neither cemented the Prime Minister's power-base nor did it bring peace to the Sudan.

On the other hand the National Alliance, despite the fact that the major party players have virtually distanced themselves from it, still drew together progressive elements in Sudan, all keen to search for peace through dialogue with the SPLM based on the Koka Dam principles; their emissaries persisted in their tireless shuttles between Khartoum and Addis Ababa, a thankless under-taking that has become increasingly fraught with danger in view of the NIF's browbeating and the government's intimidation. This identity of vision between the SPLM and those groups in Khartoum who continued to soldier on went a long way to disprove the claim that the SPLM's tenacious commitment to Koka Dam principles reflected recalcitrance on its part; on the contrary those principles were supported by a broad consensus amongst an influential constituency in the whole Sudan.

Of the documents presented below, the first is based on a speech delivered in July 1988 and catalogues the thoughts of John Garang concerning the activities of the SPLM and the ditherings of Sadiq al Mahdi during the period subsequent to Koka Dam, whereas the remainder provide clear proof of the widening contacts under-taken by the Movement subsequent to Koka Dam and the measure of support that agreement continued to have in the whole Sudan, at the very time when it was described by the government as "John Garang's Conditions". The Joint Sudan African Parties/ SPLM document is typical of many at that period, and the joint statement issued by the Koka Dam Liaison Committee (of which the Umma Party was a member) exposes the erratic manner in which the Prime Minister was handling issues.

Excerpts from the Policy Statement made by John Garang on 12 July 1988 following the failure of peace efforts

The Government's Warmongering

In my recent statement over radio SPLA on 16 May 1988, marking the 5th anniversary of the founding of the SPLM/SPLA, we under-lined our commitment to join hands with the other forces of peace, democracy, justice, equality and progress to confront the devisive forces of sectarianism, disunity, bigotry and doom, and to search for a just and honourable peace within the context of a New United Sudan. Again, during the recent 25th anniversary cel-ebrations of the Organization for African Unity (OAU), we further elaborated on our peace initiative to certain members of the international press. But alas, the warmongering sectarian bigots in Khartoum, who masquerade as national leaders, chose to distort and misread our genuine call for peace. Not surprisingly the *de facto* Government of the Unholy Trinity[1] took our call for peace as a sign of weakness. Instead of taking the olive branches that we offered, the regime turned the branches into guns and the olives into bullets. The Regime launched a futile ill-advised rainy season military offensive based on the mistaken and wishful thinking that the SPLA was weak, finished and would be wiped out once and for all. The regime even set a time limit as to when the SPLA would cease to exist. They said two months from the date of formation of the Sadiq III Government the SPLA would be finished. That puts our death date to 15 July 1988. Nothing could be further from the truth, and the Regime could not be more wrong. The SPLA is neither weak nor can it be wiped out. What force can wipe out a people's revolution? It is unfortunate, but predictable, that the Government of the Unholy Trinity should scorn our peace initiative and mistake it for weakness. Far from being a sign of weakness, our quest for peace and justice is our strength and the reason we took up arms in the first place. We took up arms to bring about peace; peace with justice in the place of a peace in injustice. The SPLM/SPLA quest for peace did not begin now; it has a long history. It is on record that our quest for peace dates back to 22 March 1985, before the fall of Dictator Nimeiri, when the SPLM Chairman called for direct talks with the Sudanese Army fighting in War Zone I, and at the national level for a National Congress involving all Sudanese political forces to discuss and resolve our country's fundamental problems.

Before I go into the history of the Movement's quest for peace and our positions on the peace process, those who beat the drums of war in Khartoum, those who scorn our peace initiative, those who dream that the SPLA is weak and finished, those who delude themselves of achieving military victory over the SPLA, those backward people deserve to be given a cold shower of facts regarding the real economic political and military situation on the ground, lest their imagination and hopes carry them away from reality and from peaceful solution to the conflict. So what are the facts?

Let those who beat the drums of war in Khartoum be reminded that in the last five years the SPLM/SPLA made unprecedented achievements. Indeed, with due modesty aside, one can say that few modern liberation movements have made such giant strides

1 Sadiq's coalition government at the time was made up of his party, the Umma, the DUP and the NIF.

in such short a time. Starting with a few rifles in 1983, the SPLM/SPLA has now built a formidable army of peasants, workers, students and revolutionary intellectuals, an army that now stands at several tens of thousands, equipped with modern weapons; an army that I dare say is stronger than that of many African countries. The political and military achievements of the SPLM/SPLA before the 1985 Intifadha are summarized in my speeches of 9 April 1985 and 26/27 May 1985 and I need not go into them again in detail. But let those who beat the drums of war in Khartoum be reminded that the rail and river transport in War Zone I remain closed; that the SPLA has sunk more than 15 Nile steamers; that the SPLA has virtually grounded Sudan's Air Force by downing 37 helicopters, 2 Buffalos, 2 C–130 Hercules transport planes, 2 F–5 and 3 Mig–23 jet fighters; that the SPLA has shut down Cheveron Oil, Total Oil and stopped the construction of the Jonglei Canal; and that the SPLA has overrun more than 50 army garrisons. Most of these victories were during Nimeiri's and Swar al Dhahab's times: but Sadiq in his two years as *de facto* Prime Minister, has fared far worse than Nimeiri and Swar al Dhahab. A quick glance at the facts quickly shows that Sadiq's warmongering arrogance and hopes for a military victory are groundless and ill-advised. Let those who beat the drums of war in Khartoum be reminded that during Sadiq's two years as Prime Minister and Minister of War the SPLA liberated the most strategic garrison towns since the war started. These are Pibor, Jekou and Kapoeta in War Zone I. Even a non-military person looking at a map of Sudan would agree with us that these towns are indeed very strategic. Despite Sadiq's short-legged stories that he was going to recapture these towns, we have now held Pibor for 16 months, Jekcu for 13 months and Kapoeta for 7 months.

Let those who beat the drums of war in Khartoum be further reminded that during Sadiq's two years in office the SPLA, for the first time, effectively took the war to what used to be called the "North". In Southern Blue Nile Province the SPLA overran the strategic garrison towns of Kurmuk and Geissan and advanced to within artillery range of the Roseires hydroelectric dam, while in Southern Kordofan the SPLA overran the garrison town of Omdorein. Although these towns were later on retaken by the regime, the SPLA had achieved its strategic objective of establishing a firm and permanent foothold in the North. As I talk to you today, SPLA forces remain in siege of Kurmuk and Qeissan and make deep penetrations to within 15 kilometres of Damazine.

To date the SPLA has recruited thousands of youth from Southern Blue Nile and Southern Kordofan. Today, the major garrison towns of Juba, Wau, Malakal, Torit, Bentiu, Aweil, Rumbek, Gogrial, Nasir, Akobo, Yei, Bor, Maridi, Mundri etc. are under siege and threatened. While we call for peace any of these towns can and indeed will fall to the SPLA.[2] Let those who beat the drums of war in Khartoum be reminded that in the last two years Sadiq, as the Minister of Defence, actually became SPLA's chief Quarter-Master General and still continues to be generous. During these two years of Sadiq's unfounded arrogance the SPLA captured thousands of small arms with millions of pieces of ammunition. We underline to the warmongers in Khartoum that during Sadiq's time, the SPLA for the first time captured many heavy weapons in good working condition. Today, and during Sadiq's time, the SPLA has acquired through capture 10 tanks including 3 T–62s captured in Kurmuk, all in good condition; we have 8 pieces of 122 mm Mortars, 49 pieces of 81/82 mm Mortars, 96 pieces of anti-tank rocket launchers (RPG–7 and RPG–2), 44 pieces of 60 mm Mortars, 37 Grenov heavy machine guns, 50 mg–42 machine guns and tons of explosives. All these weapons and more were captured in good condition during Sadiq's two years as Prime Minister and Minister of Defence.

From this brief record, I present to you that Sadiq's arrogance and war-mongering are baseless as they are not supported by the real military situation on the ground. The government of the Unholy Trinity in Khartoum is composed of people who have never known hardship all their lives. To them death and human suffering in war are mere statistics, not concrete realities in their experience. This is probably why they scorn our peace initiative and delude themselves about SPLA's weakness and the imminence of their military victory. If we put any of the three Unholy Trinity in a trench under fire even for 24 hours, I am certain they would begin to talk sense; the sense of peace. Let those who beat the drums of war without going to war themselves be informed

2 In effect of those garrison towns Torit was captured by the SPLA on 26 February 1989, Nasir on 26 January 1989, Akobo on 11 April 1989, Bor on 17 April 1989, Kapocta on 11 January 1989 while all the others remain under seige.

that SPLA's quest for peace is based on our genuine concern for the suffering of our people, a suffering that is not statistics to us, but that we ourselves live every day we wake up and every night we go to sleep.

Problems within the SPLM/SPLA

Before I continue, I do not want to leave you with the impression that the SPLM/SPLA has achieved only victory after victory without any problems; that could not be possible. Indeed that would be unnatural. Nothing in nature or in society develops or moves smoothly without resistance; and of all phenomena, a national liberation movement, like ours, that is based on revolutionary armed struggle must, of necessity, mean struggle both from within and from without. That is the only way it could move forward. There has, therefore, been; there had to be; and there will continue to be; internal as well as external factors that impact adversely on the attainment of our objectives. Internally, for example, we had to contain the elements of separatism, tribalism and opportunism. Externally, we had to grapple with problems created by the enemy in their futile attempts to infiltrate our leadership with the aim to salvage and preserve the old Sudan by accommodating the SPLM/SPLA through some form of sham peace. In the fog of their sectarian non-objective thinking, the rulers of Khartoum misread the dialectics of revolution as symptoms of SPLA's weakness. Again, they could not be more wrong. Far from weakening the SPLM/SPLA, these problems and challenges have enriched and strengthened the Movement. With each new problem, each new challenge overcome the Movement reaches a higher qualitative level in its growth and draws closer to its objective of national renaissance and national liberation, which we subsume in our slogan of the "creation of a New Sudan". Far from being the cause of alarm or worry to members, supporters and sympathizers of the Movement the correct resolution of these problems are indicators of theMovement's solidity and strength; they indicate that the Movement has come of age and is here to stay. Our strength has always been and will remain the firmness, the steadfastness and the persistence in the goals we have set ourselves to achieve. This resolve is steeled in us by the support of the masses of our people and the growing level of awareness of the SPLA soldier. The SPLA soldier has been vigilant, and his vigilance has been the Movement's strongest shield.

This vigilance is based on the correct and concrete realization by the rank-and-file of the SPLA that the Movement belongs to each and every one of them and to all the Sudanese people, not to certain ethnic or regional groupings as the enemies of the revolution would like to believe or make others believe, nor does it belong to individuals such as John Garang or any other members of the political-military High Command. The SPLA rank-and-file believe and are convinced that the SPLM/SPLA is their only hope to restore their dignity, democracy, justice, prosperity and greatness. Any internal or external attempt to abort the people's revolution should, therefore, be collectively resisted by the SPLA rank-and-file. This explains the growing solidity and cohesiveness of the SPLM/SPLA since its formation in 1983.

Merger of Anya-Nya II[3]

I have endeavoured to show that our peace initiative is genuine and not based on Sadiq's imagined weakness of the SPLM/SPLA, either internally within the Movement or externally as a result of military pressure by Khartoum. I have shown that the SPLA is strong and growing stronger than ever. In this connection, I am happy to announce to you that this strength has been recently consolidated by the Movement's tireless efforts to merge the Anya-Nya II into the SPLA. While the sectarian Unholy Trinity government in Khartoum will continue to divide the Sudanese people for its own selfish unpatriotic ends, the Movement is committed to unite the Sudanese people everywhere. I congratulate the former Anya-nya II leaders, Comrade Gordon Mong Chol, for his brave and patriotic decision to heed the Movement's call to abandon the regime of doom in Khartoum and to join hands with the People's Movement. The merger of Anya-Nya II into the SPLA has further greatly weakened the regime, depriving it of human cannon fodder that is used around its garrisons in Upper Nile. Today, as I talk to you, more than 80 per cent of Anya-Nya II forces have already been incorporated into the SPLA, and Comrade Gordon Kong Chol himself has been appointed alternate member of the SPLM/SPLA Political-Military High Command.

3   The Anya-Nya II movement was originally espoused by the army, under Nimeiri, to provide a shield to its garrisons against the SPLA; they were later used by Nimeiri's heirs despite their denunciation of Nimeirism.

This development should further convince Sadiq to accept peace as well as a rude reminder that arming the Sudanese people against each other is a futile and dangerous double-edged sword. Sooner or later the government-sponsored tribal militias will find out that they are being deceived, that the military ranks accorded them such as Brigadiers and Sultans are meaningless, and they will, like Anya-Nya II, turn the criminal's guns against the criminal. The Movement has in this connection already won the Murle, Taposa and Didinga tribal militias and will continue to do everything to win the Mandari tribal militia and the Fertit and Rezigat tribal militias despite the wanton atrocities committed by these militias. A government that arms its own people against each other in order to survive can only succeed to dig its own grave, and such is the fate of the Unholy Trinity Government in Khartoum.

War and the National Economy

The economic crisis facing our country is at best very grim, and this is compounded and exacerbated by the war, which the regime is determined to escalate. It is the Government of Sadiq that does not want an end to the war, and as long as the war lasts there can be no stability and no socioeconomic development and the suffering of our people can only increase. By today's end the regime will have already spent more than one million US dollars, as it does daily in its futile attempt to achieve military victory over the SPLA. But this is your money; it is the people's money, not Sadiq's. It should be spent on your health, the education of your children, construction of roads, purchase of public buses and other basic needs of the people. The external debt of the Old Sudan of the Sadiqs, the Turabis and the Mirghanis rose from 10 billion US dollars in 1986, when they took office, to more than 15 billion US dollars today. The Sudanese child that will be born tomorrow will be born into debt of some 4,000 US dollars. What explanation do we give our children as they grow up and find out that some invisible person in some foreign capital demands that he or she pays 4,000 US dollars? Is this the inheritance we leave to posterity? The Sudanese pound has been devalued to a point where what one pound could buy five years ago now costs more than ten pounds. One kilo of meat costs about two pounds five years ago when the war started, today it costs about 25 pounds, an increase of 1,250%. And as if this was not enough hardship caused by the Sadiqs, the Turabis and the Mirghanis, another devaluation of the Sudanese pound is imminent this year, and with it the cost of survival will rise. In the Sudan the vast majority of our people in the cities and countryside no longer live; the problem is not to live but to survive. The economists, in their jargon and textbooks, should substitute the term "cost of surviving" in place of "cost of living" in order better to reflect the real situation. It is common knowledge to you that basic commodities such as dura, bread, sugar, soap, kerosene for lighting houses of the poor, meat, benzene, drugs and many other essential commodities are no longer available, and whenever they are available they are to be found in the darkest corners of the black market and at exhorbitant prices beyond the reach, even the smell, of the vast majority of the Sudanese people. The black market has become the order of the economy and even the Prime Minister and his ministers (at least their servants) buy on the black market, sometimes from their own black market agents, as public officials, especially ministers, have shady businesses that largely control the black market. Public transport is a daily nightmare for the working people. One wonders whether Sadiq, Turabi or Mirghani has ever been to a bus station in their life, at least to see how these noble people are forced to scramble into a bus, some going in through the windows and some trampling over their mothers and fathers, with the dignity and respect accorded to our elderly completely lost in the heat and dust of waiting for public transport. Health services, education, frequent cuts in electricity, which affect major operations in hospitals, have become the order of the day. Even cheap life-saving drugs are not available. Our countryside has become a desolate forgotten world where the nation's economic and political crisis has degenerated into armed robbery and slavery. The Unholy Trinity Government of the Sadiqs, the Turabis and Mirghanis is a nightmare, a cancerous growth that urgently requires the surgeon's knife.

While these problems, the grave economic and political crises mercilessly grind at the heart of our young nation in formation, the few who control the affairs of the state in Khartoum live as if they did not belong to the same country we share or should share. While the few rich struggle to live, the vast majority struggle to survive. While the sons of the rural and urban poor are the ones who are fighting this costly war, the sons and daughters of the rich and powerful few attend higher education abroad, so that when they return they take over the machinery of the state from their fathers on the basis of the vicious circle argument that the affairs of state must be run by people with good formal education. Thus the systems condemns father and son or daughter to perpetual poverty. While their sons and daughters study and enjoy life abroad, at home the ruling clique ride in luxurious cars and jeer at the long queues for public buses under the sweltering heat of our country. For how long can this intolerable situation continue? For how long will the Sudanese people continue to finance the comfort of a rich few to the detriment of their own development?

Tribal Militias and Government-sponsored Pogrom

In addition to the crisis in the economy our country is threatened by three other crises connected with the economic and political crisis. I must bring them to your attention. One is the very serious problem of Government-sponsored robbery in the form of tribal militias that are organized and armed by the Government. The Regime has the arrogance to call these bandits "Friendly Forces". Since these militias are organized along tribal lines, by implication the Government means that there are "Unfriendly Tribes". What monster of a National Government divides its citizens into "friendly" and "unfriendly" tribes. This is unprecedented in Africa and indeed anywhere else in the world. Today, these Government butchers and thugs that variously go by the names of "Tribal Militia", "Friendly Forces" or "Marehiliin", operate with impunity, spreading terror, wanton killing of innocent unarmed civilians, looting and burning of whole villages and crops, taking with them cattle, sheep, goats and slaves. The Government has evolved an evil policy of depopulation and genocide in Bar el Ghazal, Benitu, Southern Kordofan and Southern Blue Nile Provinces. The mechanism Sadiq's Government employs to achieve this un-Sudanese goal is the "unpaid" services of these tribal militias. Sadiq's Government gives guns and bullets to the militias, and the militias get their pay in the forms of the loot they get in the field, a loot that is lucrative enough to provide sufficient incentive for these unfortunate tribal militias who, in the course of their dirty trade, become dehumanized and lose all sense of being Sudanese. This Government policy of genocide is no longer a secret to the outside world. Recently in the London *Financial Times* of May 1988, independent reporters compiled a report confirming Government sponsorship and endorsement of rape, looting, torture and wholesale murder of civilians in Bahr el Ghazal as legitimate tactics against the SPLA. When he took office in 1986, the Prime Minister Sadiq al Mahdi, without a shudder of shame, publicly announced over the BBC that if the SPLA did not stop the war he was going to exterminate Southerners. Now Sadiq's extermination campaign has been extended to Southern Kordofan, Southern Blue Nile and Dar Fur. His next target will most likely be Eastern Sudan. In the Government-sponsored pogrom in Bahr el Ghazal, old people flee to Khartoum, which they consider their capital, find the way blocked and are summarily slaughtered on account of their age. Able-bodied persons and children are sold into slavery internally and abroad. The price of a slave is now reported to have dropped from some 500 Sudanese pounds to about 10 pounds, the equivalent of one US dollar! By sponsoring this genocide, this madness of slave raids and slave markets to the absurd point where a fellow Sudanese is sold for one US dollar, does the Prime Minister not realize that his own value as a human being also depreciates to much less than one US dollar?

Foreign Intervention in Western Sudan
The economic, political and moral bankruptcy of the Unholy Trinity Government in Khartoum and its desperate attempts to hang on to power at all costs have left the doors of our country open to foreign countries to violate our territorial integrity. This is a serious threat to the unity of Sudan. In Western Sudan there are foreign military forces that came to our country uninvited and that do not fall under the control of any Sudanese authority. To be precise these foreign forces now number 6,500 officers and men, and they are increasing. They roam the area at will, spreading panic and terror among the citizens of that region. The Government is silent about this foreign penetration of our territory because the presence of these foreign troops in Darfur is one of the prices paid to foreign powers who have paid money and weapons to some of Khartoum's sectarian rulers. These foreign troops in Darfur are instigating Sudanese communities in the area against each other. They have already armed certain tribes against others. They are connected with the recent battle for Jebel Mara, in which the Fur people repulsed an attempt to dislodge them from their ancestral home. The Prime Minister, Sadiq al Mahdi, is responsible and accountable for the fighting in Darfur. The

161

SPLA supports the call of the people of Darfur on Sadiq el Mahdi to see to it that these foreign forces leave Darfur. These foreign forces must go; they are dangerous to the stability and unity of our country.

Sectarianism; an Antithesis of Democracy

The last important problem I want to bring to your attention is the question of DEMOCRACY. The Prime Minister talks loudly and noisily about democracy while at the same time his dictatorial grip on the country mounts. The state of emergency is still fully in force, peaceful demonstrations are banned, political leaders of opposition parties are detained and harassed from time to time; Sayed el-Turabi is drafting another version of his Nimeiri September 1983 religious sectarian laws. Under the new Turabi/Sadiq religious sectarian laws, the hands and legs of the small thieves will again be amputated while the hands and legs of the big thieves in Government will grow fatter than before. The regime knows that the majority of the Sudanese people are against these laws, even including the Honourable Members of the Assembly. The regime has therefore decided to have these laws passed in the Assembly through a standing ballot instead of the usual secret ballot characteristic of democracies. Since these laws are pseudo-religious no member of the Assembly would want to be seen standing and voting against these laws. A normal secret ballot would certainly go against these laws. I take the opportunity to appeal to the Honourable Members of the Assembly to insist on a secret ballot on these laws, this is their right and they should never be intimidated into this so-called standing vote. I further appeal to them in the name of the Sudan to vote against these laws, as their passage can only further drive our country into chaos. Sayed al Turabi is also drafting or has already drafted the so-called Party Organization Law intended to eliminate other parties that are not in the Holy Trinity government of UMMA, NIF and DUP. Sayed el Turabi is also drafting the so-called "New Press Laws", intended to curb the freedom of the non-sectarian press. I ask what democracy is this, but sham democracy, which amounts to dictatorship? Parliament is increasingly being rendered ineffectual as matters of serious business are decided by the three Sayeds, Sayed Sadiq el Mahdi, Sayed Hassan al Turabi and Sayed Mohamed Osman al Mirghani. If there is anything close to a democratic change in the Sudan it is that the Sayeds have expanded their number from two to three, with Sayed al Turabi taking second place and Sayed al Mirghani thrown into third place. The three Sayeds wheel and deal outside parliament, turning parliament like Nimeiri did into a rubber stamp. This dictatorial attitude and trend is not a surprise to those who know Sadiq well. In 1977 and after taking a solemn oath before Nimeiri, as a member of the Political Bureau of Nimeiri's Sudanese Socialist Union (SSU), the sole political party then, Sadiq declared without mincing his words that multi-party democracy has no place in the Sudan and that the country can be ruled only through a one party system. These are documented statements and there is no way Sadiq can deny them. This is the same Sadiq who nowadays prides and deludes himself supervising what he calls, in one of his statements, an "oasis of liberal democracy in Africa and the Middle East".

We are not amused. There is nothing democratic in sectarianism. Sectarianism of any type in politics, by the weight of its own inner logic, bends towards opportunism, dictatorship, oppression, tyranny and fascism. It had done so in Hitler's Germany; it has done so in racist apartheid South Africa; there is no reason why it cannot do so in a religious apartheid Sudan. This is the ominous shape of things to come if the Old Sudan is allowed to flounder to its logical conclusion. But the shadow of Dictator Nimeiri looms ominously from behind.

How to resolve Sudan's Multiple Problems

The very grave problems that I have been discussing, the problems of the economy, the crisis in government, armed robbery and government sponsored militias, foreign troops in our country that came uninvited, the question of democracy, drought and famine, relief and rehabilitation; all these problems can be solved only if the war ends and there is peace, peace with justice ushering in economic and social development. But the Unholy Trinity Government in Khartoum does not want peace, they want a military victory, which they cannot achieve. They only talk and double-talk about peace while in fact they prepare for yet another military offensive to, as they say, wipe out the SPLA once and for all. But you all know the truth; all Government military offensives not only failed but also led to more SPLA victories. Khartoum's record on genuine desire and actions to bring about peace is as poor as their performances in the field. In order to fully appreciate why peace has been eluding us ever since the Intifadha, it is necessary to briefly explore the history of attempts at a peace settlement.

Starting with Nimeiri, you all remember how Nimeiri used to deceive the people about peace talks he allegedly was having with the SPLA and with Anyanya–2. At one point Nimeiri said that he was conducting talks with several rebel groups. At another point he said that talks with the SPLA had reached a delicate stage. The truth, of course, is that there were no such talks. Nimeiri was simply playing with the people's emotion and desire for peace. But SPLM/SPLA called for peace through dialogue even before Nimeiri's fall. On 22 March 1985 (14 days before the fall of the Dictator) the SPLM/SPLA called for direct talks between the Sudanese Army in war zone one and the SPLA, while at the National level we called for convening a *National Congress* to be attended by all political forces in the country to discuss the formation of a New Sudan, a New Sudan with a new non-sectarian personality. Verbatim, in a Radio SPLA broadcast, I said on 22 March 1985 and I quote:

> I end by appealing to the Sudanese Army to start talking directly with the SPLA in war zone I, not through the Dictator. The Dictator, Nimeiri, has nothing new to offer. Forget about him and all those generals and bourgeoisified elite around him, who have bled our country for the last 16 years. You form your own committees in your respective garrisons and contact the nearest SPLA unit to convey your views to SPLA GHQs. We envisage a National Congress to be organized by the SPLM/SPLA, progressive and patriotic elements in the Sud-anese Army and other democratic forces in the country for formation of a New Sudan and its New Army consistent with its new particularity.

Following Nimeiri's fall, this SPLM/SPLA call for a National Congress was lost in the dust of euphoria and the scramble for ministerial positions. After formation of the Transitional Military Council (TMC) and its civilian council of ministers, the SPLM call for a National Congress was further lost in a massive disinfor-mation and mystification campaign by the TMC. The TMC, in its first 24 hours in office, concocted a malicious story that Dr. John Garang was in a plane on his way to Khartoum, when in fact I was at that time in Central Upper Nile and had no contact with

Khartoum whatsoever. This lie was fabricated by the Generals to raise the people's emotions and to disappoint them when I did not show up in Khartoum, thus discrediting the Movement and painting a negative picture in the minds of the public that the SPLM/SPLA did not want peace. When the lie of Dr. John's going to Khartoum had outlived its usefulnes, the TMC invented yet another lie. They announced that they were conducting peace talks with the Movement. At one point the TMC even announced that the talks had reached a delicate stage. Again, as in Nimeiri's time, the truth was that there were no such talks. Like Nimeiri, the TMC was raising the people's emotion and desire for peace and to disappoint them when no peace materialized and thus turn public opinion against the Movement. Records are there to prove that the first communication between the TMC and the SPLA was after 61 days from the date they assumed power and this was after the TMC had made sure public opinion had been mobilized against the Movement. The truth is that to date no Government in Khartoum has ever been genuinely interested in peace, and as I will show, the Government of Sadiq El Mahdi has been worse than those of Nimeiri and the TMC. Sadiq has actually persistently worked against peace and continues to work against it, putting obstacle after obstacle in the path of the Koka Dam peace process.

The SPLM/SPLA 22 March 1985 call for a National Congress was not completely lost; it was picked up by the National Alliance of National Salvation (NANS). A series of meetings took place between the SPLM/SPLA and the NANS, and these contacts culminated in the Koka-Dam Conference. The four-day conference reached an agreement on how to approach the solution of Sudan's fundamental problems. That declaration set out in detail the necessary prerequisites for the convening of a National Constitutional Conference and the agenda of that conference. The Koka Dam Agreement was a major watershed in the Sudanese genuine search for a just peace. Concluded on 24 March 1986, on the eve of the first anniversary of the Intifadha that overthrew Dictator Nimeiri, the Koka Dam Declaration was signed by the SPLM/SPLA, and except for the DUP and NIF, by all the other Sudanese political parties, including the Prime Minister's UMMA party and by all the major professional and Trade Union organizations. The Koka Dam Declaration provided, for the first time, a real basis for just peace. For the first time Sudan's Political forces were serious about peace and were sincere. But the leader of the

UMMA party, Sadiq El Mahdi, became Prime Minister three months after Koka Dam, and Sadiq immediately started to campaign against the peace process to which he was signatory. The campaign against Koka Dam was so intense that to date the majority of the Sudanese people do not know what was agreed at Koka Dam. Sadiq's Government went out of its way to hide the Koka Dam Declaration from the Sudanese people, and instead Sadiq started to talk about his so-called popular national Committee and to draft useless charter after useless charter. All these one-man, one-party committees and charters can only bring illusions of peace in the mind of Sadiq but not to the Sudanese people.

I feel obliged by our commitment to genuine peace to remind you of the six points that were agreed upon at Koka Dam. All the participants, and this includes the Prime Minister's UMMA party, and here I quote from the official text of the Declaration:

> Agree that essential pre-requisites which would foster an atmosphere conducive to the holding of the proposed National Constitutional Conference are:
>
> 1   A declaration by all political forces and the government of the day of their commitment to discuss the *Basic Problems of the Sudan* and not the so-called problem of the Southern Sudan, and that shall be in accordance with the agenda agreed upon in this Declaration.
>
> 2   The lifting of the state of emergency.
>
> 3   Repeal of the "September 1983 Laws" and all other laws that are restrictive of freedoms.
>
> 4   Adoption of the 1956 Constitution as amended in 1964 with incorporation of "Regional Government" and all other such matters on which a consensus opinion of all the political forces shall be reached.
>
> 5   The abrogation of the military pacts concluded between Sudan and other countries and which impinge on Sudan's national sovereignty, and
>
> 6   A continuous endeavour by the two sides to take the necessary steps and measurements to effect cease-fire.

You may still remember that I met Sadiq in Addis Ababa on 31 July 1986, when each of us went there to attend the OAU

Conference. The SPLM/SPLA side went into the meeting with an open mind and concrete proposals, and alternative proposals of how to accelerate the peace process as stipulated by the Koka Dam Declaration. This serious sense on our side was met with persistent reluctance from Sadiq to commit himself to specifics, and to our surprise, Sadiq wanted to strike a bilateral deal between the UMMA party and the SPLM/SPLA. We told Sadiq, in no uncertain terms, that that was a non-starter, and that neither the SPLM/SPLA nor the UMMA party, nor indeed any other political force had the right to tamper with the Declaration. It was the work of all the Sudanese political forces and it is only they who can collectively amend it or throw it away if they so choose. The Sudanese people have the right to know this fact. It was our position then and it is our position now. After a long nine hours of meeting with Sadiq and just before the two sides could part, I especially told Sadiq in a frank sincere talk, and in the presence of all, that "Mr. Prime Minister, if I were you, I would on my return to Khartoum hold a press conference at the airport and announce the immediate implementation of the six prerequisites for convening of the National Constitutional Conference as agreed upon at Koka Dam." "If you do that", I told Sadiq, "then I assure you that the following day I would declare a cease-fire to pave the way for convening the National Constitutional Conference." When Sadiq went back to Khartoum we were expecting him to build on the common points raised in our discussion. But, alas, we couldn't be more wrong: Sadiq, as some of you may remember, went to parliament and described us as "labouring under illusions" and immediately set in motion his military plan. Instead of creating conditions for a cease-fire, Sadiq increased fire in his ill-fated 1986/1987 dry season military offensive, which cost him the loss of Pibor and Jekou to the SPLA. And as if that lesson was not sufficient to teach Sadiq the futility of seeking a military victory, he again launched another disastrous dry season military offensive in 1987/88. This time it cost Sadiq the loss of Kurmuk, Qeissan, and Kapoeta to the SPLA. Now that the dry season is over, Sadiq has fallen under yet another illusion. Sadiq and those around him think that the SPLA has run out of ammunition and that the Movement suffers from internal division, and consequently he thinks that this is his opportunity to defeat the SPLA. One of the Sadiq's southern ministers was recently asked in an international conference in Geneva how negotiations between the government and the SPLA were progressing. True to form, the fool rhetorically asked "what negotiation?" The SPLA, he said is finished. So intensive is the illusion of SPLA imminent defeat in Khartoum that Sadiq committed his troops in an ill-advised rainy season offensive this last June in hopes of wiping out the SPLA. His tanks, artillery and trucks are now bogged down in Eastern Upper Nile and Eastern Equatoria fighting first with our friendly forces, i.e. rains, mud, mosquitoes and snakes before the SPLA wipes them out. The SPLA has already wiped out one of Sadiq's brigades between Juba and Torit in the last 14 days, and his other forces await the same fate. His so-called Deterrent Brigade, now stationed in Juba, will soon be destroyed. The SPLA knows what to do with it; we know their next move and we know where to destroy them. Sadiq is best advised to abandon warmongering and to sue for peace; otherwise, he is in for bigger surprises and bigger defeats.

The commitment of the SPLM/SPLA to peace is unequivocal and irrevocable. Despite the many obstacles created by the *de facto* Government in Khartoum to abort the Koka Dam peace process, the Movement had never abandoned and has never tired in the search for peaceful resolution of the Sudanese conflict. Many other patriots, such as those in the Alliance have also worked day and night to bring about peace. In this endeavour we met last year with a delegation of Sudanese Bishops to be followed by a series of meetings in Ethiopia, Uganda and Kenya with a delegation of the Sudan African Parties that was led by Honourable Mr. Eliaba James Surur, substituting for the Honourable Rev. Philip Abbas Gaboush. Last week the Movement met again with a delegation of the Union of Sudan African Parties, led by the Honourable Dr. Andrew Wiew Riak. In all these meetings the necessity for peaceful solution was underlined with the Alliance, the Sudanese Bishops and the African Parties. But to our disappointment the Prime Minister always blocks all peace moves, calling those who come to meet the SPLM/SPLA 5th columnists, instead of Sudanese patriots genuinely searching for peace. At one point the Prime Minister even went to the extent of forbidding contacts between Sudanese political forces and individuals with the SPLM/SPLA under threat of harassment and charge of the so-called 5th columnist. Nevertheless the Movement was able to meet all these parties and even the DUP and NIF, the two parties that chose to absent themselves from Koka Dam.

At an international level, the Movement met and exchanged views on peace with such respected leaders as the former Nigerian Head of State, General Olesugeun Obasanjo, who tried his best at mediation and through whom the SPLM/SPLA conveyed specific peace proposals to the Prime Minister, but all to no avail. The Movement was recently invited to and attended the inter-action council of former heads of states that met in Harare, Zimbabwe. The Government was also invited. Instead of taking advantage of this meeting as a starter to re-open the Koka Dam peace process, Sadiq chose to send a propaganda delegation, headed by a three-quarters crazy Southern politician. Finally, in our quest for peace, I recently presented a peace initiative in a press statement during the 25th anniversary celebrations of the founding of the OUA in Addis Ababa. The Prime Minister first complained that the peace initiative should have been conveyed through proper channels, not the press. This is surely absurd; what proper channels do we have with Sadiq when he calls the Movement a terrorist organization. Subsequently Khartoum launched a major campaign of distortion and misinformation regarding our latest peace initiative with the intention to kill it.

Although the prospects for peace are not bright for as long as the Unholy Trinity Government of the Sadiqs, the Turabis and the Mirghanis sit in Khartoum, still I must end my address to you today by calling for peace. If the Unholy Trinity is not interested in peace as they have indicated from time to time till now, it falls on the Sudanese political forces to bring about peace with or without them. The Sudanese people made a giant step forward towards peace when the Koka Dam Declaration was signed more than two years ago. This Declaration and the subsequent meetings of the Joint-Liaison Committee have laid a solid foundation for the peace process. Koka Dam is a purely Sudanese experience which will go down in history as a magnificent achievement of great significance, for it proved to the whole world that the Sudanese alone can discuss their problems freely and arrive at concrete proposals regarding their resolution. The resolutions of Koka Dam are as pertinent today as they were 27 months ago when they were adopted as the blueprint to achieve peace in the Sudan. As I have shown, the only obstacle standing in the way of the convening of the National Constitutional Conference is the *de facto* Government in Khartoum, and more specifically, the *de facto* Prime Minister, Sadiq El Mahdi, who is more preoccupied

169

with securing the Imamship of the Ansar and his temporal powers than with the welfare of the Sudanese people. It is the responsibility of the Sudanese political forces to reinforce and strengthen Koka Dam. The Prime Minister has persistently refused to implement the prerequisites stipulated in that declaration as necessary prerequisites for the convening of the National Constitutional Conference. The major argument of Sadiq is that the declaration is not binding on the DUP and the NIF because they did not sign it. If the only argument against Koka Dam is that the DUP and NIF were not signatory to it, and if otherwise the government is genuinely wanting a peaceful resolution to the conflict, then I here repeat the peace proposal which I gave to General Obasanjo to convey to Sadiq and which I recently declared in the press. Let us convene another Koka Dam type National gathering, Koka Dam II, preliminary to the National Constitutional Conference, and in which all the Sudanese political forces will be present including the DUP and NIF who chose not to attend Koka Dam I. This proposal entails strengthening, not abandoning the Koka Dam Declaration and peace process by widening it to include the absentees, the DUP and the NIF. As to the other political forces, they are bound by the Koka Dam Declaration and peace process. The necessary measure is to bring into Koka Dam the DUP and NIF.

The peace we aspire to is attainable provided that patriots and nationalists in our country join hands in a serious and genuine search for a just and permanent peace. In this context and in order to give substance to the peace process under the Koka Dam Declaration, the SPLM/SPLA makes the following suggestions and proposals:

1 The SPLM/SPLA calls on the National Alliance for National Salvation, as the neutral national body, to initiate the preparation for a national gathering, Koka Dam II, which will include all Sudanese political forces, and in particular to ensure the attendance of the DUP and NIF. This National gathering, Koka Dam II, will build on Koka Dam I and form the basis for the holding of the proposed National Constitutional Conference.

2 The SPLM/SPLA has already contacted several countries, and at least three of them have expressed willingness and readiness to host Koka Dam II. We call on the National Alliance to consult with the various Sudanese political forces. The Movement is now

ready to receive representatives of the Alliance to discuss all matters related to this peace initiative including time and venue.

3   As a gesture of goodwill on the side of the SPLM/SPLA we are now releasing, without pre-conditions, the prisoner of war, Lt. Col. Izz el Din Osman Saraj, captured in Southern Kordofan last year. We request the ICRC to help in the return of Lt. Col. Izz el Din to join his family and relatives. The release can be made through Kenya, Ethiopia or Uganda.

4   We renew our earlier offer to exchange prisoners of war through the ICRC, and this for humanitarian reasons as well as to create necessary conducive atmosphere for Koka Dam II.

5   If the Khartoum Government is not willing or ready to exchange POWs held by SPLA the Movement suggests that the relatives of the POWs come to SPLA POW camps, accompanied by members of the National Alliance, so that they can see and meet their beloved ones. The SPLM/SPLA guarantee safe conduct to and from the POW camps for the relatives and members of the National Alliance accompanying them. The POWs are under command of Lt. Col. Salim Said, of Batch No. 24, and former Commander of Jekou Garrison, which we captured in 31/5/1987.[1] This measure also will help in providing conducive atmosphere for holding Koka Dam II.

6   As a gesture of goodwill from the Khartoum Government, the Movement asks that Amnesty International be allowed to look into human rights violation in the Sudan, and especially in Aweil, Gogrial Districts and Wau town.

7   As a gesture of goodwill, I call on the Minister of Defence, General Abdel Magid Hamid Khalil, a person most of us in the SPLA who know him respect, to disassociate Major General Abu Gurun, the commander of Bahr el Ghazal, and Major General Fadhalla Burma, the commander of the Marahliin Tribal Militia, from the Sudanese Army. These officers have killed or caused the death of thousands of innocent unarmed Sudanese citizens in Bahr el Ghazal. They are murderers and criminals who should be arrested and brought to justice. General Abu Gurun, for example, forced 6–10 year old boys to kill their parents with spears while he watched in amusement; in Wau at Grinti garrison, he put 62

---

1 Lt Col. Said was captured by the SPLA when his garrison fell to that army. Offered to choose between release on the terms indicated above and joining the SPLA, he chose the latter.

civilians in an empty ammunition storeroom and gassed them to death by carbon monoxide poisoning passed into the storeroom through an exhaust pipe connected to an armed personnel carrier. These are documented facts, reported by witnesses and in the latest issue of *New Africa*, No. 250 of July 1988. These are not Sudanese Army officers, but criminals running amok in army uniform. General Abdel Magid has the responsibility to take measures against these two officers; their actions stain the image of the Sudanese army. Action against them could also create a conducive atmosphere of Koka Dam II, and finally,

8   The Movement believes that it is not the international relief organizations alone that should provide relief assistance to the people displaced by war and drought in the Sudan. This should be started at home, by Sudanese people. The SPLM/SPLA therefore calls on concerned Sudanese patriots in Khartoum to organize themselves into a chapter of the Sudan Relief and Rehabilitation Association (SRRA), Khartoum Branch, and to solicit funds, food, clothing and other material in the name of SRRA. The SRRA is a voluntary humanitarian association and there is no reason why a branch cannot be registered in Khartoum. Such concerned citizens are to contact and coordinate with the Secretary General of the SRRA, Dr. Richard M. Mulla, in the Nairobi Head Office.

The Addis Ababa Peace Forum
5–7 July 1988

Joint Communiqué by the Delegations of the Union of the Sudan African Parties and the Sudan People's Liberation Movement/Sudan People's Liberation Army (SPLM/SPLA)

–   Persuant to the Addis Ababa Peace Forum, Kampala Quest for Peace and Nairobi Search for Peace communiqués issued by the SPLM/SPLA, Anya Nya Two and the Union of the Sudan African Parties in August and September 1987;

–   Aware of the Sudan Government's persistent attempts to internationalize our domestic problems as manifested by the recent speeches of the Prime Minister, the Minister of Defence, and the Minister of Foreign Affairs, accusing some neighbouring countries, humanitarian and religious organizations of their involvement in our internal affairs;

– Convinced of our capability to solve our internal problems without foreign interference, reject these attempts which implicate some foreign countries and international organizations;

– Considering the effects of the on-going war in the Sudan which increasingly claim many lives and the destruction of properties of the Sudanese citizens on both sides including innocent citizens who have been displaced and exposed to famine, disease and misery;

– Determined and committed to bring about meaningful and just peace, stability, justice and equality to our suffering people;

– Convinced that the only way to solve our national problems is through dialogue, have therefore agreed and adopted the following:

1   The National Constitutional Conference shall be held before the end of 1988, as expressed by all the political forces in the country.

2   Call upon and urge the forces of the 6 April 1985 Uprising including the SPLM/SPLA and all the other political forces in the country to hold a preliminary meeting in the spirit of Koka Dam Conference of 1986, to discuss the programme, agenda, venue, and the time for the convening of the National Constitutional Conference.

3   The SPLM/SPLA will consider cease fire during the aforesaid preliminary meeting depending on the prevailing situation at the time.

4   The SPLM/SPLA reaffirms the guarantee and willingness for safe ferrying of relief supplies by the international organizations to all Sudanese citizens in affected areas, both under the SPLM/SPLA and Government controlled areas. The assistance rendered so far by some international organizations to the victims is appreciated. However, due to the immensity of the suffering in these areas and in the refugee camps, the SPLM/SPLA and the Union of the Sudan African Parties appeal to these organizations for more aid.

5   The SPLM/SPLA reiterates its commitment to the realization of a secular state in the Sudan.

6   The SPLM/SPLA repeats its earlier offer for the exchange of prisoners of war with the Government through the International Committee of the Red Cross.

Signed in Addis Ababa on the 8th Day of July in the Year One Thousand Nine Hundred and Eighty-Eight.

For the SPLM/SPLA,   *For the Union of the*
                                        Sudan African Parties,

Commander Yousif Kuo Mekki,
Alternate Member of the   Dr. Andrew Wieu Riak,
SPLM/SPLA Politico-Military High   USAP's Spokesman, and
Command, and the Leader of the   Leader of the Delegation.
Delegation.

Chapter Six:

Food as a Weapon

Closely related to the eruption of hostilities is the victimization of innocent citizens caught across fire-lines, particularly the most vulnerable among them; children, women and the aged. Hundreds of thousands of people in rural areas within the war zone fall into this category; the fortunate amongst them were those who managed to walk, cadaverous and atrophied, to havens beyond the war zone; the rest perished unnoticed and uncared for.

Throughout the first two years of Sadiq's government, the SPLM/SPLA were continually accused, sometimes by the Prime Minister himself, of callously neglecting those people and even of using hunger and access to food as a weapon. The SPLM/SPLA, the government claimed, was trying to bring the Southern provinces to their knees by starving out the local inhabitants. The movement was also accused of deliberately ensuring that whatever aid was available to relieve the horrific famine in the region, did not get through. In support of those accusations incidents such as that of 16 August 1986, the downing of a civilian plane in the war zone by SPLA troops, were given wide prominence in the press, while much mileage was made of the government's own efforts to procure external aid for the people of the region.

This picture put out by the government was by no means true or complete. In some respects it was a gross distortion of the truth, designed to aid the government in what it perceived to be a propaganda war. In the same way as some viewed the peace initiative, not as an end in itself but only as a political ploy, so too, for many in Khartoum, the issue of relief in itself was of little concern to them; it was only given prominence because it was an emotive subject that could be used to gather support for the government and heap ill repute on the SPLM/SPLA. For example, often times the Prime Minister accused John Garang of "starving his own people"; as a statement emanating from the Prime Minister of Sudan, it was both galling and revealing. Such statements reveal the thinking of some Northern politicians to whom there are two brands of Sudanese, those who are primarily of concern to the government in Khartoum (Northerners) and those who could be discounted to Garang (Southerners). The truth of the matter is that few political actors in Khartoum cared much about the real people behind the numbing statistics of death and famine in Southern Sudan.

Faced within the Sudan, by the government's overwhelming propaganda machine, both at the time in question and in the subsequent period, the SPLM endeavoured to set the record straight and to establish its own position on this vital issue. The SPLM's efforts to attract the attention of the world to the plight of the South predated any steps taken by the government, and far outstripped any initiatives offered by government humanitarian agencies. It is worth pointing out that the scale of the problem had already become apparent even before the fall of Nimeiri in 1985; the whole Southern region was at that time in the throes of a severe drought that left millions of people on the verge of starvation. In his first speech after the fall of Nimeiri, Garang addressed the issue and revealed the magnitude of the crisis in the South and the damage it brought on human and animal life as well as the natural environment. He also disclosed how the TMC was trying to exploit the situation for their own ends, which were, at that time, ensuring that food supply reached the government army garrisons.

In order to emphasize its concern with the fate of the thousands threatened with starvation the movement, as early as 1986, elected to bring the issue to the attention of the United Nations who were increasingly drawn into that issue. For that end a high-ranking delegation was detailed to meet Mr. Winston Brattley, the Personal Representative of the Secretary General in Khartoum. That meeting took place in Addis Ababa in February 1986. On the side of the Movement were Lt. Col. Karibino Kwanyin Bol, Major

Arok Thon Arok and Mansour Khalid. Brattley made sure that the authorities in Khartoum were apprised of his mission; both before coming to Addis Ababa (and reportedly after his return to Khartoum); in both cases he met with both the Prime Minister and Head of State of the day, General Swar al Dahab and Dr. Jizouli Dafaa' Alla. The purpose of those discussions was to work out a formula for an equitable apportionment of aid to civilians on both sides of the fence, delineate the modalities for bringing relief to those who were most in need for it and ensure that the whole operation would be strictly managed by neutral agencies such as the UN. Accordingly a plan was drawn up, whereby, government cooperation permitting, a number of controlled routes would be opened up through which supplies of food would safely be brought into the war zones under UN flag and control.

Typically, that plan was rejected by the newly installed government of Sadiq al Mahdi because, according to them, the proposals compromised the sovereignty of the state and equated the "outlaws" with the "lawful authority". By that time, "Operation Rainbow", a plan that had been set up in agreement with several relief agencies, under the auspices of the World Food Programme (WFP) was launched. Brattley agreed with the SPLM that deliveries of food aid would be made to non-combatants in SPLA-controlled areas including air transport to Yirol. That was enough to make Sadiq's hackles rise, so he ordered the discontinuance of the operation. The representative of the Secretary-General was openly accused of collusion with the rebels by Kamil Shawgi, Sudan's Commissioner for Relief, and ordered to leave the country as *persona non grata*, (the first time for a UN staff member to be thrown out of Sudan) for no reason other than his "authorized" meeting with the SPLM. That was hardly the way to treat a man like Brattley, an honourable and dedicated international civil servant who was especially picked for the Sudan job in view of his resounding success in handling the refugee problems of Indochina.

The movement, however, continued to draw the attention of the world to the predicament of innocent civilians in the war zone including "those still resident in the Khartoum-controlled towns". In a statement made on 19 September 1986 the SPLM underlined that its appeal was made for the benefit of non-combatants whether they were living in garrison towns in the South or displaced from their natural habitat, and now eking out a starved living in Khartoum shanty town. That was reiterated in the SPLM's final communiqué with Sudan African parties referred to above. Unlike the government, the movement has never tried to use these ill-fated persons as a showpiece or call them "Sadiq's" people. It may also be recalled here that Dr. Garang has announced, in his speech of May 85, the creation of a humanitarian arm for the SPLM, the Sudan Relief and Rehabilitation Association (SRRA) mandated to sensitize the world community about war-related and natural disasters, mobilize help, negotiate and coordinate aid deliveries with donor agencies and, for that matter, cooperate with humanitarian agencies including those working under the aegis of the Sudan government. The Prime Minister was aware of the existence of the SRRA and in a statement to the BBC maintained publicly that his government was ready to cooperate with the SPLM in the humanitarian field. Nonetheless the same Prime Minister reprimanded and recalled Sudan's ambassador to Rome when he agreed to appear on a television show, on humanitarian aid to the Sudan, with the representative of the SRRA; the trusting ambassador believed that Prime Ministers mean what they say publicly.

In truth, the government at that time, viewed all relief operations as convenient ways of reinforcing its beleaguered troops in the South, and it was this, more than anything else, which started off recriminations about who was holding up relief. On the orders of the government, relief agencies were not allowed to operate unilaterally in the war zone, despite assurances from the SPLM that they would not be harmed. Instead, the government persisted in its demand that relief convoys be accompanied by "military protection", a good excuse to combine badly needed humanitarian aid with lethal weapons. For example, in its issue of 5 January 1987 the independent Sudanese English language daily the *Sudan Times* reported that a United Nations sponsored convoy of seventy-three Italian Food Aid trucks carrying food supplies and medicines to the war zone was reported to have been taken by force by government troops. According to the newspaper's report, based on accounts of eye witnesses, the convoy left Khartoum on Christmas Day and was accompanied by fifteen soldiers posing as "security guards". At Jebel Aulia, South West of Khartoum, more than 200 hundred members of the government soldiers took over and loaded the trucks with 20 tons of heavy artillery. That action was later deplored by the Italian government through its Ambassador in Khartoum.

The government's non-cooperative attitude, indeed its hostility to the engagement of neutral observers, as indicated by the expulsion of Brattley, was induced by its desire not to allow eye witnesses to see and report misuses of humanitarian aid. Evidence was also accumulating that the government was using civilian aircraft for the transport of military personnel and material. One such case was the attempt by the government to force a private carrier, Transarabia, to carry armed and uniformed soldiers on one of their flights between Khartoum and Juba with absolutely no compunction; the government did not even try to hide its soldiers behind civilian clothes. Were it not for the opposition of the aircraft's captain, Sir el Jizouli, who engaged international rules on air safety to refuse the soldiers access to the plane, the government could have got away with it. However, the government continued, with impunity, to use publicly-owned civil aircraft for that purpose.

In the face of all this callousness the SPLM/SPLA had no way but serve notice to all and sundry that such activities would not be cost-free. Both government and relief agencies who agreed to work under those dubious conditions, were warned that all unauthorized flights in the region would be forcibly stopped. Instructions to this effect were given to field commanders and from then on it was a matter of judgement for those commanders in the field.

To underline its concern about the government's blatant misuse of relief operations, the SPLM/SPLA issued the following statement on 26 September 1986:

1 The SPLM/SPLA calls upon the UN-WFP and the international community at large to condemn the government for blocking relief and insensitivity to the suffering of the people in Southern Sudan.

2 Sadiq maintains that the airport at Wau is closed and that as a result "Operation Rainbow" cannot send in any flights. Khartoum could never get any more absurd than this. Wau Airport is closed not because Khartoum desired its closure but because SPLA forces are within a 3 km radius around the town. The SPLA assured the WFP that it would not shoot down the Rainbow relief plane. From where then does the danger come? The inescapable

conclusion is that Khartoum seeks to use Relief as an instrument of political blackmail against the SPLA. Sadiq himself in a recent BBC interview said that he would not mind if relief organizations dealt with the SRRA. He is on record on that but obviously he was not serious because when SPLA reciprocated by genuine, concrete action and not promises, Sadiq backed down. The discrepancy between Sadiq's statement and his government's supposedly corresponding actions can only be attributed to lack of seriousness.

3   Sadiq's real position is now fully exposed. According to him International Relief must be channelled through Khartoum exclusively for the government held garrison towns. This of course does not take into account the fact that the 2 to 4 million people estimated to be at risk from starvation are not in these towns. On the other hand the position of the SPLA is clear. The SPLA is concerned with the well-being of all those who are *genuinely in need on both sides* and it believes that for the relief to be truly humanitarian and non-political the *victims on both sides must be served.* Otherwise the relief assumes political dimensions. This basic SPLA stand is underlined by the 4-point message by the SPLM/SPLA leader Col. Dr. John Garang de Mabior to Mr. Staffan de Mistura the WFP Director for emergency operations in Sudan via the Director of the office of the Commander-in-Chief and Chairman of SPLM/SPLA. The text of that message which is dated 19 September 1986 reads as follows:

"To the people of the South the SPLA has shown its good intentions and genuine concern for them including those still resident in the Khartoum controlled towns. Now these people know for sure who stands against them and who is for them".

4   Given Sadiq's intransigence, and with a clear and clean conscience, the SPLM/SPLA High Command hereby places all SPLA forces in war zone one in a maximum state of war. All SPLA Commanders and Air Defence Units in Wau, Malakal and Juba and in all other areas are reminded that *the initial order to shoot down any unauthorized aircraft* flying in war zone one, still stands. Similarly, any unauthorized convoys by land, river or rail to Wau, Malakal or Juba are to be ambushed and their contents seized and distributed to the population.

5   Sadiq's government and the International Relief Organizations

are hereby warned that any loss of life and material arising as a result of ignoring this order will be *purely their responsibility*. It is true that the South is vast and from time to time a convoy may slip through SPLA lines and safely reach Wau, Juba or Malakal. Sometimes a plane may also manage to land. However, it is only a matter of time before the SPLA will destroy a convoy, sink a steamer, derail a train or shoot down again another plane. In any of these cases responsibility will be borne by Khartoum and the relevant relief organization for choosing to run the risk rather than pursue dialogue and agreement with the SPLA and the SRRA.

In reality, these airports, including the fields at Wau and Malakal lay within territories controlled or reachable by the SPLM, and it was no longer safe to fly in shipments without the SPLM's prior agreement. The SPLM, we recall, had previously told all the relief agencies that they were welcome to discuss the question of the distribution of humanitarian aid with the SRRA.

1987 was a tenebrous year, not only because of the intensification of war, but also because of the government's lack of concern for those citizens who were presumed to be its subjects; the government would rather have those people perish than risk seeing part of the aid given to them falling into the hands of the "outlaws". For example when the Sudan Council of Churches worked out a formula with UNICEF for the vaccination of children in the South, after that organization had completed the vaccination of eighty per cent of the children in the North, the government responded by a flat "No". That government was not even discomfited when one of their numbers, Dr. Pacifico Lado Lolik, member of the Council of State, visited Wau and discovered thousands of people dying of hunger. Pacifico had the courage to report publicly what he had seen. But Sadiq's response was to come out with yet another one of his overwrought ideas; the creation of a Sudan Mercy Council bringing together Muslim and Christian organizations and headed by Dr. Pacifico himself. Mercy was not what the hungry needed; what they did need was food and medicine and those who had both were able, ready and willing to deliver them were it not for the government's effort to dissuade them from working in the SPLA-controlled areas.

Since ironies never cease in the "Democratic" Republic of Sudan; three years after the expulsion of Brattley the same government of Sadiq al Mahdi accepted a proposal identical to his, under what has come to be later known as Operation Lifeline, Sudan (OLS). That change of heart was not accidental; it took two important events to bring the Prime Minister to his senses. The first was the collapse of sixteen military garrisons in the South. That was a humbling experience, the Prime Minister now realized that his government's control of the South was, at best, tenuous. The second was the position taken by the donor community who were exasperated by what they had been seeing; thousands of people were dying while the government kept dragging its feet for nothing but petty vanity. Thus early in 1988 the SPLM met with Ken Brown of the U.S. Department of State who discussed with the movement the question of dual operations, one with the government, the other with the SPLM. Shortly thereafter the U.S. Office of Foreign Disaster Assistance (OFDA) openly declared that, due to the gravity of the situation in the South, food would go to the needy irrespective of what the government said.

It was at this juncture that the U.N. decided to put pressure on the government and the government half-heartedly acquiesced. The Secretary-General named James Grant, the Executive Director of UNICEF, to supervise a special relief operation in Sudan, who immediately decided to meet with Garang personally; that meeting was held inside the Sudan at Kongor. The two parties came to an agreement on a dual relief operation under which eight carefully chosen routes were opened to UN-sponsored relief agencies for the transmission of food supplies to the war zone in the South. The UN has, thus, succeeded in what the International Committee of the Red Cross (ICRC) has failed to achieve; that organization reached an agreement with both the government and the SPLM to undertake airlifts to both sides at specified airports agreed to in advance. For that purpose the SPLM identified three airstrips within the area under its control. Deliveries to the government-controlled airports were carried out, uninterrupted by the SPLA, while those destined for the SPLA-controlled areas were discouraged by the government, a matter that was severely castigated by the SPLM in one of the speeches of its leader.

The movement, however, continued to express its concern for the beleaguered citizens and appreciation for the work of the international governmental and non-governmental agencies. It also kept reminding the international community and aid organizations of the magnitude of suffering in the SPLA-controlled areas, and reiterating that the only way to reach out to the afflicted was through cooperation with the authority in place; that authority happened to be the SPLM/SPLA. One such statement was made on 8 March 1989 on the opening in Khartoum of the International Conference on Southern Sudan Emergency Relief, to which the Movement was not invited.

The statement read:

1 The SPLM/SPLA has learnt that an International Conference on Southern Sudan Emergency Relief will be held in Khartoum with the following objectives:

a) To determine food, medical and other needs among the populations at risk in the Sudan;

b) To inventorize existing supplies and logistical resources; and

c) To designate responsibilities among UN and other agencies for the urgent implementation, during the month of April, of procurement, transport and distribution activities.

Since the SPLM/SPLA is not represented in the Khartoum Conference, we seize this opportunity to state our position on the vital matters under consideration.

2 The Movement appreciates the concern of the International Community and their wish to help the needy people in Sudan. This concern is indeed commendable. It is common knowledge that the country has been afflicted by natural disasters in the last few years such as drought and floods. As a result population and cattle suffered much, and many lost their lives. The SPLM/SPLA was from the start very much concerned about the plight of famine-stricken population and has put one appeal after another so that the International Community could come to their rescue. Our call was heeded by a number of agencies but there were difficulties, arising from Khartoum's reluctance to help these people. Despite this, something got started, albeit in very small quantities. It is therefore to be reiterated that the Movement is very keen to seek ways and means to ameliorate the situation and it is our wish that this conference will come out with concrete proposals and practical suggestions so as to do what is possible in the sixty days left of the dry season. The needs are immense and time is almost running out.

3   We would like to remind the meeting in Khartoum that more than 90% of the affected population in South Sudan are under SPLA administration. It is therefore, logical that the meeting should devote a proportionate amount of attention to the situation in SPLA-administered areas and earmark assistance to them accordingly.

4   As the United Nations Secretary-General, Javier Perez de Cuellar, spoke of a "race against time" it is imperative that the conference should pay great attention to transport by land; relief can now be transported by land from Kenya, Uganda and Ethiopia through SPLA lines and the whole population East of the Nile can be reached by land. Food can also easily be stored in warehouses in Kapoeta, Torit, Farajok, Pibor, Nasir, Kongor, Pochalla, and many other places under the SPLA. All these places can be reached by road transport over the next sixty days left of the dry season.

5   In addition to the above places, food can be transported to within ten kilometres of Juba town by land from Uganda and Kenya.

6   The SPLM/SPLA is willing and ready to discuss all the above with the organizations and agencies now meeting in Khartoum either as a group in a conference similar to the one now being held in Khartoum or singly.

7   We conclude by wishing all concerned to have the will and determination to see that this humanitarian undertaking succeeds in order to save lives.

Operation Lifeline worked well for a while and indeed continues to operate even at present. Yet again, relief efforts were often hampered by authorized and non-authorized interventions by army officers in the South. For example, numerous relief planes have been destroyed, sometimes as they parked on the ground, by "unidentified" fighter planes. One such case took place during Sadiq's rule, in June 1989 when a German relief carrier chartered by the World Lutheran Federation was bombed at Torit airport while John Garang was on an official visit to Germany, addressing the Human Rights Sub-Committees of that country's Parliament. The incident was viewed by some commentators as a protest by those "unidentified" sources against that visit.

Another aerial attack was made in early December 1989 during the Junta's rule at Waat airstrip (one of the airfields specified by the ICRC for relief deliveries to SPLM-administered areas). That attack took place on the same day SPLM/SPLA was meeting in Nairobi with representatives of the military Junta to discuss peace in Sudan, under the chairmanship of Former President Jimmy Carter. The junta has surpassed Sadiq's government in their lack of concern for the afflicted population within the war zone; they ordered closed all flights to airstrips in areas within the purview of the SPLM authority, threatened with expulsion from Khartoum all non-governmental organizations working with the SRRA and accused the U.N. of using its food deliveries from Kenya for running arms to the SPLA. So it was no longer the U.N. representative in Khartoum who was helping the rebels; now it was the organization itself, that is the level of absurdity to which an insecure and unexposed government would go. The junta also asked the Kenya government for the stationing of military monitors at the Kenyan border town, Lokichogio; the request was as audacious as it was absurd, for not only did it amount to an accusation to the Kenyans themselves, also the Khartoum junta do not control a single iota of land along the whole borders between Sudan and Kenya.

For many people outside the Sudan, the Sudanese conflict has been newsworthy chiefly for the cost in human suffering caused by famine. Unsurprisingly, a great deal of political capital is involved in any discussion of this terrible tragedy, and the successive Khartoum governments were not slow to criticize the SPLM for causing all the suffering and hardship. News reporting of the issue both outside, and especially inside the country, was often hideously distorted. It is therefore imperative to put the record straight on this issue, as on so many others. The excerpts below come from a policy statement made by Dr. Garang in June 1988 on the tortuous negotiations on relief that had taken place between the SPLM/SPLA, the government and aid organizations. Those are followed by excerpts from the interactions that took place between Garang and members of the U.S. Congress on the issue of relief, in the course of Garang's visit to that country. Some of those congressmen visited the areas under SPLA-control in 1989 led by congressman Micky Leland, Chairman of the House Sub-Committee on hunger, to whom this book is dedicated. Leland lost his life for the cause of Sudan, in an air crash during

185

his visit to camps of Sudanese refugees on the Ethiopian borders. Those camps and other concentrations of Southern refugees beyond Khartoum were never visited by any of Sudan's so-called commissioners of relief who were so jealous about their turf; that drudgery was left to the Grants and Lelands of the world, without whom the world would have been bleaker than it really is.

Excerpt from John Garang's Policy Statement, 12 July 1988

Famine, Natural Disasters and the Government's Callousness

Another problem that confronts us is partly the responsibility of the Government, but it is mostly visited on us by nature. It is the problem of drought, caused by nature, and the problem of desertification about which the Government can do something. Many parts of our country are threatened by famine as result of the drought, and this is exacerbated by the war. A responsible Government should do everything possible to produce and stock food reserves against drought, while in the immediate short-term it is necessary to appeal to the international community for relief and rehabilitation assistance. In the South alone about 3 million people are threatened with starvation. In southern Blue Nile and southern Kordofan about 1 million people are affected, bringing the total in the drought and war affected areas to about 4 million. On our side, the SPLA has tried its best using the limited information media at our disposal to bring this tragedy to the attention and conscience of the world. The International Committee of the Red Cross (ICRC) has been working with both the SPLM/SPLA and Sadiq's Government to find ways and means to bring relief to war displaced and drought affected people of Southern Sudan. It was in early March 1988, that the ICRC presented to the Movement a programme of action to provide relief both to Government and SPLA towns under security guarantees by the two sides. It did not take the SPLM/SPLA more than one day to endorse the ICRC relief programme. After securing SPLM/SPLA approval and security guarantees, the ICRC went to Khartoum to secure a similar understanding and security arrangement. But those who rule from Khartoum do not understand nor feel the plight of the people. The Prime Minister, Sadiq el Mahdi, dragged his feet and double-talked for three months. It was not until the end of May 1988 that the ICRC informed us that Khartoum had finally given its blessing. Although Khartoum delayed unnecessarily, the approval was a positive sign that a humanizing trend might have set in at Khartoum. But the breeze, if it was there to begin with, was short-lived. Sadiq quickly reversed his position when it came to actual implementation of relief programme. The ICRC programme stipulated a start with survey flights to three Government-held towns and to three SPLA held towns. The SPLA honoured its part of the agreement and allowed the ICRC to make the survey flights to the Government held towns of Juba, Malakal and Wau in early June 1988. When these survey flights were completed on the Government side, the ICRC asked for Government approval to make similar survey flights to the SPLA held towns of Akon and Yirol, both in Bhar El Ghazal and to Kongoor in Upper Nile. Mr. Sadiq reneged on the Agreement, and gave the ICRC a flat NO, telling them that instead, he would only allow relief supplies to Government-held towns. Sadiq, true to character, dishonoured an agreement he had made with the ICRC within days of reaching that agreement. To us in the Movement and those who know the man well, it came as no surprise that when it came to real action of providing relief Sadiq had to go back on his word. In one of our talks with the ICRC we asked them a straightforward question as to why they thought Sadiq would agree to relief assistance to reach the people of Southern Sudan when it is the Prime Minister's declared policy to starve and exterminate the people of Southern Sudan. Mr. Sadiq had said this openly over the BBC in 1986 and should he respond positively to the ICRC relief programme, this would surely be in contradiction, we argued. The ICRC official in question said that they would try their best and added that, based on earlier preliminary meetings they had with the Government, they had reason to be hopeful.

Conference with Col. John Garang, Sudanese Peoples' Liberation Army, regarding the relief crisis, Room 137, at U.S. Capital, Wednesday, 7 June 1989

Rep. Leland:

All of us here this morning had the opportunity to meet Colonel

Garang earlier this year in Africa. Those members of Congress, I mean, Congressman Bill Emerson from Missouri, who is here as Vice-Chairman of the House Select Committee on Hunger, and, of course, Congressman Mike McNulty who is from upstate New York. At that time we invited Col. Garang to come to this country to give his point of view about the troubles in Sudan. We are very pleased that he has acceded to our invitation and came and is in the process of talking to people to try to educate them from his perspective as to what is going on in Sudan.

Let me take this opportunity to publicly acknowledge Col. Garang's help in providing safe passage in humanitarian relief in the Sudan. The recent cooperation of Colonel Garang and his organization recognizes the importance of international humanitarian aid. When respect for the rights and well-being of innocent civilians is forgotten, hunger is inevitable and exacts a terrible toll. Last year, more than 250,000 people died of starvation and over the last six years more than a million people have died of that same starvation because of cataclysmic confrontation due to the civil war in the Sudan. This is also an appropriate moment to call on the government and people of the United States to maintain a generous flow of aid, both emergency relief and the tools and seeds needed for further development. More than 200,000 displaced and starving people in Sudan depend on this country and other donor nations; so do hundreds of thousands of Sudanese in refugee camps in Ethiopia and Uganda. Incredible difficulties have confronted the private voluntary agencies attempting to transport relief under the banner of the United Nations. Without the active assistance of the Sudanese Peoples' Liberation Army under Col. Garang, much of the 50,000 metric tons of food and medical supplies that have been delivered would not have arrived. We are most grateful for Col. Garang's cooperation and the bravery of his staff who have escorted aid through hostile territory.

Let me now, before I introduce Col. Garang, introduce to you the members of Congress who are here. And I see that Congressman Howard Wolpe, who is Chairman of the Sub-Committee on Africa of the Foreign Affairs Committee is here also and I will introduce him. Let me first introduce, as Chairman Wolpe comes up, the Vice Chairman of the House Select Committee on Hunger for a statement.

Rep. Emerson:

I am delighted to have this opportunity to welcome Col. Garang to Washington and to the United States. I have felt, having visited Sudan earlier this year with the Chairman and our delegation of the Select Committee on Hunger, that one of the things lacking in this United States is adequate information about how to judge and assess the situation in Sudan that is so complex it; almost defies a verbal description. So it is good to have the Colonel here to tell the story that he has to tell.

And I also want to thank him for the part that he has played in helping to maintain the cease-fire without which people would be starving. This year, for the first time in five or six years, because of modest cooperation of the weather and monumental efforts by the United States government and other governments and the wonderful assistance of many PVOs, there is no starvation at this time. This does not mean that the people are healthy and well. It means that, opposed to the last five years, contrasted with the last five years, to this point in time, this year, they aren't starving.

Rep. McNulty:

I would like to associate myself with your remarks and those of the Vice-Chairman in saluting Col. Garang for his current efforts in providing relief to the innocent civilian population in Sudan. But I would be less than candid if I did not say to you, Colonel, that I am somewhat disappointed that there is not more emphasis on the long-term solution to this problem, and that's the end of the civil war. I was somewhat distressed yesterday during the period of time in which I was present at your meeting that you recounted the history of the differences which divide you from the government in the Sudan. Those are the same issues we discussed when we were with you in Addis Ababa and I think that it's time for us to change the focus to a possible common ground that can unite the SPLA and the government in Khartoum to bring an end to the fighting, which is the only real long-term solution to the famine conditions in the Sudan.

So, I would urge you, Colonel, to, if you would, start talking a little bit more about the future and what the future can hold rather than about differences that divided you and your adversaries in the past. And I think if we do that and make that focus the focus of our attention in the future, we will come closer.

Rep. Wolpe:

I am delighted with the leadership you and your Committee on

Hunger have really brought to bear on this critical human tragedy that has been occurring in the Sudan. I want to join in welcoming Col. Garang here today and I think his visit on the Hill provided all of us with an opportunity to hear the views of the SPLA, both as it relates to the immediate human emergency that faces that country, and also as it relates to the broader question of the political settlement that in the end can be the only lasting means of providing peace and stability to that desperately torn country. If there is ever to be a settlement to the Sudan's tragic internal conflict, a war which has left an estimated 1 million Southern Sudanese dead since 1983, the legitimate historical grievances of the Southern Sudanese must be addressed in a genuine and comprehensive way.

I travelled to the Sudan a couple of years back and spent time in talking with leaders of every element of the society. I was struck by how so many even well-intentioned Northern Sudanese who really were committed to the concept of a one Sudan, of a united Sudan, had very great difficulty in comprehending the sense of discrimination, the sense of second-class citizenship that was all pervasive among Southern Sudanese. It was difficult. It felt a little bit like in the United States trying to bridge the racial differences within our own country. There are many parallels in the kind of dialogue that I participated in in the Sudan.

So, those legitimate grievances must be understood more fully, more comprehensively, if there is to be a long-standing political settlement. At the same time, it's critical that both sides, the government of the Sudan and the Southern opposition, confront these questions openly, honestly, and flexibly and that a premium be placed on the saving of human lives. And that means that neither side can break the cease-fire that has been agreed to at this point, and both sides must work diligently to try to bridge those differences to resolve the long-standing issues.

There is much that can be done also, I think, to advance the relief process in the short term, and I hope that in the course of our conversations today we might explore with Col. Garang other means that might be taken within particularly that portion of the country that is controlled by his forces to ensure that speedy, efficient delivery of food and assistance to those that are so desperately in need and are facing such a desperate situation. I am particularly concerned about the situation in Juba and hope that some means can be found that will make certain the people in

Juba are not ultimately jeopardized and that greater suffering occurs.

Col. John Garang de Mabior:

I would like to thank you, the U.S. Congress and Congressmen Leland, and Wolpe who just talked and other Congressmen who visited us in the Sudan. Congressman Wolf is not here, Senator Humphrey who also went to Sudan is not here. As Congressman Leland said, I am not a stranger to the United States; I have lived here 9 years. And if I live to be 90 years old, I will have spent 10 per cent of my life in the United States.

I have lots of personal friends I am happy to meet again after eight years. I will be meeting them while I am here.

I will talk briefly because this problem gets better understood in an interaction rather than in a monologue. I will make brief remarks to underline the problems and I will talk briefly on the core problem itself because this is what we want to solve. I will address attempts we have made so far at solving this problem before talking about the question of relief and human suffering that is going on in my country. I will also talk about human rights in my country, which are very important; the international community is becoming more and more together; human rights are now a vital concern of all human beings, and this also needs to be addressed in the Sudan.

Briefly, the Sudan is a very large country, the largest country in Africa – 1 million square miles. We border 8 countries; Ethiopia, Kenya, Uganda, Zaire, Central Africa, Chad, Libya, Egypt and Saudi Arabia across the Red Sea. This places the Sudan in a very strategic position in Africa. We have lots of resources; lots of educated manpower. It is estimated that we have over 200 million acres of potential agricultural land. We have only used 10 per cent of this. We have lots of mineral resources including oil in Mujlad, oil that Chevron was working on. We have oil in Bentiu, in the Southern parts and in Bor and Pibor. We have other minerals, yet we rank among the least developed countries in the Third World.

We have been at war with each other for 23 years of the 33 years of our independence; the Sudan became independent in 1956. Until now, we have had 23 years of war. And the first war, which was led by Anyany, lasted for 17 years – from 1955 until 1972 when it was resolved by the Addis Ababa Agreement, granting local autonomy to the Southern Region. War erupted again in 1983 and continues to the present. Now there is another six years of war. So one may ask the vital question as to what is wrong, why should any society be fighting amongst itself for 70 per cent of its independent life; 23 out of 33 years?

The Sudan's major problem, I believe, is that the policies that we have adopted since independence have been inconsistent with our historical and contemporary reality. The Sudan has over 400 ethnic groups speaking more than 150 different languages; we have a multi-nationality country. But the practice of policies in Khartoum by all the governments since 1956 has treated the Sudan as a mono-nationality, one nationality country; that the Sudan is an Arab country. I am officially defined by the foreign policy of my country to be an Arab. This is not true. The Sudan is composed of all sorts of nationalities, this includes our fellow citizens of Arab origin, includes people of African origin, and they are all Sudanese without discrimination, without favour; they belong to one country. This is one major problem.

The problem is also of our own history. Sudan is an old country; it goes back to Biblical times. We have three major civilizations in Africa – we have Egyptian, we have the Kushite and we have the Ethiopian. Kush is approximately the present Sudan. Ethiopia is approximately the present Ethiopia; though the boundaries were porous at that time. Egypt is well-known to you. Our civilization is stretched – after Christ we had Christian Nubia, and then came the Islamic and Arab period, came the Turks and came the British. All these elements are parts of our heritage and we value all of them. This is a reality that is ignored in our country.

The other problem is that of religion. The Sudan is a multi-religious country. We have Muslims, and among the Muslims there are different sects. We have Christians, and among Christians there are different denominations. This is the reality of the Sudan. But the policy of the Sudan of all governments that have come to power in Khartoum is to favour one religion, that is Islam, and this was capped in 1983 by the imposition of Sharia Laws by President Nimeiri, a military dictator. This again, is an inconsistent policy, inconsistent with our reality.

One other reality is backwardness. Sudan is a backward country, although it has vast natural resources, and the practice and the policies in the Sudan have been assuming that the Sudan is developed. We have adopted consumerist policies with very little emphasis on rural development where more than 80 per cent of our people live.

These problems have interacted with each other to cause the grave crisis that we have. So, I want to sum up this by saying that we have in the Sudan a geographical state; we have not evolved in the modern period into a nation state, something with which we all identify. As a result, sectarianism has characterized the politics of the country. Some people say the Sudan, in order to be the Sudan, must be an Arab country, some say it must be an African country, some say it must be Afro-Arab, that is, Africans becoming Arab. Some say it is just a bridge connecting the Arab and African worlds. We have not evolved a viable identity that transcends all the various localisms so that the localisms are there but there is something bigger to which all Sudanese identify. This has been a major problem.

On the outside, in the SPLA, when we established the SPLA in 1983, we addressed these issues very concretely, very frankly, and we still address them in order to have a viable Sudan. We must have a multi-nationality state, a multi-religious state, to which we all identify.

The SPLM stands for the unity of the country, unlike the first movement of Anyanya that called for separation of the South from the rest of the country. We don't believe separation is the correct solution. We believe that the correct solution lies in justice; as long as there is justice for all the nationalities, justice and freedom of religion for all the religions, there is no reason why we cannot have one viable Sudan.

The United States, for example, was peopled by many nationalities. The English came, the Germans came, the French came, the Italians came, the Africans came, and you in the United States created a concrete foundation from the very beginning on which the United States is built. This is our challenge in the Sudan. We are determined to bring this about, and we shall have a peaceful and prosperous Sudan.

On the side of what we have done to bring about peace, we started at Koka-Dam; we came to agreements addressing these fundamental issues of nationality, of religion. And at Koka-Dam, we agreed to abolish the September Laws, the Sharia Laws that were imposed by Nimeiri. We agreed to abrogate treaties with foreign countries, military defence treaties with foreign countries.

Koka-Dam came and went and this is history. Recently we

came to another agreement that was reached with the Democratic Unionist Party; that was in November 1988. This was more or less a subset of the Koka-Dam Agreement. It called for suspension or freezing of Sharia Laws, lifting of the state of emergency after which we go for a National Constitutional Conference to resolve the fundamental issues of our country. This is the agreement that is now under discussion. We are meeting on 10 June in order to discuss how to implement this agreement. And if it is implemented, we will go for the National Constitutional Conference. We are hopeful that this increases prospects for peace because most political parties in the Sudan agree on the basic issues. We agreed at Koka-Dam that the Sharia Laws of 1983 be abolished. We agreed on the necessity of a multi-nationality country. We agreed on basic issues. The task is to sit down and put these things together into an operational peace formula.

On 10 June, we shall meet, we shall discuss, and we have extended the cease-fire so as to enable this process to go on. The cease-fire was unilateral on our side. The other side has accepted the cease-fire. It expired on 31 May, and we extended it another 15 days. We are ready to extend it again if there is progress towards peace. So, it is not on the 15th that the cease-fire will end, but if there are prospects – and we hope there will be prospects – we will extend this for another 15 days.

On the question of relief, a combination of natural disasters, floods and drought and the war have combined to cause enormous suffering. Hundreds of thousands of people have died. Children are at risk, pregnant women, the elderly; these are victims of these natural disasters and of war. There are also tribal militias that have been armed by the government that are destabilizing the rural economy, and these also have led to intense suffering.

There was difficulty before in finding a workable formula whereby relief could reach people at risk on both sides of the conflict; people under government administration, people under SPLA administration. But as of last December, all the sides reached an agreement to facilitate relief to those who are in need. The government is cooperating. The SPLA is cooperating. The international relief organizations are working. So is the International Committee for the Red Cross. We have Operation Lifeline Sudan under UNICEF. We have the Norwegian Peoples' Aid Organization. The SPLM will continue to facilitate their work without any hindrance, as it has been suggested by some papers. I want to assure you that this is not true.

The people are in real need. We need food. People need medicines, they need blankets, and these needs are enormous. They cannot be done by a few organizations. We need more organizations to be involved and we welcome them. We appeal to the people of the United States, the peoples of other nations to help in this relief. We are also stressing rehabilitation. We are hoping for 125 new schools this year in Kapoeta, Torit, Bor, in areas that are under our administration. The area we now administer is bigger than the area of Ghana, it is bigger than the area of Uganda, and this is an area that is not contested. It is peaceful, and we can have schools, we can open schools, and we are going to open schools. They need very simple things, exercise books, chalk, blackboards. And these things can be provided. And the youth – the children are the future for the New Sudan we want to create. And we very much appreciate assistance to them.

We need agricultural implements because you cannot depend on relief always. People must grow food for themselves. There are large concentrations of people in places like Juba. There are no industries in Juba. The long-term solution is that these people cultivate for themselves in the countryside. We have discussed this with the International Committee of the Red Cross as to how they can be resettled in the countryside. Khartoum says that the SPLA blocks them in Juba, the SPLA says Khartoum prevents them from coming out of Juba because it is using them as a human shield.

So, we say this is a simple problem. We welcome international observers to go to Juba under some organization and see the movement out of Juba and follow up wherever they go under the SPLM, follow them, follow up to their resettlement in the countryside. We are willing to provide security for such international observers. This is the only viable, long-term solution.

In terms of relief, I want to say that these needs are enormous. They do not only depend on a cease-fire. We have made it open-ended; as long as there are needs, we are ready and willing to provide security for relief to reach those who are at risk, both on the government side (if they pass through our territory). The people are free to work in a peaceful atmosphere.

A last point is the problem of human rights. We have enormous difficulties with respect to human rights. Some of you might have read or heard about resurfacing of slavery in the Sudan. Two lecturers of the University of Khartoum have independently verified this, journalists have verified this. It is directly connected with the government armed and tribal militias to fight the SPLM, and this has degenerated into lawlessness, it has degenerated into slavery. These militias are given guns, are given ammunition by the government and they are told that their pay is in the South. Nobody of course, works for nothing, and they come and take children, they take cattle. Areas such as Aweil, Gogrial, Bentiu have been devastated by these militias. That is a clear case of human rights violations.

The second case is that of prisoners of war. We are not a party to the Geneva Convention, we are a guerrilla movement. But we have to date over 1,000 prisoners of war that we hold. These include more than 30 officers the rest are NCOs and men. The government, to date, has not a single prisoner of war, and we have appealed to international humanitarian organizations: to take care of the prisoners we are holding. It is a problem feeding them in the bush, and the International Committee of the Red Cross is undertaking this. We have requested an exchange of prisoners of war if the other side has any; we are willing to exchange these prisoners.

We believe that human rights must be respected both during war and during peace. So, the prisoners of war have their human rights to be respected. The object of war is not to kill, it is to make the other side non-combative, for once the soldier has no gun in his hand, he must not be killed. We are against the use of food as a weapon. This has been talked about a lot. I want to say that we are against the use of food as a weapon in any war; and we will, as I said before, cooperate, facilitate, seek relief assistance to go to those who are at risk on both sides.

Chapter Seven:

The Year of Change

The year 1989 was one of profound political change, from Eastern Europe to China. For Sudan, too, this could have been a momentous year; change was triggered by one important new development; an agreement reached, after a year of secret negotiations, between the SPLM and the DUP. Traditionally that party had not negotiated with the movement, and was only conspicuous by its absence in Koka Dam. However, the agreement they concluded with the SPLM was as significant as Koka Dam, if only because the signatory of the agreement, on behalf of the (DUP), was Mohamed Osman al Mirghani, the spiritual leader of the Khatmiya sect. The repercussions of that agreement were immense including increased pressure on Sadiq to bring an end to hostilities. The NIF were disconcerted by the decision of the most honoured Islamic leader in the North accepting to freeze the Islamic penal laws, to the point that they accused al Mirghani of heresy and launched an armed attack on his house. On the other hand Sadiq narrowly survived a nascent military coup in February, three months after the agreement, when the army presented him with a twenty-one point memorandum. Prior to the presentation of that memorandum the army, represented by the Minister of Defence, General Abdel Magid Khalil (a man who was hand-picked for that job by none other than Sadiq and whose integrity was recognized by Garang in his May 1985 speech), declared its support for the November Accord. Khalil resigned his post when the Prime Minister vacillated about the Peace Initiative and later made things worse by replacing his DUP coalition government with another coalition; this time with the NIF. However, the situation created by the army memorandum gave the Prime Minister his worst hour; his "Southern Policy" was standing on its head, his chosen aides had deserted him and the peace process that was initiated by his party, among others, at Koka-Dam, was now steered by al Mirghani, a political leader with no official position in the government.

That peace initiative was hailed by all the Sudanese people; their demonstrations in the streets of Khartoum in support of al Mirghani's breakthrough was a telling gesture to the NIF who often claimed to be the spokesmen of the silent Muslim majority. But the deafening shouts of those demonstrators were not exactly music to the ear of the Prime Minister. Instead of capturing the initiative, by virtue of being the man at the helm, Sadiq chose to play a spoiling game. His new marriage of convenience with the NIF, who joined the government after the break with the DUP, can only be seen in that light. That disastrous step was Sadiq's nemesis; not only the SPLM but also the army and the trade unions were disenchanted, and they began to put pressure on the Prime Minister in order to make him part ways with the NIF and form a broader government committed to peace. That government was duly formed and brought in, for the first time in Sadiq's rule, representatives of the left and the trade union movement. And were that action taken three months earlier Sadiq would have saved himself humiliation and saved the nation immeasurable suffering. Besieged on all sides, and seemingly incapable of any decisive action, Sadiq was finally brought down by a putsch led by Brigadier Omar Hassan al Beshir, which promptly installed a new military government.

These changes were strongly connected not only to developments in the course of the fighting, with the SPLA increasingly on the offensive against demoralized government forces, but also, more importantly, to renewed political pressure that had been brought to bear as a result of the SPLM/DUP Agreement seen by many as a harbinger of the sort of breakthrough Sudan had been seeking. Tragically, however, it also brought out into the open the most committed opponents of any type of change, extremists within the central establishment who clearly connived to bring a section of the army once more into power, precisely to avoid having to confront these changes head on.

Thus due to Sadiq's prevarications the war continued in spite of the peace agreement and by the beginning of 1989 it escalated to a point where the government could no longer sustain its efforts. SPLA forces retook a number of important garrisons in the South in January 1989, and it was partly this pressure that eventually led to the army memorandum and, ultimately, the downfall of Sadiq's regime. At the same time, pressure emerged on Sadiq in the political front, following the conclusion of the peace agreement and the hesitancy of the government to see it through. With the DUP and the SPLM in agreement, Sadiq had little choice but to sign on the dotted line and that was too much for the Prime Minister's mighty ego.

The initiative that the SPLM gained from this agreement was immense, as it represented the first genuine progress since Koka Dam. In order to keep the momentum of the peace initiative rolling, John Garang undertook several visits abroad, to Germany, Switzerland, U.K., U.S., and addressed parliaments, the media, church groups and academic centres. At all those fora he delivered speeches designed to outline the SPLM's commitment to the peace process, and its efforts towards finding a permanent solution to the nation's problems through the recently concluded peace agreement. That was also an occasion for the SPLM leader to articulate the movement's thinking on relief, human rights and democracy.

Sadiq fought tooth and nail against the agreement to the point of getting Parliament to reject it. To achieve that end he colluded with the NIF, first to undermine the agreement by overplaying the issue of Sharia and stressing the "impossibility" of abolishing or freezing the September laws through Parliament, and second by splitting hairs on the meaning of words. But events were against him. A trade union insurrection in December 1988, in which massive anti-government demonstrations crowded Khartoum with vociferous calls for an end to hostilities, made it impossible for the Prime Minister to ignore the issue. Finally, the open army memorandum that was handed to Sadiq in February 1989 pushed him into action. The note was a thinly veiled threat to the effect that the government should bring an end to the war, either by winning it outright, or by concluding a peace agreement.

Sadiq, with his flair for surprises, came out with a new stratagem to dodge the issue; he expressed reservations about certain items in the agreement. Because they were allegedly not clear to him; those came to be known as "clarifications". On 10 March 1989 the Prime Minister despatched his Minister of Interior Mubarak al Mahdi to seek "clarifications" on two points in the Sudanese Peace Initiative signed with al Mirhgani.

(i) What did the SPLM mean by the defence pacts impinging on sovereignty;

ii) The correlation between the lifting of the state of emergency and the cease-fire.

To the SPLM, the two questions were stunning; as they were to the rest of Sudanese who were being told all along that the problem of the agreement was the issue of Sharia and the difficulties encountered by the government in freezing, through parliamentary legislation, the penal aspects of it. To the SPLM the two questions raised by the Prime Minister were non-issues because the former was a reiteration of a similar clause in the Koka Dam agreement that the Umma Party signed; the latter was already discussed by Sadiq with Garang in their meeting in July 1986 and both agreed that the lifting of the state of emergency and the cease-fire would go hand in hand, i.e. be simultaneous. It was, thus, clear that the Prime Minister was looking for a face-saving device to justify his earlier rejection of the peace initiative even at the cost of embarrassingly conceding that he had rejected, and got Parliament to vote down, an agreement that he did not understand in the first place. The response of the SPLM's representatives to Sadiq's emissary was terse; in a public statement made after the meeting the movement had this to say:

(a) The "Sudanese Peace Initiative" jointly worked out by the SPLM/SPLA and the DUP was hailed by almost all political parties and trade unions as the sole avenue to the National Constitutional Conference and hence lasting peace. Therefore its rejection through a resolution of Parliament on 21st December 1988 was an amazing development.

(b) Given the fact that the Sudanese Peace Initiative is in essence a refinement of the Koka Dam Declaration which the Umma Party had endorsed, the instrumental role it played in turning down the Initiative was quite unwarranted.

(c)   The Sudanese Peace Initiative is not susceptible of partial acceptance as reservations currently attached to it by the Umma Party clearly suggest. Therefore if the Initiative has not found favour with the Umma Party, the Movement suggests, as an alternative, the implementation of the Koka Dam Declaration to which the Umma Party and SPLM/SPLA among others are signatories.

Eventually al Mirghgani's Peace Initiative was adopted as a basis for the programme of the new government formed by Sadiq and from which the NIF was excluded. Action was initiated to implement the agreement including the freezing of Sharia through legislation and the Council of Ministers was due to meet on the 30 June 1989 to consider a draft law aimed at abolishing the contested laws in preparation for the joint meeting with the SPLM scheduled for 4 July. That would have been the last step before going into preparations for the convening of the National Constitutional Conference, scheduled for 18 August 1989. In response to those positive measures Garang declared a unilateral cease-fire on the first of May, which remained in place till the overthrow of the regime in Khartoum. The correlation between the acceleration of the peace process and the NIF's *coup d'état* is obvious; the hardliners now saw that Sadiq's will to prosecute the war was gone, and that if nothing was done, peace would finally be concluded; a peace that would create a new Sudan united in diversity; and that would have been antithetical to what the NIF stood for. Sensing the urgency of the moment the increasingly desperate NIF chose to intervene through their cohorts in the Sudanese army.

The selection of documents which follows includes the text of the SPLM/DUP Agreement (as an annex) together with excerpts of Garang's statements prior to and after that agreement in which he, once again, emphasized the nature of the SPLM's struggle for fundamental changes in Sudan's body politic rather than quick fixes. In addition to those speeches the material includes extracts from some of the interactions Garang had with policy-makers, academics and concerned Sudanese in the course of his visits in the summer of 1989.

Excerpts from the Speech of John Garang to the Media and the Sudanese Community in London (Africa Hall) June 1989

Search for National Identity and Unity

I will give a very short synopsis of the problem and I would rather have an interaction than a monologue. What I will do is to provide a complete conceptual framework within which the situation in Sudan can be better understood, better discussed and better resolved. I believe that our basic problem in the Sudan is that, since independence in 1956, the various regimes that were in power in Khartoum had to provide a community, a paradigm, a basis for a New Sudan. To illustrate this, sometimes we refer to ourselves or to the Sudan as an Arab country. Some say an African country. Others say it is Afro-Arab, that's Africans becoming Arabs, and I would also add that some call it Arabo-African, i.e. Arabo Africans, that is Arabs becoming African. In all this, the Sudanese have been left out in the cold; that is, there has been no situation where there is that common Sudanese identity to which we all pay an undivided allegiance irrespective of our tribal background, race, or religion. Having failed to do this, we take refuge in sectarianism and use our differences (instead of enriching the Sudan) for political purposes. This, I present to you as the basic problem of the Sudan that needs to be resolved.

We in the SPLM did discuss this in 1983 when war broke out again. As you all remember in the first war, which was fought by the Anyanya, that war was a separatist war that wanted the separation of the South from the rest of the Sudan. Separation of the South was the primary objective of the Anyanya Movement. The success of a movement can be judged in relation to its primary objective – if it does well that is good, but if it does not, it has to reach a compromise; in strategic terms it would have failed because it failed to achieve its primary objective. And that is what happened to the Anyanya Movement. Other things can be said, good things, bad things, but I am talking here about primary objectives of any Liberation Movement.

Now in our situation the SPLM/SPLA in 1983 was discussing this issue for six months. Some said that we should fight for a separate Southern Sudan while others, including myself, argued that the problem in the Sudan is not that of the South separating or the West separating or the East separating, it is essentially a problem of justice. If justice is brought about then nobody would wish to separate and so we would build a unity of the country.

That is the primary objective of the Movement and we have been consistent in this regard since 1983. That unity must be within the context of justice, so that the type of questions that are often asked, for example, what does the SPLM want? What does Dr. John want? All become irrelevant. If Sudan's problem is understood in the context in which I presented it, such a question will no longer be what should be given to the south or to any other region, essentially the restructuring of political power in Khartoum, which has been dominated by small sectors of the Sudanese community; a restructuring of power in Khartoum which results in a socio-political mutation which I had characterised as the New Sudan. The New Sudan as a socio-political mutation will be qualitatively different from the Sudan that we know. The idea as to what should be given to the South in this context does not arise because that stage would have been bypassed. Power sharing is what happened in 1972. In 1972 power was shared; the bulk of it was left to Khartoum and some of it was given to the South, which was a very tiny proportion indeed. So we have a situation where Khartoum gives and Khartoum takes, that is the Lord giveth and the Lord taketh.

The Centre and the Peripheries
Now we have developed a situation where this thing will no longer be the case, where the SPLM/SPLA, other nationalities, and Sudanese will have an effective say in Khartoum. Having resolved the problem in Khartoum we will then go to the regions because Sudan is a large country that cannot possibly be administered from the centre. We will then talk about a decentralized form of rule, *whether these are federal states or autonomous; the relationship between the regions or federal states and the centre will have to be resolved in the first place.*

Going back again to the 1972 scenario here we had an incongruent situation where you have one region, the Southern autonomous region and then the central government. This is constitutionally inviable because essentially, this depicted the government in Khartoum as the central government and at the same time the government of the North; the two things were combined in one. You, therefore, had a situation where Khartoum gives Regional Autonomous rule to the South which did not depend on a constitutional status but on individuals, and in 1982–83 Nimeiri was able to say that the Addis Ababa Agreement was neither the Koran nor the Bible and sure enough he tore it into pieces and threw it away. He had a right to do this because the agreement was personal.

I am talking about an interplay of political forces that results in a socio-political mutation that is called the New Sudan that nobody can unilaterally change. Can we achieve this? I believe so. As I said before we have defined our problem within the context of a multi-nationality, within the context of separation of Mosque and Church on the one hand from the state, and giving Mosque and Church complete religious freedom provided that they don't infringe on sovereignty or on the political situation.

We are talking about the restructuring of power in the centre so that no individual can unilaterally change such a constitutional set-up. This vision I am providing here is the vision of the New Sudan. I am talking about an end; it is this vision that I am talking about that has been lacking. Since 1956 we have been talking of an African Sudan, or an Arab Sudan or an Afro-Arab Sudan or an Arabo-African Sudan or simply as a bridge, a connection between the African world and the Arab world. I have been fighting since 1983 to get rid of this sectarianism and to have in its place a new socio-political formation. Now, is this achievable or is this just a dream? Is it possible and how is it possible?

How to bring about the New Sudan

In terms of the SPLM/SPLA and what we have done, because of the definition of our objectives, we define ourselves in the Sudanese political process. The Anyanya Movement defined itself as separatist Movement. We, by defining ourselves as standing for the unity of the country, have defined ourselves into the Sudanese political process and we have maintained this stand since 1983. We have interacted with the other Sudanese political forces since that time. So before Nimeiri was overthrown we were in contact with all Sudanese opposition groups making a common front against the Nimeiri regime. Afterwards we were in contact with the Alliance, with the Umma, DUP, and all the Sudanese Political Parties.

These contacts resulted in the Koka Dam conference that was held in 1986, and attended by all the political forces except the DUP and the National Islamic Front. We were able to agree on fundamentals, the idea of a National Constitutional Conference came out from the Koka Dam meeting. This was a meeting of the most reputed political forces, so you can see the new vision in practice, because if this vision was not there the meeting of Koka Dam would not have been possible. But because of the vision that we presented it was possible to sit with political forces, who, otherwise would not have possibly sat with a separatist movement as was the case in the Anyanya situation. We agreed at Koka Dam that the September Laws should be abrogated, we agreed that defence treaties with foreign countries that impinge on Sudan's sovereignty should be abrogated, we agreed on the lifting of the state of emergency, we agreed to work out a permanent cease fire, and to hold the National Constitutional Conference to resolve the fundamental problems of the Sudan such as nationality problems, relationship between religion and state and what some people call power sharing.

I totally disagree with this concept of sharing power, for it is not something in a "siniya" (food tray). I use the words restructuring of political power in Khartoum rather than power sharing because the latter brings to mind immediately the question, who is sharing power with whom? And the answer is usually North and South, Arabs and Africans, Christians and Muslims. It has the connotation of the old paradigm. Thus we were able to reach this historic agreement at Koka Dam.

The SPLM and Parliamentary Elections

We also added at Koka Dam that Parliamentary elections should be deferred, because holding elections at that time was like putting the cart before the horse. Also if other political parties go for elections without the SPLM we will have a constitutional problem later even if we come to an agreement because there is a government in Khartoum that has been formed as a result of these elections. The SPLA would not contest an election because it is an armed movement and there was a law by the Transitional Military Council that any armed group cannot contest elections.[1]

---

1 The refusal of the SPLM to go into elections was not only due to this legal prerequisite but also to its implication. The SPLA, according to that law, would have been constrained to lay down its arms even before the realization of the Koka Dam conditions for the creation of an atmosphere conducive to cessation of hostilities let alone disarmament.

Whatever the outcome of the elections the SPLM would have zero seats in Parliament; and the question would be how to graft the SPLM onto any system of rule in Khartoum? We said no, this is doing the same as before. Let them defer the elections and help agree on fundamentals on the restructuring of power and we in the SPLM would be a part of the election commission because, as you all know, the way the election law is drafted goes a very long way towards determining its outcome. For example the graduates' seats,[2] which were drafted into the election law, gave the graduates about 30 out an assembly of 272. So you don't have one man or one woman vote, the graduates are more equal than the others – they have more than one vote. They had 20 or 30 votes depending on their ratio to the rest of the community. But the other parties went for elections as you know, the Umma Party got 101 seats, the DUP 63, the NIF 51 seats, 28 of which were graduate seats out of 30 graduate seats.

Revival of Koka Dam

Now Koka Dam as a process leading towards peace and the creation of a New Sudan was lost in the dust of the elections. Koka Dam could not be implemented because a major coalition partner in the new government, the DUP, was not a party to Koka Dam, which is a logical argument. The situation was created in November 1988 last year where we agreed with the DUP to essentially something similar to Koka Dam with the one major exception, instead of calling for the abrogation of the September Laws we used the word freezing. But our position is clear, the SPLM stands for separation of religion from the state and granting of religious freedoms – liberties to all religions without favour and without discrimination. That position remains firm up to now and it will remain so in the National Constitutional Conference.

In order to go to the National Constitutional Conference, however, we will tolerate the freeze because there are other sectors of the Sudanese Community that are opposed to these laws – there are Muslims that are opposed to these laws, there are western Sudanese who are opposed to these laws and so it will not be the SPLM/SPLA alone who fight the battle for a secular state.

2   The graduates' constituences were reserved for those Sudanese who completed post-secondary education in addition to their polling right in territorial constituencies.

There are others who have no place to air their views and the National Constitutional Conference would provide such a forum. So if the laws are frozen, it is as good as not having them even though they will still be in the books as statute laws. Between their freeze and the National Constitutional Conference, they will not be in effect, or when we go to the other Sudanese political forces. This is the background to the compromise that we made. On the other hand the DUP, which is a religious party, made a compromise too by accepting the freeze. This was a step forward. Instead of moving by one leap we decided to move in small steps. Our objective remains the same.

That agreement caused political crisis in Khartoum and again I understand that this indicates a problem because I asked a question before. Is it possible to have this vision of New Sudan? Can we bring it about when we reached this agreement with the Democratic Unionist Party and they were sincere in their talks with us. On his return to Khartoum Sayed Mohamed Osman al Mirghani was met at the airport by tens and tens of thousands of Sudanese across the party line, across the regional line. We took that as a referendum for peace – the Sudanese wanted peace. That was clear from the reception that was given to Sayed Mohamed Osman al Mirghani. The NIF tried to organize a counter demonstration against this agreement but it faded out. This again indicated the desire of the Sudanese people for peace. The Umma Party endorsed it. The Prime Minister said he accepted it and that there were positive elements in it. Therefore, the peace initiative reached last November was accepted by the broad masses of the Sudanese people.

However, on 28 December, this agreement was literally voted down; the Umma majority and the National Islamic Front voted against this agreement in parliament. This forced the DUP out of the government and a new coalition was formed between the Umma and the NIF, forming a new majority. That government was not viable and events quickly showed its unviability. I have to underline also that when we reached this agreement in November, we were accused by certain quarters of opportunism in the sense that November was the beginning of the dry season. It was said in Khartoum that we reached this agreement because the government was launching a dry season offensive. We said no; this is not the case, we just want peace; peace within the context of the New Sudan that I presented to you as our conceptual framework. We were misunderstood in November, and parliament voted against the agreement. A new government was formed and military operations intensified as a result of voting against the peace agreement. The result was that the SPLM/SPLA ended up, within the period of six months during the negotiations and after the agreement with capturing the following garrisons, Kiyalla, Torit, Ikotos, Katire, Upper Talanga, Parajok, Khor Inglis, Liria and turning North we took Magalla, which is only 40 miles from Juba, Gemeiza, Bor, Akobo, Waat and Adong. We took all sixteen garrisons.

In reality we proved that it was not because of our military weakness that we signed the November Peace Agreement. This was after the fact, however, as I said before the Sudan government that was formed was very fragile. The army made its move and presented a 21-point memorandum to the Prime Minister giving him an ultimatum that either the government accepted the November Peace Agreement or it gave the army sufficient armament to fight the SPLA efficiently. It is not in the order of normality for an army to give ultimatums to Prime Ministers. The truth of the matter is that the army wants peace, the other clause about giving sufficient armament is the sugar-coating. Again we took this as a vote by the army for peace. That ultimatum resulted in the formation of a new government. This time the National Islamic Front were out of government and the DUP came back into government. That government publicly said that they accept the 16 November Peace Agreement between the DUP and the SPLM/SPLA. When this development happened in Khartoum, the formation of the new government and the acceptance of the November Peace Agreement (that was the end of the dry season and nobody could have accused us of opportunism) – we immediately declared a unilateral cease fire to cover the whole month of May and we said the following: it is not sufficient that the government accepts the 16 November Peace Agreement but we must go ahead and implement it; before the month of cease-fire ends the government must implement the November Peace Agreement. That was extended subsequently and it is in force as I talk today, though there have been minor violations e.g. the government bombed Ikotos on 30 May, Labalwa on the 31 May, and Torit on the 1 June. But I have said these are minor incidents.

The ceasefire is holding. We met on the 10 June and the government was saying, though they accepted the peace agreement, there were other things that were not clear, that there were clarifications to be made. We thought that the agreement was clear enough because Parliament voted against it on 28 December. Presumably they could not have voted against something they did not understand. But since they said there were things that were not clear, we said alright let us sit and discuss those things that were not clear. The meeting of 20 June was called in order to discuss those clarifications and the implementation of the agreement itself so that we go to the National Constitutional Conference. I was informed when I was in Washington that the meeting had finished on a positive note. A new meeting is scheduled for mid-July and a date for the Constitutional Conference had been set, 18 September provided all the requirements are met.

What I am underlining here is not the process but the dynamic interaction of the Sudanese political forces and thereby the possibilities of achieving a New Sudan, the vision of a New Sudan, the paradigm I did refer to at the beginning of my talk. Again in terms of the political interactions that are taking place, some people argued that this is not possible, because of religious fundamentalism and because the North and South are different. I said this is not true if we take the case of September laws, for example, these were decreed by Nimeiri. When he came to power in 1969 he declared himself a Marxist by self-acclamation, then he traversed the political spectrum since 1969 when he said he was a Communist, to 1983 when he imposed September Laws and wanted to become Imam. Miracles happen but not this one. I wanted to present to you that Nimeiri's decision to impose Sharia was not on religious grounds but it was a political decision. Nimeiri was running out of cards, and religion in the form of Sharia Law or September Laws was one of the cards left for him. He returned to the differences that made him or that would have made him the great Nimeiri: he started to use differences between the North and South, he used religious differences and imposed Sharia as the last available political card. Again when Nimeiri imposed these laws the present Prime Minister Sadiq al Mahdi was himself opposed to them; he said they were not worth the paper on which they were written and Nimeiri threw him in jail for this opposition.

The Struggle for Secularism

I want to present to you that opposition was political. The Prime Minister himself in the 1960s was a secularist. He stood for the separation of mosques from the state. He stood for that and he quarrelled with his uncle. He had taken a political line consistent with what I am saying just now. At Koka Dam we agreed to abrogate the September Laws. This was one of the agreements we made with several parties including the Umma Party. Three months later elections were held. The Umma Party won the elections and got the largest number of seats. A government was formed with Sadiq al Mahdi becoming the Prime Minister and it became politically convenient for him to hold Premiership on the one hand and the Sharia on the other.

The Sharia Laws are a hot potato, so if he could hold the two together much the better. But if enough political pressures are brought to bear on the situation, I have sufficient reason to believe that one of them must give way. Here again we are talking about a political process. Last November the SPLM and the Democratic Unionist Party, a religious-based party, agreed to freeze religious laws. The question is, thus, what political pressures must be brought to bear on the situation so that all of us appreciate the necessity of a multi-nationality state? What political pressures need to be brought to bear on the situation so that all of us appreciate the necessity of separation of Mosque and church on the other hand, from the state? If these political pressures are brought to bear on the situation, I assure you that people will move and they will move politically. They have done so in the past and they will do it in the future. So how the political process in the country has been working out itself is an indication of the correctness of our vision and of the possibility of realizing this vision.

How to create a New Sudan

We are here talking about a social situation, a socio-political mutation to get the New Sudan. So we are not going to have the situation where the question will be posed as to what must be done in order to create the New Sudan. We cannot say one, two, three, four, five because as I said, this is a socio-political situation; it is complex situation that cannot be reduced into numbers of 1, 2, 3, etc. No, it is not a cabal. This is a political situation, this interaction of the political forces that is necessary. And they have been interacting and we have been going in the direction of the New Sudan. We are now closer to it than we have been at any other time in our history. Now in the SPLM/SPLA we are receiving lots of people from the North, we have people from al Heisheisa (something that could not have happened before). We have people from Rufaa, we have people from Shendi, we have people from Port Sudan joining the SPLM on a common road. Well, they have come in smaller numbers but they will increase.

Sometimes, Southerners have been asking the question: why should we shed blood for the whole Sudan? This is a demagogic question that has been asked and actually it is a matter of understanding the process and how it works itself out. It is not the South invading and liberating the North because the question has also been asked: How can these Southerners come and liberate us? This is certainly unrealistic. But when we fight in Southern Blue Nile (and if we are able to fight in Southern Blue Nile) then the dynamics of the situation will have made it possible for the people of Southern Blue Nile themselves to be engaged in the fighting. When we go to Southern Kordofan, the people of Southern Kordofan will themselves be engaged in the fighting. It is not a mechanical process of Southerners moving Northwards and Northerners waiting for their liberation with their hands folded. No, this is not the process. If we fight in Medani, I assure you that there will be people in Medani fighting in this battle. Of course some people will say: but the North is a desert, there cannot be guerrilla warfare there. Algeria has more desert than the Northern Sudan; this is an untenable argument. The Polisairo is fighting in a desert, which is worse than the Northern Sudan. This is untenable, it is unhistorical, it is not true.

This idea of identity has been bothering us since we went to Southern Blue Nile and we asked the population there to join us, which they did. When under training they were asked why did they join the SPLA? They replied that they wanted to fight the Jalaba. We then asked: where is the Jalaba? They pointed Northwards! The divisions have been created for people to maintain their rule in Khartoum, and a whole superstructure of fiction and disinformation has been erected in order to keep these people in power. The SPLM/SPLA along with other Sudanese political forces, is determined to demolish this superstructure of fiction, this edifice of fiction, and in its place, as I said before, to create a New Sudan. The possibilities are there as I have indicated in a discussion of how the political process has been interacting, how it has been working itself out, and it is through this process that we will achieve a New United Sudan.

From the Bullet to the Ballot

If we go to the sphere of the ballot rather than the bullet, the prospects also for the vision of the New Sudan that I have for you, are great. The bullet has enabled us now to be in control of most parts of the South and we are in Southern Kordofan and Southern Blue Nile. If there are elections today and you assume the scenario of the last elections we can get most of the seats in the South – 68 seats. We can get some seats in Southern Kordofan; the SPLM can also get some seats in Southern Blue Nile; possibly in Port Sudan we could get some seats; in Khartoum itself the SPLM can get some seats from those who are resident there and from the large number of Southerners who have migrated to Khartoum who will be franchised. Now if we add these, we are actually talking about a minimum of 100 seats (which is about what the Umma Party has now – they have 101 seats). Then that would make us the major partner in government. We could form a government with any party who accepts our vision of the New Sudan. I am not saying that this is what we will do, but I am only pointing out the possibilities because the question raised before was: is this vision of New Sudan possible? I am saying that through the bullet it has been possible and people are joining the SPLM. We stood our ground for the last six years and expanded. Through the ballot, i.e. through democratic means converting the bullets into ballots, this is also feasible. So what I have done is to give you the conceptual framework or paradigm of how the SPLM views the Sudan. I have given an indication of how the political process has been working itself out, and have given the tip of the iceberg of the possibilities that are there.

I will leave this here so that we have an interaction. My intention was to present to you the vision of the SPLM/SPLA but not to discuss item by item – it is a global view. Thank you very much.

Seminar with John Garang de Mabior at the Brookings Institution, Washington, D.C. Friday, 9 June, 1989

Creating the New Sudan

Rather than defend this or that position, or try to propagate, I would want to begin by saying that the basic challenge that is facing us, and has been facing us, in the Sudan is the failure to have what I may call a socio-political mutation within the present geographical Sudan. What do I mean by that?

In Africa, you have various entities that are yet to be transformed into nation-states; take Central African Republic, for example, where somebody masqueraded as the emperor of the state; that was Bokassa. So we have inherited entities that we are trying to form into viable nations, nation-states. Since 1956, at our independence, what we have been witnessing in the Sudan was an attempt by vested interest groups to define the Sudan according to their interests, whether these be religious or ethnic groups. This does not mean that there have also been groups that have risen above sectarianism.

This has been our basic challenge. Sometimes the questions are asked; what does John Garang want? What does the SPLM want? And then the answers are given: they want greater autonomy for the South. It is a fight between the Christians and Muslims. It is a fight between Northerners and Southerners. It is a fight between Africans and Arabs. The basic point is missed; it is none of these. It is not a fight between Northerners and Southerners. It is not a fight between Christians and Muslims. John Garang does not want anything special as an individual.

It is, therefore, necessary to give the SPLM's version of the Sudan so that these questions are no longer asked. Our vision of the Sudan is to create from the historical Sudan, from the contemporary Sudan, a New Sudan in which all the nationalities, all the religious groups, coexist. There must be a commonality to all those groups with which all of them identify. In the present situation, you are either identified as a Southerner, a Northerner, a Christian, or a Muslim. But there is nothing to which you can be involved as a Sudanese, pure and simple. So we are involved or engaged here in a process of national formation. I have been once asked what is your ideology? I said, "My ideology simply is *Sudanism*". That is, "*neocleationism*', if you wish, to neoclate or coalesce into a nation. This is the basic challenge. The SPLM was formed in 1983 with this paradigm in mind, that is, not to fight for a separate Sudan – a Southern Sudan was the basic objective of the first movement, the Anyanya Movement that lasted 17 years. That Movement defined its objectives as separation of the South.

Any Movement is characterized, or is known, for its basic objective. The basic objective of the Anyanya was separation. It was

213

dissolved in 1972, and that basic objective failed. It failed because the South did not become independent. Instead what happened was a compromise between the leadership of the Anyanya and the leadership of the government that was in Khartoum. Now, our Movement's, the SPLM's objective, is the creation of the New Sudan, which I said might evolve, might mutate. Of course it is difficult to say that, "If you do one, two, three, four, five, six, and up to the end, then you will have your New Sudan", because here we are dealing with a social situation that is in flux. But once you have your objective straightened out, then the rest becomes strategies and tactics. I will give examples to illustrate this point.

The method which we have chosen in order to achieve the objective of a united Sudan, is to struggle to restructure power in the centre so that questions as to what does John Garang want do not arise, so that questions as to what does the South want do not arise, because when you ask a person what does the South want, or what should the South be given, that presupposes that there is somebody who gives. And, as the saying goes, "the Lord giveth, the Lord taketh". What has been happening all this time was the presumption that Khartoum will give, and somebody will receive, the South will receive. What we want to create is a situation where the questions of somebody giving and somebody receiving would be out of the question.

All the various parts of the Sudan will be part of the new power structure in Khartoum, where power is redefined, so that nobody gives and nobody takes. I don't see myself as a Southern Sudanese to be given nor do I look at some Northerner as a giver. I don't look at Brother Sadiq al Mahdi to give me anything, because I don't expect to be given anything. I am part and parcel of the Sudanese body politic, and if there is a decision-making, I shall have an equal right, like any other Sudanese, to participate in this process of decision-making.

Convergence of Political and Military Struggle

We decided in 1983 to fight for a united Sudan along these lines. The first fight for a united Sudan was not between the SPLM and the Sudanese army, it was within the SPLM itself because there were people who argued that we should fight for a separate Southern Sudan. Our group said no to that, because it was untenable; untenable in principle, untenable in strategy, and untenable given any other consideration. This issue was resolved through dialogue and eventually armed struggle. Our side of the argument won both intellectually, and physically. This was how the SPLM was started; the SPLM was started as a unionist movement, and it was started by fighting within itself for unity.

After that, we went on to the process of armed struggle with the protagonists of the Old Sudan. The situation on the ground now is such that, to a large degree, there are two *de facto* administrations in Sudan. This is no news; the SPLM, over the last six or seven months overran 16 armed garrisons. We are establishing administrations in the areas under our control; we have established schools and we are going on with this process. We have gone now to Southern Kordofan. We have gone to Southern Blue Nile. And we are entrenched there. The question of separation no longer arises. There are Southerners who say: "Why should we fight for the whole country?" I say, "Well, if you are willing to fight, if you are ready to fight, follow me. When you reach Medani where you think the South ends, then stop there. I will go ahead with the rest of the people from Medani itself." There are Northerners who say how can the South come and liberate the North? This is a mechanical way of viewing the situation. When the SPLM reaches Medani, our vision is that the people of Medani themselves will be involved in this struggle because they believe in a United Sudan. It is not a mechanical issue of the SPLM as a Southern Sudanese Movement; today there are people from Hasa Hisa who are members of the SPLM. We see this as a dynamic or as a dialectical situation going northwards. The SPLM descended from the South, this is true, and there are going to be peculiarities about the Movement that are connected with the South; but as it evolves, it will engulf the whole of the country; this is what we say in our Manifesto.

I would like the discussion to be focused on this, seeing whether this is attainable. Is it attainable to have one Sudan under these circumstances? In Sudan we have sectarianisms; is it possible to transform the country, in the light of this, into a democratic Sudan? I say it is possible as our own experience has shown. The Movement, since 1983, kept contact with all political forces in the country from the left to the right because we do not believe that the SPLM will operate the Sudan alone. We envisage the situation as a convergence of the armed struggle which we are waging, and the political struggle which is being waged in other parts of the country. We had an Intifada (popular uprising) in 1964 against military rule. We had an Intifada in 1985 against Nimeiri.

This political struggle over there and the armed struggle on our part, amount to a convergence of different forms of struggle in order to achieve the basic goal, of a New Sudan. This had happened. We have kept contact with the principal political forces and agreed on talking freely on basic issues, things like the relationship between the religion and the state. Again, we agreed recently with the Democratic Unionist Party in order to freeze the September laws.

Now, it is important to put this in the context of the struggle which we are waging, because our ability to come to an agreement with Sudan's political forces shows that we are in the mainstream of Sudanese politics. In Anyanya I, it was not possible for Dr. Mansour here to be sitting with me, Garang, on the same side of the aisle, because "they" were Northerners, Arabs, Muslims. And "we" were Southerners, Christians; and there was just no way for the two to come together.

I was a member of the Anyanya Movement and when the combatants of that Movement heard Radio Omdurman speaking in Arabic, they shot at it; because that was the enemy. But it was just a radio. We have bridged this gap, and the contribution of the Movement's media was such that it has erased this North-South divide. Thus the idea of a separate Southern Sudan, is behind us. In 1983, we were accused of being anti-Arab, anti-Muslim, separatists and all that. I have been depicted in a cartoon in Khartoum wearing the flag of the United States with the inscriptions including the words CIA, the star of David, and the Russian sickle and hammer. There was also a big cross on my chest and even a German swastika. This was supposed to describe me. I have been accused of being, in one sentence, an agent of international communism and the Church. But that was not me.

On Religion, Politics and Peace

This is a summary of the contradictions that are there, but our focus is very, very clear. We will achieve this one Sudan; the tactics that we have used up to now have taken us a long way. Let us give an example of the present peace process that is going on. We are meeting tomorrow with the government representatives, that is on June 10. There will be a meeting at Addis Ababa between the Ministerial Peace Committee on the government side and Dr. Lam Akol Ajawin on our side. How did this come about? You all remember Koka Dam. Koka Dam called for abrogation of Sharia Laws, September Laws. It called for abrogation of defence treaties with foreign countries that impinge on our sovereignty. It called for lifting of the state of emergency. It called for a cease-fire before going to the National Constitutional Conference. Koka Dam died a natural death following the premature elections, which we opposed. We said that; let us go first to a National Constitutional Conference, agree on the basics, and then all go for elections, including the SPLM. This was not agreed upon.

I want to stress the dynamics of these agreements, because there is an element in people's mind that there is religious fundamentalism in the North stopping people from moving forward. I want to say that this kind of approach is untenable. You take the September Laws for example; those Laws were passed by Nimeiri. Who is Nimeiri? Nimeiri started in 1969 as an avowed Marxist by self-acclamation. This is what he said; he said he was a Marxist and a Communist. He even said that he was going to turn the Sudan into the Cuba of Africa, whatever he meant by that, but that was his self-description. This man then trasversed the political spectrum; come 1983 he wanted to become Immam of the Sudan, to impose the September Laws on the country. I want to present to you that this was not religious inspiration. Yes, there are miracles, but I am not persuaded that Nimeiri was suddenly con-verted from the Marxist he was in 1969 to the Immam – prospec-tive Immam of the Sudan in 1983. The September Laws were the last card of Nimeiri in order to hang on to political power. This is politics, not religion. Nimeiri bankrupted himself by centralizing power in the palm of his hand so that all Sudanese political forces were coverging on him. He played on these differences, the political and now the religious differences, and he declared the September Laws. On the nationalities differences, he divided the South.

I maintain, therefore, that this was a political division, not a religious division. The Prime Minister Sadiq al Mahdi at that time was opposed to Nimeiri politically. Nimeiri threw him in jail for this opposition. Those are matters of historical records. Sadiq al Mahdi himself was in favour of the separation of religion from state, and this was his basic argument with his uncle in the 1960s. He wanted his uncle to have the spiritual leadership of the Ansar, and he Sadiq, the political leadership; in other words he wanted religion separated from the state since it was untenable to be a sectarian leader and to want also to be a national leader. One of the two must give; you either be a leader of the Ansar which involved a specific religious group or a leader of the whole nation, which involved everybody. Sadiq was very clear in the 1960s on this issue. He was in opposition to the fusion of religion with politics in the 1960s; he was also very clear on this thing at Koka Dam. The Umma Party was opposed to the September Laws and they agreed with the SPLM and other political parties to abrogate those laws.

But then, after 3 months, elections came and Sadiq al Mahdi became the Prime Minister. He found it convenient to sit on two stools, to have both, be Prime Ministership and the September laws; this is the best of both worlds. But if there are sufficient political pressures on him, then he will have to choose between the two. Again, these are political not religious decisions.

Last November we agreed with the Democratic Unionist Party, which is also a party based on the Khatmya sect. We agreed to freeze the Sharia laws, not because Mohammed Osman Mirghani was not religious, but because he wanted to maintain the unity of the country. Again, this was a political decision, not so much fundamentalism involved here.

Accordingly I want to present to you that the shifts you see; shifts in grounds from Nimeiri to Sadiq al Mahdi to the Democratic Unionist Party, were a result of political pressures. The approach, therefore, is to ask the questions, what political pressures are there that can be brought to bear on the political situation so that people move? And I know people can move because people have moved before, and we are going to move them. This is our strategy.

Now, that agreement we had in November, what was its background? The National Islamic Front had a bill in Parliament which they wanted to push through. People wanted me to come to Kampala at the time when there was a vote in Parliament on this bill that contained a new version of Islamic Laws. The meeting in Kampala between Sadiq and Turabi and myself was meant to be a handshake, a handshake with Dr. Garang. And then people go to parliament and say, "Even the infidel Dr. agrees, you see his picture here, he is greeting Al Mahdi, he is greeting Al Turabi" so what is this fuss all about? I said no, there is no deal, I am not going to Kampala to vote by proxy in favour of Sharia.

We then came to an agreement on 16 November and immediately caused a political crisis within the government. The DUP-SPLM's Peace Initiative was opposed by the Prime Minister, even though publicly he said he was for it. On the 28 December, he came out openly against the Peace Initiative and got Parliament to vote it down. That sent out the DUP from the government; the National Islamic Front came in. It was a fragile government; that could not last. The army came in and handed a 21-point memorandum to the Prime Minister; either accept the Peace Initiative or give us guns in order to fight. The fact was that the army wanted peace. So you have the situation here where the Prime Minister was under pressure from the army, under pressure from the Sudanese public in order to arrive at peace. He was also under pressure from the SPLM; we had captured 16 army garrisons. The Prime Minister had to accept political reality.

The meeting we are having tomorrow is not because the Prime Minister wants peace (he had voted against this agreement in December); it is because of the political pressures from the army, and that pressure is still there; the pressure from the SPLA, and that pressure is still there; pressure from the Democratic Unionist Party, other Sudanese political forces and from the Sudanese public, at large, because people want peace. This is why we are going for a meeting tomorrow supported by the majority of the Sudanese. Our idea is to increase those pressures so that we arrive at peace. Through these pressures, we are going to arrive at a New Democratic Sudan that is secular, that is democratic, and in which power is restructured from the centre. Power is restructured from the centre by whom? By all of us, including the SPLM. We will be part and parcel of that political power in Khartoum, and therefore, the idea of what will be given to the South does not arise, because we will be part of that political process.

Sudan is a big country, and you cannot administer it from the centre. It will need to be decentralized whether you call them federal states or local autonomous regions, but the crucial thing is not the federal states or the regional autonomous entities (which are matters of form) it is decentralization. We have done this before; the South had a regional autonomous status before. Nimeiri came and cancelled it. He said that the agreement that created autonomy was neither the Koran, nor was it the Bible. So it is not sufficient just to have a federal or decentralized status, it is necessary also to have checks within the system so that no crazy man comes tomorrow and says, "From now on there shall be no constitution. I Nimeiri, am the constitution". Having those guarantees will help the restructured power system in Khartoum; guarantees not by the good wishes of individuals, but by the physical interplay of forces. This is important. After we have taken care of the power structure in Khartoum, then we come to the powers of the regions and those too must have checks and balances.

This is the Sudan we envisage. This is the Sudan we see, this is the Sudan we have been fighting for in the last six years. This is the Sudan we will continue to fight for and the Sudanese people are open minded enough to see that and struggle for it. I am confident that the Sudan is not a microcosm of Africa or a bridge between Africa and the Arab World. No, we are not a bridge. We are not Arabs, per se, we are not Africans, per se. We are not Afro-Arab, a term being thrown around a lot. "Afro-Arab" of course, means Africans becoming Arabs, but you can turn it around and say, "Arabo-Africans"; that is Arabs trying to become Africans. But you see the complexity of the situation when these terminologies are thrown around. Some people say, "We are Arabs", some people say, "We are Africans", some people say, "We are Afro-Arabs". Now I am adding a fourth category "Arabo-Africans". Would it not be easier to say that we are Sudanese. At the end of the day, we shall have a mutation that has a specificity based on our historical heritage that goes way back to Kush, to Christian Nubia, to the Arab migrations to the Sudan, to Islamic influences in the Sudan, to African Kingdoms that were born, to the Mahdist state. This is our socio-political reality.

Question:

My name is Hussein Afijellih. My question is that one of the main obstacles standing between Sudan and peace is the issue of Sharia Laws versus secular laws. To solve such an obstacle, would the SPLM agree to the principle that each region or province in Sudan should democratically choose its own criminal law codes?

Col. Garang:

When we talk about each region democratically passing its own laws, there is a catch to it, it can be very misleading. One might belong to a region that has no Sharia criminal code but being citizen of the same country he may be subjected to them else-where; I would be equally concerned if somebody's hand in Darfur is being cut off. It is not a democratic right to cut off the hand of a thief who has stolen $10. I don't agree with that line of argu-ment. The criminal law should be universal to all Sudanese; we are one country. Personal law can be private. I will allow our Dr. Mansour to elaborate on this point.

Mansour Khalid:

I think the questioner must have in mind the proposition of the government to introduce what is called alternative laws to the Hudud. Of course, Sharia is a body of law that covers all human activities and has its civil and criminal aspects.

Now, the proposed laws go, in a way, against the constitution. What do I mean by that? If you look at the said alternative laws, you find, for example, a new crime called ridda "apostasy", which had not been introduced by Nimeiri in his Sharia laws and, in fact, though, the late Mohamoud Mohammed Taha was con-demned under that charge, there was nothing in the law to justify his condemnation to death by the judge.

However, the new crime of apostasy, I mean, condemning a Muslim to death because he converted into another religion is unconstitutional when you are talking about a constitution that guarantees the freedom of faith. I mean, people can profess what-ever religion they want to profess, which also means your right to change your religion or not to have a religion at all. The contradiction appears also in that those very people who call for hanging a Muslim who apostasizes, tolerate the existence of "infidels" within the body politic, I mean, people with no religion which is against the tenets of Islam. I mean, if the state they are constituting is a truly Islamic state, then that Islamic state should wage Jihad against those infidels since Jihad is ordained by Islam. But if you are ready to accept, living with the infidels, simply because those infidels are carrying arms, then why cannot you tolerate, for a Muslim living in the North to change his religion if he so wants. And if you can give yourself the right to abrogate Jihad which is dictated by the Koran why cannot you abrogate Hudoud? All that shows you that the whole thing is political, there is absolutely nothing religious about it.

Questioner:

I am interested in redefining the position of Garang's Movement in the context of the American foreign policy. Now he is a guest of the United States and if we see his Movement through an African perspective, and the relationship between the African revolution and the U.S. up to this moment the U.S. doesn't shake hands with the true leaders of African nations. In the case of the Congo, they participated in neutralizing Patrice Lumumba and supported General Mobuto. In the case of Ghana, the unique leader, Kwame Nkurumah, was overthrown by General Ankara, through an American plot. So now John Garang is seen by the African and by everybody in the area in the list which includes Tshombe, Kasivubu, and Mobutu. My question, Mr. John Garang, is "Who is the more important to the other in terms of Sudan – John Garang to the United States or the United States to John Garang?

Garang:

I don't know who made up the list: Kwame Nkurumah, heading the one list, and Tshombe heading the other. If you made it up then you put me wherever you choose, it is your prerogative. But we are in an international arena where interaction among nations, among the liberation movements, among states is increasing. Gorbachev comes here and shakes hands with Reagan. Mugabe comes here and shakes hands with Bush. Interaction among peoples is increasing. Our position is clear, and it is clearly printed in our Manifesto. It is upon you to judge where the SPLM fits in your paradigms, in your thoughts or in your divisions. We have come to the United States as a delegation to put forward our point of view. We requested to come. We have the right to request to go anywhere we choose. Khartoum, with which you are aligned, has talked itself into believing that John Garang can never go to the United States because he is Communist.

When I came to the United States finally, the question now is; "But why does he go to the United States"? When I don't go to the United States, they say "Ummm. That's a Communist, that's why he doesn't go to the United States". When I come to the United States, they say, "Umm. He is a stooge of imperialism, that's why he goes to the United States." Either way, I will be accused of something. And to tell you the truth, I don't give a damn. I know what my objectives are. I know what the objectives of the Movement are. The objectives of the Movement are to create a New Sudan and this New Sudan cannot be created in a vacuum, it will be created as a result of the correct utilization of the contradictions that there are, both internally and externally. There are international contradictions, which I must use. I have internal contradictions which I must use. And my aim is to create a New Sudan.

Question:

You have met with the Assistant Secretary for Africa and you have met with other officials here. Could you talk in a broader-based way about the attitudes and what you see in terms of U.S. policy, what you would like to see? Have you asked the United States government to do anything? What are the attitudes that you are finding in what has been a very important visit here to Washington, and one that's received quite a lot of attention and press coverage?

Garang:

It is not a secret that the United States government has been a good friend of the Khartoum administration. The United States government has given lot of military assistance, lots of financial assistance, and other material assistance to the government in Khartoum all along. When I say the "government in Khartoum", I don't speak only of the present government of Prime Minister Sadiq al Mahdi, I speak of the government in Khartoum as a continuum from the days of Nimeiri and before the days of Nimeiri until now. What has changed in Khartoum is the form, not the content of the government.

So, my coming here is to establish a dialogue with the administration; one of the points which comes up is obviously the assistance that is given by the United States Government to Khartoum. This assistance, military, financial and otherwise, translates into moral assistance, and makes the other side intransigent, because Khartoum prides itself in having the support of the Arab world, and having the support of the Eastern world. This is the reality. I am a person who is conducting armed struggle. I want to explain my course to everybody, to the United States, to the West, to the East, to the Arab world. I will send delegations now to Egypt. I am prepared to send delegations to Saudi Arabia. I want to

223

explain to the Arab people that the SPLM is not the enemy of the Arab people. I want to explain to the American people that the SPLM is not the enemy of the people of the United States. This is one of the things that I have been discussing.

Second, I have been discussing the necessity of relief assistance. Relief, humanitarian assistance where there is war or where there are natural disasters, is a phenomenon that is of concern to everybody in the international arena. There was an earthquake in Armenia, and the people of this country and other countries contributed to alleviate that human disaster. There is a disaster in the Sudan. I am requesting people of goodwill everywhere to assist in this. These two items have been on the agenda. Peace has also been on the agenda. I have explained the point of view of the SPLM that peace will come to the Sudan when justice has come to the Sudan, justice in the context of the New Sudan on which I talked before.

Question:

When you spoke of the vision for the New Sudan, you mentioned two concepts which in my mind are related, but they can be dealt with separately, one identity and the other one democracy. On identity, it sounded very much like what I heard my good friend, Dr. Mansour, almost 20 years ago, say, and others in the early May group, and that is that the New Sudan must transcend tribal, ethnic, sectarian, linguistic problems. And I, as a student of the Sudan, always felt this is a wonderful idea held by a few intellectuals, but not by the great masses.

My first question is, when do you think that enough of the masses will share that view?

The second part of the same question is, you spoke of democracy. And the government, as you, of course, know and we all know, says we have had elections. What better way to find out what the people want than to give them a chance to vote for 42 parties?

Garang:

The two are really interrelated, identity and democracy.

It is true, intellectuals have this grand idea of everybody coalescing into one identity that transcends sectarianism, whether this is based on religion or on ethnicity. I am conducting a revolution with this idea as an objective to implement. We can, as intellectuals, sit in this room and discuss Sudanese identity. We can take a week; we can take a month. At the end of the day, we shall disperse. The issue of identity and of this new thing being formed, is a goal.

Having set the goal, the next thing is: how do you achieve this goal? In our case, going back to 1983, the issue to be resolved was very fundamental, do we want a separate South or do we fight for one country? That issue was resolved and it is a step towards creating common identity. Now as I said before, we have moved to Southern Kordofan, we have moved to Southern Blue Nile. There are people within the SPLM from Hasa Hissa. There are people from Rufa'a who are now coming to the SPLM. The coming of these people to the Movement enriches the Movement. There are certain things in the Movement, whose members are predominantly from the South, that were not clear before because these interests were not there. It is a process of mutual education. The issue will be resolved through time and as a process. But the important thing is to have the goal of Sudanese unity as the corner-stone. Other things, then, will fall in place.

Democracy depends again on the context in which it operates. Let us take the present democracy. There is a call for an Islamic Republic and, at the same time, people talk about liberal democracy, and pride themselves on this. But this is a contradiction in terms; you cannot have liberal democracy with several parties, and you also call for Islamic Republic. By definition, there is only one party in an Islamic Republic, that is the party of God, Hezbollah. Now, you cannot have the DUP, the Umma, the National Islamic Front, the Communist, the SPLM, all the 40 parties you attended to. These are inconsistent with the basic paradigm which is being pursued, that of an Islamic Republic. Our democracy, which people are after, cannot work, within this context. For democracy to thrive, it must do away with sectorialism and parochialism.

In Europe, and here, liberal democracy did away with feudalism and parochialism. After the American War of Independence there was an idea to make George Washington King; if that was done, you would not have had a republican party.

We believe in democracy and in order for this democracy to thrive, parochialism must go, feudalism must go, the rule of families must go. You know, in the Sudanese Parliament, people vote as to whether you are Ansar or you are Khatmiya. We believe in democracy, but then, in order for democracy to thrive, the conditions for its flourishing must be there, and that is what we are creating now.

Question:

At the moment, Sudan's economy seems to be in near collapse, and there are those who feel that in the coming decade the environmental situation will not be much better. What would you say now if you had influence on economic and environmental policy, what would be the basic outlines of what you would do to rescue the economy in a sustainable way?

Garang:

With respect to the economy and the environment, let's concentrate on the economy. We shall come to the environment. We have a general problem with international economy. There are advanced capitalist and advanced socialist economies. There is Third World, the so-called Third World, made up of poor countries.

The process of development in the advanced capitalist countries took a historical route which we will not follow. It is a history of expansion by those countries to the rest of the world. It is a history of colonialism. Europe expanded out to America, eventually to Africa, Asia. There was quantitative accumulation of wealth from other parts of Europe; these are historical realities. The development of Europe, the industrialization of Europe was not an easy affair. It involved colonialism, it had involved exploitation including that of child labour. The Labour Party in Britain, for example, struggled for the rights of workers. The working day was progressively reduced until it has become 8 hours now.

Now, we are in a situation where you have the industrialized West having reached this stage as a result of lots of difficulties, internally and outside in the colonies. We are in a situation where the Third World has lots of linkages with the advanced capitalist countries. The issue is how do we delink and move forward to establish an industrialized society. In Africa, we cannot go out to colonize other places; this is out of the question; there is nobody else to colonize.

How do we move forward? Europe has achieved a consumerist society. Underdeveloped countries are now aspiring to consumerism. This is unattainable because the necessary base, economic base, is not there to support a consumer society; the consumer society of the West had its own history of development. A similar thing can be said about socialist economies, that is, having a certain level of development and wanting a certain level of consumption. This is a basic contradiction, and symptoms abound in socialist countries as to how to achieve the same quality of life that has been achieved by the capitalist world.

The issue is really how to organize our resources, so that we start at grass-roots level development and be self-reliant. Our development is going from cities to rural areas. I envisage development going from rural areas to cities, so that I don't have a problem of people demonstrating for wheat bread when there is grain produced locally, when there is dura, when there is sorghum. The lifestyle that has been reached by Europe and we aspire to is simply untenable.

We are also concerned about environment issues. There is a contradiction between the protection of the environment and the economic development pattern we pursue. My country is not an exception to this. I don't have hard answers to your question, because the development process is going to be complex, given the fact that we are living at the same time when there are very industrialized societies and very poor societies that want to emulate them. It will definitely need a new world order, in which the developing countries will have the opportunity to develop, because if they don't it will affect everybody.

Question:

With a view toward tomorrow's talks in Addis Ababa, I understand you are terribly optimistic about a breakthrough any time soon. Do you see a role for the United States at some point to mediate talks between the SPLA and Khartoum, as it did with the Brazzaville talks that led to the Angolan-Namibian accord?

Garang:

Well, I am optimistic about peace in the country, based on the interaction of mostly internal factors. The Brazzaville talks involved sides that were supported by both superpowers, Moscow on the one side, the United States on the other. In our case, we have a situation where the SPLM has not been supported. It is not supported by the United States or by the Soviet Union. I see the role of the United States as bringing pressure to bear on its ally, that is Khartoum.

In that context, it is possible for the United States to play a role, because our course is very clear, and I will explain it in any form in the same terms as I am talking now. Now, the United States can bring pressure to bear on Khartoum because Khartoum is an ally of the United States. With respect to the SPLM, there is nothing that the United States provides to the SPLM to be able to twist its arms, as arms were being twisted in Brazzaville. For this to happen, the United States government will have to give us a few arms, a few bullets, as it has given to Khartoum, and then it can pinch a little here and pinch a little there and say, "You guys agree?" At the present time, it is one-sided.

Question:

Federalism is proposed as a way out for Sudan, why do you think the Northern parties are opposed to federalism and power restructuring?

Garang:

Who is afraid of federalism, power-sharing, freedom of religion? Certainly the sectarian parties. This has been our failure since 1956. Since 1956, we inherited a colonialist structure, we did not make something of our own. We inherited a colonial structure and those who took over the reins of power were coached by the colonial system. This is true in many African countries.

Now, in the sense of indirect rule, Britain developed certain families, the Mahdi family; Egypt developed families, the Mirghani family. So, at independence, we really took off with sectarianism, based on families, based on religious sects, based on nationalities. The agenda which we proposed, I agree with you, directly threatens the interests of sectarian parties, and it has to. If it doesn't, we will continue along the same path that we are now. It is a radical agenda that will bring about a restructuring of power, in Khartoum. Those interests that are threatened have no choice but to change or perish. And this is a historical process that must go on.

We have formed the SPLM. We are now 6 years old. We have prevailed. And we are appealing to the other Sudanese political forces to join in the struggle for change. We cannot possibly bring about this change alone. So there are other political forces in the country, in the North itself, that agree with this agenda. It has taken us this long because the interests have been entrenched. People ask the questions as to what the SPLM wants? What we want are these minimums. We have allies in the North, and these allies will work with us. They have been working with us, and they will form this new union.

Question:

But how do you educate a less-developed population where you have geographic, religious, tribal, language, so many divisions? How do you begin this process of political education, because what you are talking about is a concept that maybe many people don't understand? And then, let me ask you also if, in fact, you do indeed have 42 political parties, is there not a way to find some coalition-building so that you might have a more manageable number of four or five or ten parties that would be more manageable where there could be some big ideas that could bring people together?

Garang:

We have 42 political parties. The SPLM, for example, shall fight elections, and we are prepared to do this. We believe in democracy, and we believe we can win these elections. So why should we be afraid? And it will be part of an education process even in the South. If we go to elections tomorrow, I am confident that we can win all the seats in the South; in the present assembly, this would mean 68 seats.

We can also win seats in the Nuba Mountains. We are there. We can win seats in Southern Blue Nile. We shall fight the elections in Northern cities. I am talking in practical terms about Khartoum where it is reported that there are over 1.5 million Southern Sudanese that have migrated to Khartoum. These will be franchised. And we have other supporters in Khartoum itself. In Khartoum we would win a number of seats. In terms of the present Parliament, which has 272 members, if we go to elections tomorrow, we can get a minimum of 100 seats, 68 from the South and the rest from here and there in the Nuba Mountains, in Blue Nile, in Khartoum.

So, in terms of political parties, we can go for elections and make coalitions with any of these parties. We are willing to go into this exercise, and this is part of the reason why it is difficult to get peace, because it is the other side which is threatened. They see that if people go for universal elections, they will lose. The base of the Umma Party is Western Sudan; Kordofan, and Darfur. There is a lot of fighting in that province and there is no SPLA there. These are the contradictions of the situation. The Umma Party has undermined itself, without SPLA, and they stand to lose in Darfur because of that. The Umma Party needs to put its act together before they go for elections. So in terms of coalition parties and using the ballot, we are prepared to do this if there is peace.

In terms of education, the education process is going on. Everyday people are getting educated into the situation by the dynamics of the situation itself.

Dr. Khalid:

I want to take up this question on education. I think the best way to educate people is by example. And I think if people continue in the Sudan to be parochial in their outlook, it is because the leadership has so remained since independence, thereby perpetuating the divisions that exist in the society.

I always refer to the Indian Example. India has definitely much more problems than the Sudan – bigger in size – but if India succeeded in maintaining its unity and democracy, it so did because it had the type of leadership that was able to transcend the divides that existed; the religious divides, the ethnic divides, the linguistic divides. In fact, Mahatma Gandhi lost his life because of that. If you look at what India has done, for example, what Nehru has done after independence, appointing as head of state, as President of India a Moslem, Zakir Husain, and that was after the division with Pakistan, and when the Moslems did not represent more than 10 per cent of the population. That was a signal if not a message sent by Nehru to the Indian people.

The same thing you can say about Indira Gandhi. I mean Indira Gandhi was killed by a Sikh though Indira had been advised by her security people to remove all Sikhs from her personal guard. Her answer was, "If I want to be the Prime Minister of all India, how can I really exclude an Indian from his job on the basis of his ethnic origin". So education depends on type of leadership you have. This leadership never existed before in the Sudan.

Chapter Eight:

Prospects for the Future

The coup, which brought Brigadier Omar Hassan al Beshir to power in July 1989, was the direct result of the inadequacies displayed by Khartoum's government. That is why several external observers had pinned their hopes on the new regime, particularly in view of some promising remarks made by the Junta during their first few days in control. But the army officers who seized power were neither free agents nor honest brokers, they were there to stop the peace process at the behest of the NIF. That junta, though calling itself the national salvation government, did exactly that when it shelved the peace agreement of November 1989, the only frame of reference for peace, acceptable to all Sudanese political forces save for the NIF. In other words, the NIF wanted to achieve through the brute force of a military dictatorship what they failed to achieve through the democratic process.

This "Salvation Army" soon engaged in a vendetta against all politicians and trade unionists known for their opposition to the NIF and ardent support for the peace process. Draconian measures were taken that swept away political parties, trade unions and the independent press. As for peace, the junta's alternative was as naive as it was dubious; the novel idea the junta came up with was the holding of a national referendum on the issue of Shari'a. Credulously they must have thought that the Muslim majority would uphold sharia, and the non-Muslim minority would have no other alternative but to yield to the will of that majority; and that was the end of that. This is the level of the junta's foolhardiness.

It was apparent right from the start that the new government had put no thought to questions such as: what does the SPLM stand for? How has it consistently argued its case with northern parties? And, therefore, how would dialogue with the SPLM be continued? Worse still, it backtracked from all the progress that had been made, and called for new talks without prior conditions. This language was not new; the SPLM/SPLA heard it from the NIF when they denounced both Koka-Dam declaration and the Peace Initiative with the DUP as SPLM's pre-conditions. Evidently the NIF was assuming that their word was as emphatic as the word of Allah, otherwise how on earth would they have arrogated to themselves the right to veto national consensus on such a major issue? That was, of course, a hefty agenda; and for the NIF to achieve their political aims and fulfil Allah's purpose they should have looked for a more competent government; of all Khartoum governments in the last thirty years, this one gets the lowest marks.

The response of the SPLM to the new government was as careful as had been its greetings to the II May regime. Unlike in the case of TMC, the rejection was not as prompt; it came one month later as if the SPLM wanted to give the junta the benefit of the doubt or allow them enough time to show their real colours. There was little evidence that the soldiers had prepared any policies as regards the SPLM, or that they were particularly sincere about bringing peace to the country; caution was thus the order of the day. So by the end of that one month period of grace the SPLM, in a major policy statement by John Garang, came out with its position on the events in Khartoum. In that statement Garang reasserted the Movement's commitment to peace in line with the two basic agreements accepted by all the Sudanese political forces and only rejected by the NIF. He also dwelt on the issue of democracy, which was brought to the fore by the junta's onslaught on popular political and social organizations. Nonetheless Garang was positive in his response to the junta's request for the resumption of negotiations.

Two rounds of negotiations have taken place; the first was in Addis Ababa in August 1989. Nothing came out of that meeting in view of the divergent positions of the parties; the SPLM stood tenaciously behind the November 1988 peace agreement; the junta echoed the NIF. Any other position by the SPLM would have amounted to a betrayal not only of its allies, but also of the whole cause of peace. One thing that clearly transpired from that meeting was the strong desire of the junta for the SPLM/SPLA to make a deal with them, to the exclusion of everybody else. The NIF, we recall, were seeking to achieve through military putchism what they had failed to achieve through the due processes of politics. That offer was both ill-considered and scandalous, the junta should have realized that the SPLM/SPLA would and should be the last to help them achieve that end. If such a compromise was not made with Sadiq al Mahdi whose legitimacy was not challenged by the SPLM except in so far as it was deemed a partial legitimacy, it would be ludicrously unreasonable to think that it would be made to those whose legitimacy was non-existent except as a *fait accompli*. Even so the meeting ended with a friendly note; a joint statement declared that the two parties would meet again to resume talks once the government in Khartoum has elaborated its position on the issues raised by the SPLM, now that they knew what the SPLM stands for. A channel of communications was agreed to by the parties.

But instead of returning to the negotiations table, as envisaged, the junta decided to hold their own national constitutional conference, a rally to which were invited academics, clerics, pseudo-politicians and, above all, political opportunists of repute of whom many litter Khartoum's political landscape. If that gathering was meant to help the junta formulate their own views on the peace process nobody would have had the right to take exception to it; however, the junta imagined that by holding that meeting they were short-circuiting the on-going peace process, particularly the call for a national constitutional conference.

That farcical "peace preparatory conference", which took place in Khartoum, not only highlighted the wisdom of the SPLM's reticence towards the junta, but also revealed the perfidy of the NIF. The final report of "The Steering Committee for the National Dialogue on Peace Issues", that sat in Khartoum during September 1989 without the participation of the SPLM and only one month after the Addis meeting between the SPLM and government representatives, was a bizarre document from any perspective. Not only did the document not take account of the proper basis for talks, which were to be found in the texts of the Koka-

233

Dam and DUP Agreements, also it mentioned the SPLM on only three occasions, each time to criticize them for blocking negotiations!

The junta also attempted to mislead the world by suggesting that that rally was open to the SPLM and, indeed, claiming that an invitation was extended to the movement. That invitation, however, was not extended prior to the meeting through the channel agreed to by the two parties only a month earlier, but through the waves in the course of al Bashir's opening address to the conference. The SPLM, in this game of wit, did not allow itself to be led on or choose to soft-pedal; they accepted the offer, and surely that acceptance was transmitted through the waves too. The Movement's answer was, "yes we shall participate, but only if the junta open up the conference to the legitimate representatives of the people and create an atmosphere conducive to free debate". This would entail, the SPLM argued, ending the ban on political parties, trade unions and the press, and allowing the legitimate leadership of those organizations, that is those who were freely chosen by the grass roots, to take their rightful place in the conference. The SPLM/SPLA did not a war fight in order to secure ministerial positions for the "boys" or have a tranquil interlude between two wars; war was fought for permanent peace. Such peace could only be achieved through national consensus, which would entail the fullest and most effective participation of all. That, of course, was an eventuality the NIF junta was not ready to face; having dissolved political parties, banned trade unions and decided to rule the country through raw violence.

But the junta would not relent; they called for another round of negotiations in order to sell their new proposals. A meeting was duly held in Nairobi, early December 1989 under the Chairmanship of President Carter. The SPLM was not sufficiently impressed with those proposals since they have failed to address adequately the issues, and also evaded the theses adduced by the SPLM, the adversary with whom they wanted to reach an agreement. One of the propositions advanced with gusto by that rally and by the negotiators in Nairobi was federalism; it was presented as if federalism was divinely revealed to them. Those who are conversant with Sudan's political evolution know better; federalism was proposed by southerners many wars ago, to the distress of northern political parties, including the Muslim brothers, who thought that federalism was an attack on Khartoum's hegemony and, to them, attacking Khartoum's monopoly of power was like an attack on motherhood.

However there was a ploy in this revival of federalism; what the NIF junta were concerned with and looking for was not good governance but an artifice whereby they would get the South off their backs on the issue of Sharia. That is why, whenever the word federalism is mentioned by the junta and their shady advisers, it is always counterpoised with the statement that under federalism each region shall have the right to legislate its own penal laws. To the NIF, therefore, Sharia shall be a *fait accompli* in the rest of the Sudan once the "heathens" of the South and their "foreign anti-islamic" supporters are contained. What the junta and their advisers failed to realize was that federalism is a system of government devised to apportion power between the centre and the regions and, accordingly, "the relationship between the regions or federal states and the centre will have to be resolved in the first place"; this citation comes from a statement reiterated by John Garang only three weeks before the NIF's coup d'etat. Probably the Islamo-Jeffersonians may not have cared to go through the federalist papers but one would fairly presume that they have combed the political literature of the SPLM in order to uncover the thinking of their adversary on all the questions at issue, including this one. Obviously the SPLM has never been solely concerned with the laws that govern the South; they were, above all, exercised in devising a more just and befitting system of rule for the whole Sudan including the South. As for the "heathens" of the North the junta believed that they would be overcowed and subdued through repression so that the NIF could implement their agenda.

Accusations of fascism should not be levelled lightly but for a government that has, in the course of less than a year, so hardened to injustice, the accusation is well deserved. In no time of Sudan's history was a government denounced, for its human rights abuses concertedly, by Amnesty International, Africa Watch, the Arab Lawyers Union, the European Parliament, the ILO Governing Council and the U.N. sub-committee on human rights. Episodes of torture were catalogued in reports submitted to those bodies, and that record alone yields enough pointers to the type of society the NIF has in store for the Sudan. That also unmasks the NIF for what they really are; a party that is irrelevant to Sudan's multifaceted problems; both their ideology and application are now proven to be politically divisive, socially subversive, economically ruinous and even lacking in any redeeming moral attribute; the unspeakable atrocities practised by NIF agents on political detainees locked up in horror chambers in Khartoum had nothing to do with Islam or, for that matter, any other religion. Bestiality does not cease to be bestiality simply because it is dressed up in quranic verses.

Society in the North may have become fear-ridden momentarily but people soon learned how to live with terror, as people often do. In less than a year hatred against the NIF junta became colossal and widespread. An alliance bringing together all political parties, trade unions and army officers was formed under the name of National Democratic Forum (NDF); its goal is to remove the junta government and "restore" democracy. A national charter analyzing Sudan's crisis of governability, and charting out the path for the future, was adopted. The SPLM/SPLA joined ranks with the NDF, but only after making its views known on both the nature of the crisis and the manner in which that crisis should be resolved. Those views were reflected in a memorandum, which was consequently adopted by the parties concerned and regarded as an integral part of the NDF's national charter (both documents are annexed). Far from being punctilious, the SPLM wanted to be true to its vocation as an engine of revolutionary change and faithful to its commitment for Sudan's rural destitutes particularly when the original NDF's charter was seen to be predominated by the concerns of the urban elite. Equally the SPLM underscored the need for the parties to go from the stage of battle cries and generalities, to that of programmes and specifics, before and not after the fact. The experiences of the October 1964 uprising that toppled Abboud's military rule and that of April 1985, which unseated Nimeiri should have taught the Sudanese some lessons. It was high time that unintended consequences of revolutionary changes ceased to become essence, as has been the case in 1964 and 1985.

Below are highlights from John Garang's speech of 10 August 1989 in which he outlined the SPLM's views on the June 1989 military coup, the reasons that led to it and the way out for the Sudan.

First Statement by John Garang to the Sudanese People on 10 August 1989; Following the Military *Coup d'état* of 30 June 1989

1   As you all know, our National Capital, Khartoum, witnessed on the 30 June a change in Government. The elected Government of Prime Minister Sadiq el Mahdi was ousted by a *coup d'état* led by a group of Army Officers sworn to bring to an end political parties, and establish a military dictatorship that they say is for national salvation. Since then the junta has followed up on its words to establish authoritarian rule; they have banned all political parties, dissolved all trade unions, shut down all non-military press, suspended the constitution, imposed martial law and vested all legislative, executive and judicial powers in one man, the Council President, Brigadier Omer al Bashir. No doubt you have been wondering about and waiting for the position of the SPLM/SPLA on these momentous developments. I wish here to assure the people that your Movement has been following the situation very closely and that we have conducted a very careful and sober analysis in order to arrive at conclusions and actions that will safeguard the interests of the suffering Sudanese and that will not compromise their hard won democratic achievements.

2   In arriving at the position that I am announcing today, I wish to assure you that we were fully conscious of the vital responsibilities laid on us by history. Today the SPLM/SPLA is the only democratic force in the country that the Junta had no power to ban, dissolve or arrest its leaders. On the other hand the SPLM/A has the power to shorten or lengthen the days of the junta. This is indisputable. In using this power, the Movement had to exercise the utmost political maturity guided by the supreme interest of our people. This is the reason for our delay in announcing our position. During the past 40 days the Movement has conducted wide contacts with broad sectors of the Sudanese community. Beginning with the Movement itself, all SPLA commanders and mass organizations have made their views known to the leadership. We have been in contact with the banned political parties, with the dissolved Trade Unions, with various opinion groups within the Sudanese Army, with Sudanese working or living abroad in various countries, and we have listened and recorded all the statements of the junta since they came to power.

3   I am aware that our delay in announcing our position was misunderstood or distorted, and that many rumours have been floated in Khartoum. Various international news media have made statements attributing them to me or to some spokesman of the Movement. It was even reported that I had a telephone conversation with Brig. Omerel Bashir, which is of course not true. It has been suggested for example that the Movement delayed in announcing its position because we had reached a secret agreement with the Junta. This is of course completely false, without any foundation. I want to assure the Sudanese people that all these rumours were unfounded and created by opportunists; they were either plain wishful thinking, or deliberate disinformation. The position we announce today is our first statement since the coup, and we are convinced that this position is the general consensus of the Sudanese people, inside and outside the Sudan and in their political organizations including the Army.

Sudan needs Peace
4   The change in Khartoum takes place in the midst of a deep economic and political crisis in the country. The economy is in ruins with the budget registering the highest deficit in history, hyperinflation has reached alarming proportions, war is raging in the country all over and foreign troops are active in some parts of our country. The war has drained our human and material resources. You cannot have a healthy economy when more than 20 million Sudanese pounds a day are devoured by the war machine. You cannot have economic stability when the natural resources are unexploited because of the war. You cannot build a giant country like the Sudan with a begging bowl in hand. Hence, the resolution of Sudan's problems should take as its starting point the reasons that led to the outbreak of war, so that a lasting peace is achieved in our country.

5   The commitment of the SPLM/SPLA to peace is unequivocal and strategic. The peace we aspire to is not just any peace but peace with justice. The basis for a permanent peace was set out in the Koka-Dam Declaration of March 1986. This was the will of all Sudanese political forces including the SPLM/SPLA; the only absentees of Koka-Dam were the DUP and the NIF. The principles laid down in Koka-Dam were further developed and strengthened in the Sudanese Peace Initiative of the 16 November

1988 that was worked out and signed by the SPLM/SPLA and the DUP, and which brought the DUP into the peace process. Thus *only the NIF had never supported peace.* The DUP/SPLA peace agreement won a huge popular support in the country, and served as a rallying point for all the peace-loving forces in our country. This is reflected by the fact that almost all the political parties and Trade Unions supported the Sudanese Peace Initiative. Peace could have prevailed in Sudan on the 31 December 1988 were it not that Sadiq al Mahdi and the National Islamic Front (NIF) rejected the November agreement and stood firmly against it. You recall that on the 21 December 1988, Sadiq and the NIF manoevred the Constituent Assembly and forced it to pass a resolution formally rejecting the agreement and insisted on the imposition of the divisive Islamic Laws. This was a big blow to the peace process but it was not the end of the story. The momentum of the peace march which had permeated and gripped wide sections of the Sudanese society could hardly be halted by a few bigots. The peace-loving forces including the SPLM/A continued to intensify the struggle for peace on all fronts until conditions were created that made Sadiq swallow his pride and he was forced in March this year to endorse the November Peace Agreement.

6   As soon as the new government of Sadiq al Mahdi endorsed the November Agreement, meetings started with the Movement in April and we declared a cease-fire on 1 May as a gesture of goodwill to enable the government to implement the provisions of the agreement. The cease-fire which was initially for one month was extended twice till it became two months in all. Within that period a meeting was held between the SPLM/A and government delegations on 10 June to review the implementation of the Peace Agreement. That meeting went a long way in narrowing the gap of difference and the two sides agreed to meet again on 4 July 1989 to iron out the remaining points of difference on the implementation of the November Peace Agreement. Furthermore, a date was fixed, 18 September, for the convening of the National Constitutional Conference that would usher the Sudan into a just and lasting peace.

7   As I have just outlined, the peace process had reached an advanced stage when the fifteen Army officers seized power on the 30 June; four days before the scheduled meeting of the two sides to the conflict. The obvious question that arises is the follow-

ing. Is the *coup d'état* motivated by the interest of bringing about peace speedily to the country? If the answer is in the affirmative, what then is the position of the new military regime on the on-going peace process, the wheels of which it stopped rolling? This is the crux of the matter that any government in Khartoum must address if it has to be taken seriously. Does the regime now in Khartoum stand up to the mark? In order to answer this question objectively and comprehensively I would like to examine and share with you the position of the junta on nine key question.

8   The first question is: What is the junta's perception of the problem of war, which they say they have come to solve, and related to this what is their programme for peace? This is a vital question because without a clear understanding of what the problem is, it is futile to talk about its solution. On this the junta considers the problem of war as "The Southern Problem". You have heard the Junta repeat this time and again that the problem is the problem of the South. Obviously the junta has a very shallow and distorted perception of the nature of the central problem of the Sudan. On this the government of the parties that the Junta ousted was much more advanced. All past peace agreements, as you all know, from Koka Dam to the 16 November Peace Initiative, affirm that the problem is the problem of the Sudan and not the so-called problem of Southern Sudan. Indeed this global perception of the problem constitutes paragraph one of the Koka Dam Agreement. Omer el Bashir's perception and contention that he has come to solve the problem of Southern Sudan misses the point by a wide margin; it is a step backwards, a retrogression, indeed a crude, and reactionary position that can only bring disaster not peace to the country. In my address to the nation on 27 May 1985 I underlined the futility of diagnosing the general problem of the Sudan as the "Southern Problem", and I quote:

Negotiations in the context of the so-called "Southern Problem" is against the national interest and a recipe for disaster. Suppose we solve the problem of the South, we will soon have to solve the problem of the Jebels because the Nuba can also take up arms; after that the problem of the Beja, and so forth. It is a national problem, not a Southern problem that we must address.

That was in 1985. I told this to General Swar al Dhahab and his TMC, and I am telling it now to Brigadier Omer el Bashir and his Salvation Command Council. This statement that I made in 1985 is more true today than it was then. The Nuba had not taken up arms in 1985; but they have done so today in their thousands, men and women. And while Brigadier Omer solves his Southern problem, more people in addition to Southerners, Nubas and Ingassanas will have taken up arms, including the people of Medani, Hassa Hisa and Shendi, Omer's home town.

9   If the junta is to be of any use to the Sudan, it must discard this perception of a Southern problem and think with the rest of us, think with the march of history, not with the archaic past. According to this archaic perception Omer thinks that he is the Sudanese nationalist and we in the SPLA are his Southerners, and according to him all that which is required is for him to sit down with Dr. John Garang, representing the South, and him representing the Sudan, and in his words talk soldier to soldier to solve his Southern problem. Has Brig. Omer el Bashir bothered to ask the question as to what is it that makes him the Sudanese and makes Dr. John Garang his Southerner?

10   Regarding the junta's programme for peace, they started on the wrong foot and ended up without a peace programme. The regime started out with the announcement that they are against all previous peace agreements reached by the SPLM/A and the previous government. Well, a simple initial question is: What is the guarantee that whatever peace agreement the SPLM/A reaches with the junta will not be cancelled by some other Omer Two who may take over tomorrow, or does Mr. El Bashir consider himself the last coup maker? But more substantively, the truth is that the Koka-Dam Agreement of 1986 and the November Peace Initiative of November 1988 were reached by the SPLM/A and the majority of the Sudanese political forces representing in one way or the other the Sudanese people. These agreements addressed the fundamental problems of the Sudan, among them the essence of the central problem of the Sudan, problems of unity of the country, religion and state, democracy, the system of rule, restructuring of power at the centre, socio-economic development, and so forth. The junta is behaving as if Sudan came into being on 30 June. It is presumptuous of these officers to throw away all previous peace agreements and peace efforts, as they

241

announced, and claim to start from scratch. There is a wealth of accumulated experience about the process of peace making in those agreements. Be that as it may, the junta has cancelled everything that was on the Sudanese political landscape before 30 June, including all previous peace agreements. Let us now look at the junta's replacement of these agreements, that is, their peace programme. Piecing together what the Junta has said so far, one can summarize their programme in four points, namely:

(a) Cease-fire
(b) Amnesty
(c) Talks with the SPLM/A without preconditions
(d) Solution to what the junta calls the "Southern Problem".

If we take the four points together they simply do not constitute a new radical peace programme that would justify a *coup d'état*. One would have expected a dramatic move towards peace to justify the takeover, such as the outright abrogation of the September Laws, lifting of the state of emergency, abrogation of defence treaties with foreign countries and immediate convening of the National Constitutional Conference. Such a programme could have been a substitute for Koka-Dam, and might have justified the coup as a necessary step towards peace and democracy.

11 That the junta has no peace programme is best illustrated by considering their four points singly. We see that each point collapses to nothing. Take the first point, cease-fire. This is not new; we had a cease-fire that had lasted for two months when Omer made his coup. The second point, amnesty, this is as naive and absurd as it is preposterous a proposition for Omer to make. Omer says he offers amnesty to the SPLA so that the SPLA returns to the Sudan in peace. Surely Omer must know that we are in the Sudan, but that is not the point; the point is that Omer is just as much a rebel as the SPLA and a junior rebel for that matter. Omer rebelled against an elected government only 40 days ago; the SPLA rebelled against Nimeiri's military dictatorship 6 years ago. What is it that gives this new and junior rebel the legitimacy to offer amnesty to his seniors? The issue of amnesty simply does not arise in the peace process and we dismiss the junta's statement on amnesty as ill-advised and in bad taste. We advise them not to mention it again. The third point in the junta's peace package, talking to the SPLM/A without preconditions is also nothing new. We have been talking with the previous govern-

ments and political parties without preconditions. In order for any two parties to talk they do not need preconditions, they simply agree to talk. This was the case when we met at Koka Dam, it was the case when I met el Mahdi in July 1986, it was the case when we held a series of meetings with the African Parties in 1987 and it was the case when we met the DUP delegation in August 1988. There were no preconditions in all these talks. Perhaps the junta is confused about, and makes no distinction between, talks and the outcome of talks. The fourth and last point, solving what the Junta calls "The Southern Problem", I have already earlier dismissed this as a non-starter. In summary the junta has no peace programme, one wonders why they took over only 4 days before the scheduled peace talks of 4 July and before the National Constitutional Conference that was scheduled for 18 September. One wonders whether the Junta did not take over power in order to stop the peace process. It is upon the junta to prove the contrary, the Sudanese people and the SPLM/A are watching.

A Coup by Deception

12   The second question is: What support does the junta enjoy within the Sudanese Army? This question is important because the Army at present is the only presumed base of the junta. From our contacts with various elements in the Army, the junta is opposed by the majority of the Sudanese Army. The truth is that the Army had agreed to a takeover when they presented their 21-point memorandum to Sadiq el Mahdi last February, and subsequently started to prepare public opinion for the takeover. At the same time the government of Sadiq el Mahdi, under pressure from the threat of an Army takeover, from the Sudanese public, from the SPLA and from the international community, started to talk peace much more seriously than at any other time. Indeed the same day of the coup, on 30 June, the Council of Ministers was going to pass all the provisions of the DUP/SPLA November Peace Agreement, after which the necessary bills were going to be passed by the Constituent Assembly before the 4 July meeting between the government and the SPLA. This was to pave the way for the convening of the National Constitutional Conference scheduled for 18 September. It was under the confusion of these circumstances that the four principal officers of the junta made their move; probably they feared that the 4 July meeting was going to lead to the National Constitutional Conference. Essentially the

four officers took over power by deception, and this largely explains why there was no fighting. They went to the Army General Headquarters and announced that the expected military takeover was underway and that they were acting in the name of the GHQS. They told all units in the Capital to remain in their places and that no one should leave or enter military barracks. In the meantime they arrested the Army High Command and Sadiq el Mahdi's Ministers, and announced the military takeover in their own name to the surprise and disbelief of the rest of the Army. The other 11 Council Members were coopted subsequently. When the trick of the 4 officers was discovered and their ideological orientation known, opposition within the Army started immediately.

13   That this is the actual situation is indicated by the fact that as I talk to you today more than 600 Army officers and 400 Police officers have been dismissed in the last 40 days of the coup, and the purges are continuing. If the *coup d'état* was a military takeover popular in the Sudanese Army why would the Junta be dismissing its own officer cadres, why so many officers dismissed? We are here not talking of a few officers, say 10, 20 or even 50; we are talking of more than 600 officers. What is the explanation to this? In all Sudan's previous three military coups (1958, 1969 and 1985) this phenomenal dismissal of officers has never happened; it is unprecedented. The likely reality is that the junta, or rather the fundamentalist political force behind it, is destroying the Sudanese Army in order to replace it with a sectarian Army intended to defend the political programme of that political force. Sectarianism in the Sudanese Army as it is in politics does not augur well for peace and unity of the Sudan, and I take the opportunity to warn the Sudanese people of this imminent danger.

14   The third question is: What mass support does the junta enjoy among the Sudanese public? It is true that the Sudanese people were fed up with sectarian politics and with the bickering of the sectarian parties. The economic situation had reached an unbearable low, life was miserable; the people wanted an end to the war and wanted peace to break out, so that the country ushers in a new era of rapid socio-economic development and prosperity. Any government that replaced the impotent government of Sadiq el Mahdi was to be preferred. Indeed the Sudanese people expected a coup, almost were calling for a coup in the absence of

any credible alternative they could see. But is this the coup the people expected or called for? I believe the answer is no. When the junta called for a mass rally in Khartoum for the public to express their support, less than 3,000 people turned up to hear El Bashir explain why he took over. In a city of 5 million people for only 3,000 to turn up, or even 10,000 as reported by some international media, this is tantamount to a mass popular vote against the junta. In the desperate situation of the Sudan, a popular military takeover should have been greeted by a mass rally of at least one million people. What happened? The people are intelligent, he who takes them for granted does so at his own peril. They know the character of the junta that has taken over. The truth is that Sudan does not need another military dictatorship (we have had them for 23 of 33 years). The people might have wanted an *interim government, initiated of necessity by the Army, that would be charged with a specific programme to prepare the way for true democracy* and the *creation of the new Sudan*. The Sudanese people did not want and certainly do not want an indefinite military dictatorship, as declared by the junta in their statements.

The Call for Democracy

15   The fourth question is: What is the position of the junta on Democracy? Without mincing their words the junta says they have come to establish a military dictatorship. This comes at a time when the wind of democracy is blowing all over the world, at a time when dictators are being toppled in popular uprisings. Can Sudan be the exception to democracy? The junta has asserted that democracy has failed three times in the Sudan; they cannot be more wrong. They probably do not know the meaning of democracy. It is true that there was what appeared to be liberal democracy from 1956 to 1958, again from 1964 to 1969 and recently from 1986 to 1989, that is, a total of about 10 years out of our 33 years of independence. On the other hand there has been a military dictatorship from 1958 to 1964, from 1969 to 1985, from 1985 to 1986, that is, for 23 years of our 33 years of independence. This one now under El Bashir, is our fourth military dictatorship. Both pseudo-liberal democracy and military dictatorship have failed in the Sudan and what is more, military dictatorship has failed in more years (23 years compared to 10 years) than the pseudo-liberal democracy that the junta has found convenient to

criticize. This compels us to concretely discuss "democracy", as applied to the Sudanese situation.

16 Democracy might mean different things to different people but, in essence, it relates to a system of government in which supreme power is vested in the people and such power is, directly or indirectly, exercised by them. So, whenever we talk of democracy we should be presumed to be talking about a *system* of government not government by whim, *people's power* and not that of a tribal chief, feudal lord, military dictator or religious Imam claiming to represent or know best the interests of the people. That power also is not a conceptual abstraction; it is a reality that affects the daily lives of people. In an address to the nation on 22 March 1985, shortly before the fall of Nimeiri, I summarized in 9 points the objectives of the Movement. The first of those points related to the maintenance of Sudan's national unity and territorial integrity. The second reflected the SPLM's commitment to "the establishment of a NEW DEMOCRATIC SUDAN in which equality, freedom, economic and social justice and respect for human rights are not mere slogans but concrete realities to be promoted, cherished and protected". The ingredients of the democracy we are striving for are thus very clear: Personal and political freedoms, social and economic justice, respect for human rights, equality of citizens before the law, equality irrespective of race, tribe, religious belief, or sex.

17 Equally clear is our conviction that such democracy does not exist and has not existed in the Sudan we know. On the eve of Sudan's independence the British had bequeathed on our country a system of liberal democracy based on multi-party rule, freedom of expression and association and independence of the judiciary. That model of government is what has failed three times in the course of the last 33 years following Sudan's independence. In effect what has failed was not liberal democracy, rather the way that democracy was envisaged or understood and then artlessly grafted onto Sudan's body politic. Worse still, it was the very champions of liberal democracy in the Sudan who had often masterminded its demise through political recklessness, social irresponsibility and archaic sectarianism. The truth is that Sudan's liberal democracy was but a hollow shell, a mere procedural exercise without substantive political and economic content to which the political players were intellectually and emotionally commit-

ted. It was thus a matter of no surprise to anyone that whenever liberal democracy collapsed under the heels of the military the first to lambast it were those who pretended to be its champions; sometimes those self-proclaimed advocates of liberal democracy were even seen hailing and welcoming the military as saviours and redeemers. I am informed, and I am not surprised, that some members of the previous government, while now still in jail, are already lobbying in favour of the new military regime. What democrats are these, who only yesterday prided themselves in running what they called an oasis of democracy in Africa and who now hail the military as saviours? Surely we are not talking the same language. Democracy to those of Sadiq el Mahdi and their like is only a tool, a procedure, not an ideal.

18 Liberal democracy cannot be a code to be copied nor a flag to be waved, it is a system of government that was borne out of a bitter struggle for freedom and justice as we are now struggling for the same causes. It was a struggle against feudalist exploitation, against centrifugal forces that threatened national unity, against the entanglement of the Church in the affairs of state, against the exploitation of the working class by capitalists against sexist domination of women by men, and so on. But that was not the case of the Sudan where the facade of liberal democracy served as a comfortable alibi concealing all manner of injustice inherent in a social system nurtured and sustained by forces of reaction who masquerade as advocates of liberalism. For example Sudan's traditional political parties, far from being a reflection of social class affiliations as was the case in Europe, were really frontages to sectarianism, sectarianism based on family, race, religion or some compound of these. Sectarianism, on the other hand, is by definition undemocratic. What sort of democracy is there in a system where political authority is hereditary, leadership immune from accountability and masses have no independent will of their own; but always trailing the "Ishara" – beck and call – of the Imam. Democracy cannot, has never and will never flourish in a situation characterized by sectarianism. There has never been democracy in Sudan and thus democracy has never failed in the Sudan. What there has been and what has failed in the Sudan was sectarianism masquerading as democracy and military dictatorship.

19 Sudan has yet to devise its own form of democracy in which

the noble values of freedom, fraternity, prosperity, justice and equality should be maintained on our cultural soil while the social aberrations and anachronisms of traditional society are weeded out. Two things should be underlined in this regard; the first is that, given the country's multiplicities, the *Sudanese political system will have to be pluralistic* within a basic commonality. It is to be cautioned, however, that such pluralism must be a reflection of social differentiation and ease of administration and development rather than religious, regional or ethnic cleavages. For while the former would ensure better interest articulation by the party on behalf of its constituents, the latter would only serve to highlight cleavages that militate against national unity. Secondly, for such democracy to take root it will have to come out through a serious national debate involving all political forces, social and professional groups including the SPLA and the Army. As regards the latter no one, in his right mind, would deny such a right to the military having seen them involved in politics for two-thirds of the life span of modern independent Sudan. On the other hand any military ruler who believes that he can remove with a stroke of a pen Sudan's political forces and social and professional groups must be living in a political wilderness and should always remember the Abbouds and the Nimeiris of Sudan.

20 Such a national debate, we have said and resaid time over time, will have to address the country's fast-rooted problems which are basically political in nature; no legal tinkering by technocrats shall suffice. In this connection the views of SPLM were emphatically expressed in my address over the Movement's radio on 26 and 27 May 1985. That address was meant, among other things, to lay at rest the persistent, though suspect question: What does the SPLM want? Quoting from the statement this dialogue must be undertaken

> by all democratic and patriotic forces in the country so that a national democratic consensus is reached on the fundamental issues. Such a national democratic consensus cannot be brought about by a bunch of generals; it can only be brought about through dialogue among the national democratic and patriotic forces in the country, and the SPLM/A is willing and ready to enter into that broad discussion.

This remains as valid today as it was in 1985.

21   On the practical sphere of action the Movement's resolve and commitment for the democratic option was reflected in both the Koka Dam Declaration and the Sudanese Peace Initiative of November 1988. In its preamble the Koka Dam Declaration affirmed our rejection of "all forms of dictatorship" and our desire "to create a New Sudan in which the Sudanese individual enjoys absolute freedom from the shackles of injustice, ignorance and disease in addition to enjoying the benefit of real democratic life; a New Sudan that would be free from racism, tribalism, sectarianism and all causes of discrimination and disparity". Thus the democracy we are fighting for has broad social, economic and cultural dimensions; it is not a hollow shell; it is not the pseudo-liberal democracy that has failed and is discredited in the Sudan. Our commitment to democracy was further emphasized in the Sudanese Peace Initiative where the preambular part also referred to the resoluteness of both signatories in consolidating and enriching Sudan's democratic practice. We assure the junta and the Sudanese people that our commitment to democracy is irrevocable and non-negotiable. On the other hand there is nothing that bars the junta from taking the democratic option and discarding dictatorship.

Religion and the State

22   The fifth question is: What is the position of the junta on religion and the state? Judging from the junta's statements there is sufficient reason for concern that Brigadier Omer has hidden agenda, with or without the NIF, to impose a theocratic state on the Sudan, or part of the Sudan. When Brig. Omer took over, it was widely expected that his first act would be to abolish Nimeiri's September Laws; instead, El Bashir outdid Swar al Dhahab in his fundamentalism, and started to talk the same language as Dr. Turabi. El Bashir declared the constitution suspended, but curiously picked one item, Nimeiri's Sharia Law, for discussion with the SPLM/A, thereby exposing his ideological colours. El Bashir said that if he failed to reach agreement with the SPLM/A on the question of Nimeiri's September (Islamic Sharia) Laws, this would be taken to the people for decision in a popular referendum. Most interesting. A self-imposed military junta has the audacity to talk of carrying out a popular referendum on Sharia Laws, when no referendum has been carried out on the junta's assumption of power. With its lack of legitimacy aside, the junta's friends in the

NIF will tell them that Allah's Laws, the Laws of God, are not subject to human opinion! Indeed it is blasphemous for El Bashir to say that God's Laws would be taken for human judgement.

23 On the question of religion and politics the SPLM, sure enough is not an anti-religious Movement; the Movement is not against any religion. The Movement's Manifesto declares that an ideal system of government for the Sudan is that where the state is separated from both Mosque and Church. Within such a system "all religious faiths in the country shall have complete freedom to practise without hindrance or intimidation, provided that this freedom to practise is not abused and used for political purposes" (Chapter 9, paragraph 24 (c)). This citation comes from a paragraph in the Manifesto entitled religious fundamentalism and the reference to fundamentalism was deliberate. To us in the SPLM/A, fundamentalism stands condemned because it is sectarian and undemocratic. Fundamentalism is also condemnable because it goes against the grain of Sudanese society as it has historically evolved.

Our country's historical evolution informs that inter-faith coexistence was the result of a process whereby heavenly religions did not only tolerate indigenous belief – systems in Sudan; also, in many instances and institutions, became fused with them. That is why, instead of religious conflict, Sudan has survived for centuries in ecumenical harmony. This tradition was carried further through the colonial period when the Sudanese Muslim leaders reconciled themselves with the secular aspect of colonial rule. In none of their political actions or reactions to the alien non-Muslim system was any leader inspired by religious responses. True to this spirit of religious tolerance the two Muslim sectarian leaders, Sayyid Ali al Mirghani and Sayyid Abd al Rahman al Mahdi continued to shun calls for the imposition of Islam on Sudan's legal system. The two Sayyids could have imposed an Islamic constitution on the country at independence, since they had sufficient majority in parliament, but unlike their more educated heirs, they obviously had the wisdom to realize that such an imposition would not have been cost-free; its highest cost would have been national disintegration. Accordingly Sudan continued invariably to be governed by secular laws except when it came to personal laws.

24 The fundamentalists, therefore, had to wait for Nimeiri's

reincarnation as an Imam in 1983 in order to carry out their designs. Thus Nimeiri, encouraged and abetted by the Muslim Brothers, decreed his version of Shaira, the so-called September Laws, and made of religious belief a determinant of political behaviour. Since then the shadow of Nimeiri has hung ominously over the country. Under Nimeiri's Sharia it is known that over 300 citizens, mostly poor non-Muslims were amputated or cross-amputated. They have formed an association called the Association of Sudanese Amputees (ASA), no other country in the world boasts a similar organization. Another 700 or more continue to languish in jails, as the state is afraid to apply the sentences since there is no appeal against God's Law.

25   When Nimeiri was dislodged from power in April 1985 one of the slogans of the popular uprising was cancellation of Nimeiri's abhorrent September Laws. But the generals who highjacked the popular uprising under Swar al Dhahab were in no mood to undo the ugly remnants of Nimeirism, including his undemocratic religious laws. Indeed Swar al Dhahab then, like El Bashir now, started to talk the language of Turabi. In his recent trip to Tripoli last week, El Bashir told the Sudanese community in Libya that "there can be no unity in the Sudan except under Islam". This is a very dangerous statement that further reveals Brig. Omer's fundamentalist inclinations and intentions to partition the country.

26   As things stand today there is no greater danger to our country's unity and stability than that posed by fundamentalism. The fundamentalists may now be entering a new stage in their manoeuvring, it is a dangerous stage. Having failed to get their way through the democratic process and through street intimidation and media villification they are now poised to use state power either directly or by proxy through El Bashir's Junta, as they did under Nimeiri.

27   Fundamentalism in the case of the Sudan is really a misnomer for, by definition, what is dubbed fundamental is so called because it pertains to the roots. The roots of our belief systems, be they traditional or heavenly, have given birth to inter-faith harmony. But what the fundamentalists of Khartoum seek to impose on the country today is an intellectual vision of Islam based on experiences alien to the Sudan, and indeed to Africa. It is a vision of Islam that is never practised and has never been practised in any

251

of our villages anywhere in our country. The call by the SPLM/A for the separation of Mosque and Church on the one hand from state is the experience of the Sudan and of Africa. Africa has known predominantly Muslim countries like Senegal, which were happily ruled by a Catholic President for decades; power changed smoothly from President Senghor (a Christian) to the present President Abdu Diuof (a Muslim). Similarly power passed smoothly in Tanzania, a country with a Christian majority, from President Julius Nyerere (a Christian) to the present President Hassan Ali Mwinyi (a Muslim). Africa has also seen almost total Muslim countries like Morocco, Libya, Tunisia and Algeria who still refuse to be drawn into the dangerous game of imposing on its citizens public laws that are religiously-based. Other African countries with Muslim majorities more than that of Sudan have not imposed Sharia Islamic Law; these countries include Egypt, Chad, Niger, Mali, Gambia and Somalia.

28   We advise El Bashir not to take the position taken by fundamentalists for that position is dangerous, unhistorical and alien to the Sudan and to Africa. We do not need a referendum on Sharia; God's Law cannot be put to a referendum. We repeat, our position is that we are not against Islam, we respect it; indeed we cannot be against God's Law. All that we say is that Sharia, or any law pertaining to other religions, should be a personal law. Religious faith is a relationship between the believer and his God. The believer is free to choose which aspects of Sharia he would observe and which he would not, and it is only that believer who would be answerable about that on the Day of Judgement; and only God will judge. This position is shared by most Muslims in the Sudan, and it is the position on religion all over Africa. Since El Bashir has absolute power and is not answerable to any parliament, the Movement calls on El Bashir to immediately remove Nimeiri's September Laws from the books, and take the country back to the pre-1983 situation. The September Laws are not God's Law; they are Nimeiri's and Turabi's; God's Laws will remain in the hearts of men and women, not in statute books. Religion belongs to the individual, and the state belongs to all of us collectively. There can be no mistaking this simple truth.

The Hidden Agenda of the NIF: Partition of Sudan

29   The sixth question is: What is the Junta's position on the unity of the Sudan? Do they believe in Sudanese Unity? We have reason to believe that the junta has a hidden agenda to partition the country. El Bashir himself has said so in various forms at least three times in the last 40 days. Although this has been officially denied by a spokesman of the junta there is sufficient cause for alarm. Separatism is of course known to be a programme of NIF as it was the programme of the Anyanya Movement in the South. On this I would once again want to assure the Sudanese people that the Movement is totally against separation. In this connection, it is to be recalled that the first blood shed by the SPLA was not against the Sudanese Army, the first battles were against separatists within the SPLA. This is a matter of public and historical record. In 1983 at its inception the SPLA fought against the separatist tendency of Akuot Atem, Gai Tut and William Abdalla Chuol. Separatism is a form of reaction and opportunism. It is known that Akuot Atem's separatists eventually ended up allying themselves with Khartoum's Army, as their so-called "friendly forces" fighting for Southern Sudan from Khartoum.

30   Our belief in Sudanese Unity and territorial integrity is axiomatic, that is, it is a principled position. In our Manifesto published 31 July 1983 we said in very unequivocal terms, and I quote,

It must be reiterated that the principal objective of the SPLM/SPLA is not separation for the South. The South is an integral and inseparable part of the Sudan. Africa has been fragmented sufficiently enough by colonialism and neo-colonialism and its further fragmentation can only be in the interest of her enemies. The separatist attitude that has developed in the South since 1955 has caught the imagination of the backward areas in Northern Sudan. Separatist Movements have already emerged with guerrillas fighting in Western and Eastern Sudan. If left unchecked, these separatist Movements in the South, East and West coupled with the stubborn determination of a repressive minority clique regime in Khartoum to hang onto power at all costs will lead to the total disintegration of the Sudan. This imminent, latent and impending disintegration and fragmentation of the Sudan is what the SPLM/A aims to stop by developing and implementing a consistent democratic solution to both the nationality and religious questions within the context of a United New Sudan.

That was in 1983. Our position remains the same.

31   Except for the NIF, the vast majority of the Sudanese people and political forces stand with the SPLM/A on the issue of Sudanese Unity and Sudan's territorial integrity. However, there is reason for alarm. I take this opportunity to alert the Sudanese people to the danger of separatism, this time not coming from the South as used to be the case, but ironically coming from the North. I am confident that any attempts at separation in any form will be opposed not only by the SPLM/A but all the Sudanese patriotic forces. In any event the North/South divide is a thing of the past; the SPLM/A is deeply entrenched in Southern Kordofan and in Southern Blue Nile Provinces, and we are there to stay. The Movement has also inroads in Wad Medani as well as in Khartoum. Anyone wishing to separate the North will find it difficult to draw the line, and will be opposed in the North itself, as Southern separatists were opposed and defeated in the South. The unity of the Sudanese people and Sudan's territorial integrity will prevail.

Economic Recovery and Rehabilitation

32   The seventh question is: What is the junta's position on the economy? How does the junta plan to rescue the country from economic collapse? Connected with this issue is the question as to what are the junta's views on socio-economic development and on social and economic justice. On this vital issue of the economic and social welfare of the people, the junta has no known vision. The anti-corruption drive and scuffles with petty traders accused of black marketeering are normal routine police work and the Army has no business meddling in police work. These anti-crime activities cannot substitute economic policy. On the economy we are told that these are very complicated issues; that technical committees of experts will be formed to study the problems of the economy. Is it not absurd for the junta to take power ostensibly for national salvation, and then to turn around and tell the nation that they do not have a programme, that all they have is sincerity and seriousness to solve Sudan's problems? The junta may have no elaborate programme for the economy, but it is incumbent upon anybody taking power in Khartoum to have a clear vision

and some general outline of an economic programme. On this the Movement has expounded its views elsewhere. Obviously any economic recovery programme for the Sudan must be rural-based as this is where the majority of our people live. It must address the basic needs of the people. Similarly any industrialization programme must also be people-based and must of necessity begin with agro-industries. Such a model must be based on the principle of maximizing individual initiative within the constraints of social welfare, while at the same time maximizing social initiative within the demands of individual motivation. Essentially the economic programme must emphasize self-reliance to achieve self-sufficiency in the basic necessities of life, food, health, education, shelter, clean drinking water for all citizens, and so on.

33   The Sudan is a rich country, yet we remain among the 25 least-developed countries of the world. We have over 200 million acres of arable land, and only less than 10 per cent of this has been utilized. Our country is endowed with tremendous amounts of water and mineral resources, and not more than 2 per cent of these have been exploited. Our economic development programmes hitherto have been oriented to the urban areas, to the cities. These cities were outlets for colonial products, or administrative centres for colonial rule. The Sudanese city, like most African cities, does not provide development services for the hinterland, for the rural areas. Most of our cities do not produce even the hoe, sickle, or panga; basic requirements of the farmer, not to mention fertilizers, pesticides, water pumps, ploughs and tractors. Out city is not a productive city but a consumptive exploitative cancerous growth living on the rural areas. And like cancer, our cities are killing the rural areas making both the cities and rural areas themselves unproductive and inducing famines, of magnitudes which have never been experienced before in Africa. In turn, the crisis of the parasitic unproductive city, the exploitation of the farmers and the neglect of agriculture have resulted in widespread social unrest in both cities and rural areas. Hence, mass uprisings and organized armed robberies have become the order of the day in both rural areas and the cities. The state out of necessity is forced to exercise more and more repressive measures to contain the uprisings of the hungry masses in both the rural areas and the cities. These are daily occurrences and the rural and urban uprisings and lootings will continue until there is a

revolutionary transformation at all levels: political, economic, social, cultural, scientific and technological, that is, until we start to lay in place the basis of the New Sudan, whose development is self-reliant and self-sustaining.

34 These ideas are not abstractions. They are achievable if we put our investment priorities right. Take for example the problem of power. The Sudan is endowed with very many rivers that can easily generate hydro-electric power. There is no reason why we cannot achieve rural electrification all over the Sudan within a period of say ten years after the war. And with electric power all sorts of possibilities become open to the masses of our farmers. There would be no reason to crowd in unproductive and congested cities if rural electrification is achieved. Take another example, our many rivers are well endowed with fish and with little invest-ment this fish can be propagated and multiplied many-fold, so that every family can have a meal of fish at least once a week. Similarly, there is no reason why we should not be self-sufficient in poultry products, so that each family can have a breakfast of eggs at least once a week, and a main dish of chicken at least once a week. There is no reason why we should not be self-sufficient in food grains and root tubers, and in meat and milk products. The list of possibilities continue, and these possibilities can be realizable within the next ten years, if we shift gears and adopt the correct economic policies emphasizing rural develop-ment rather than the fake artificial urban development and its export market orientation that has consumed our country to the bone since independence. What we are talking about is the urban-ization of the rural areas, the transfer of cities to the rural areas or rather the agro-industrialization of the country side, the rapid adoption of innovation and new techniques by millions of our small farmers in rural areas, in the place of the present elitist development or rather mal-development. We are talking about the rapid spread of education, science, technology and innovation to the vast majority of our rural people. These ideas are developed elsewhere. I only felt it necessary to underline that whereas the Junta may have no elaborate economic programme, *it is absolutely necessary, that anybody who takes power in Khartoum must have a vision of how to get bread, sugar, oil, salt, medicines, education, shelter*, the basic needs of millions of our people now languishing doing nothing in our over-crowded capital, and not only for the

city dwellers, but even more so for the farmers who constitute the backbone of our economy. The people do not care so much about the junta's or anyone else's politics, they want food, shelter, health, education for their children, and whoever says he is in command in Khartoum, should better start thinking hard how to address these issues otherwise there would be no reason for him to take power.

35   It goes without saying that the problem of war and peace on the one hand and the economy and the New Sudan on the other are faces of the same coin. The transformation of war to peace must result in the formation of the New Sudan, capable of ushering our people into a new era of rapid socio-economic development, prosperity and happiness for the masses of our people. Such a New Sudan cannot be brought about by a bunch of generals who do not have the slightest idea or vision of how to deal with the problem of the economy.

Our Vision of a New Sudan

36   The eighth question is: What is the junta's vision of the Sudan they want to evolve, what is their vision of the New Sudan that they have been talking about? On this, it appears that the junta uses the term "New Sudan" as a convenient slogan. They said nothing about the content of the New Sudan. But the junta betrays it colours and is out of step with history when it talks of partitioning the country, and misses the point when it stresses pan-Arabism, ignoring the pluralistic nature of Sudanese society. By these declared policies the junta demonstrates profound ignorance of the issues at stake in the search for peace within the context of the New Sudan. Perhaps it is too much to ask of the junta what they mean when they talk of the New Sudan, what their vision is. They have either not thought of the issue and simply use it as a slogan, or else their vision coincides with that of the NIF, and we all know NIF conceptualization of the Sudan. We will leave it to the junta to explain to the Sudanese people what they mean by the term "New Sudan". However, since this concept was borrowed from the SPLM/A and has become fashionable, I feel obliged to state the views of the Movement on the subject of the "New Sudan".

37   The New Sudan is a conceptual framework developed by the SPLM/A, within which the situation in the Sudan can be better

understood, can be better discussed, can be better resolved. I believe that the central question, the basic problem of the Sudan is that since independence in 1956, the various regimes that have come and gone in Khartoum have failed to provide a commonality, a paradigm, a basis for the Sudan as a state; that is, there has been no conscious evolution of that common Sudanese identity and destiny to which we all pay undivided allegiance, irrespective of our various backgrounds, irrespective of our tribes, irrespective of race, irrespective of religious belief. Having failed to achieve this commonality, national politics and governance took the form of sectarianism, regionalism or tribalism, all of them centrifugal forces that cannot mould a people into a nation or a multi-nationality state. This I present to you is the basic problem of the Sudan that needs to be discussed and resolved. Any credible programme for the salvation of the Sudan must emanate from this conceptualization. In the SPLM/A we did discuss this central question very seriously back in 1983 when the Movement started. We rejected then as we reject now the separation of the South or any other part of our country. We rejected then as we reject now the idea of a "Southern Problem". We diagnosed the problem not as a "Southern Problem" but as the "Problem of Khartoum", that is, the problem of power in Khartoum. We therefore resolved to struggle for a radical restructuring of power in Khartoum to bring about a new commonality, a new identity, a new socio-political formation, a socio-political mutation which we call the New Sudan. We resolved to bring about a situation where the SPLM/A, where other political forces, other regions, other nationalities, where the Sudanese people as a whole will have an effective say in the power structure in Khartoum, and having resolved the problem of the centre, we then go after the system of rule in the regions, whether this is in the South, West, East, North or centre.

38   In making this analysis we looked at the Sudan in historical as well as contemporary perspective. We went back to our roots, to as far as we could get in recorded history. We found out that we had not been the helpless people we appear to be today. We found that our ancestors several millenia before the Christian era had, among others, founded the very strong kingdom of Kush, that this kingdom flourished and interacted with other adjacent civilizations of antiquity, that indeed the 25th dynasty of pharaonic

Egypt was Sudanese and that this Sudanese dynasty in Egypt interacted with Palestine, Assyria and other civilizations of the Middle East. As we went and came down the corridors of history we found that Christianity came to the Sudan directly from Palestine at a time when Europe was still tribal and barbaric. Following the corridors of history further we came to the spread of Islam and Arab migrations into the Sudan, the founding of the strong Kingdoms of Sennar, Darfur, Shilluk, and so on; the intrusion of Turko-Egyptian colonial rule and their expulsion by the Mahadiya; the subsequent establishment of Anglo-Egyptian colonial rule and popular resistance to it culminating in the attainment of independence in 1956.

39   The rest of our contemporary history from 1956 is well known. In the 30 years of independence since 1956 we have been at war with each other for 23 years, we have witnessed four military coups, two popular uprisings and three civilian sectarian multi-party coalition governments. The main cause of these wars and of the instability and suffering our people went through have been Khartoum's sectarian rule and the failure to evolve an overall national paradigm. The SPLM/A therefore resolved to bring about, with other like-minded Sudanese political forces, this national paradigm, the New Sudan. The programme to realize the New Sudan revolves around five main inter-related projects or tasks, whose accomplishment will determine the particularity of the New Sudan. These are:

(a)   A Sudanese National Renaissance.

(b)   Democracy.

(c)   National Unity within non-sectarianism.

(d)   Economic self-sufficiency, self-reliance and social justice.

(e)   Political and military independence and solidarity with all oppressed peoples.

These issues have been debated and must continue to be debated. At the practical level they formed the basis of the Koka Dam Declaration and the November Peace Initiative. Sudanese intellectuals and academics also prepared position papers on the New Sudan and these were discussed at the Ambo Workshop. I take the opportunity to appeal to all Sudanese patriots to engage in serious debate of the parameters of the New Sudan, and to participate actively in the realization and consolidation of the New Sudan.

40   I am convinced and have always been convinced that the New Sudan is achievable. Indeed we are closer to achieving the New Sudan now than at any other time in our history. Because of the correctness of its vision, the SPLM/A since 1983 has remained, has persevered and has acted as the catalyst of the Sudanese Revolution. The possibilities of achieving the New Sudan are clearly discernible in SPLM/A's interaction within the mainstream of Sudanese politics over the last six years. Ever since its forma-tion in 1983 the Movement has kept appealing and contacting elements in the Sudanese Army and has kept contacts with other Sudanese political forces.

After Nimeiri's fall the Movement could not be deceived into being absorbed into the old Sudan in a new form. We correctly analysed Swar Dahab's TMC as Nimeiri Two, whose sole function was to prepare room for the traditional sectarian parties to take over. It was a regime that could not prepare conditions for bring-ing about the New Sudan. Under very difficult conditions when we were almost deserted by our allies the Movement continued and persisted in the struggle. You well know what happened. General Swar al Dahab handed power to the sectarian political parties who continued the Old Sudan of sectarian injustice, bicker-ing, corruption and economic decline.

The Movement continued to give hope to the patriotic and democratic forces, to the forces of the uprising in general. As a result the Movement reached a historical agreement with demo-cratic forces in the Koka Dam Declaration in March 1986. This was a major step towards the realization of the New Sudan. The sectarian parties without exception and true to form vigorously opposed and sabotaged implementation of the Koka Dam Agree-ment. Again, the Movement did not tire, we continued to interact with the Sudanese political forces. When the three sectarian parties (UMMA, DUP and NIF) allied themselves for the first time since independence to form a three-party coalition govern-ment, the Movement diagnosed this as a very dangerous develop-ment. Indeed the NIF was resolved and determined to impose their theocratic state.

It was at this point that the Movement reached another historic agreement with the DUP, the least sectarian of the three, that was, the Sudanese Peace Initiative signed on 16 November 1988. That agreement was essentially a subset of the Koka-Dam Agree-ment, designed to reinforce Koka Dam by bringing the DUP into the peace process. The November Peace Initiative immediately put the grand coalition of the three sectarian parties in crisis. As you all know, the UMMA and NIF opposed the Peace Initiative. The DUP in consequence quit the coalition, and UMMA and the NIF formed a coalition government. That government was very fragile and it was a matter of time before it would collapse.

In the meantime the SPLA intensified military operations, capturing 16 Army garrisons in a seven-month period. Following its mediocre performance in the field and near collapse, the Army intervened and issued Sadiq al Mahdi a 7-day ultimatum in a 21-point memorandum demanding acceptance of the Peace Initiative. Sadiq accepted the Peace Initiative and swallowed his pride. The acceptance of the Peace Initiative in turn caused the NIF to resign and the DUP to return to the coalition. Clearly it was the November Peace Initiative which triggered off the 30 June *coup d'état*. What I am underlining here is the process, the dynamic interaction of the Sudanese political forces with the SPLM/A as the catalyst, the salient driving force. This interaction, this interplay of political forces, which culminated in the 30 June coup, indicates the possibilities of achieving the New Sudan. It indicates that the political process in the country has been working itself out in the direction of the New Sudan, and this vindicates the correctness of our vision and shows the immense possibilities of realizing this vision, the New Sudan.

Human Rights

41 The ninth and last question is: What is the Junta's position on human rights and basic personal and political freedoms? Again this question is related to peace, for a regime that has no respect for human rights cannot possibly be expected to bring about peace. On this issue the Movement has time and again declared its commitment to human rights and basic personal and political freedoms. Among other instances, the Movement's commitment to human rights was included in the objectives of the SPLM and in my maiden speech to the nation in which I said that our struggle is to "establish a New Sudan, a democratic Sudan in which equality, freedom, economic and social justice and *respect for human rights are not mere slogans but concrete realities we should promote, cherish and protect*". We have been and we will continue to be consistent with this principle. It is because of our commitment to human rights that we go to all extents to see to it that

261

the lives of prisoners of war are spared and respected. To date we have hundreds of prisoners of war, including more than 30 officers. This policy on prisoners of war will continue. It is because of our commitment to human rights that we allow relief food to reach government controlled towns, even to Sudan government soldiers in besieged towns, for the human rights of civilians and government soldiers caught up in the war must be respected. The policy on relief and the corridors of tranquillity will continue to remain open. Operation Life-line Sudan, the ICRC, the Norwegian People's Aid and other relief organizations will continue to bring relief assistance through SPLA lines to the civilian population in need and at risk wherever they are. On the question of human rights and personal and political freedoms the record of the junta in the last 40 days of its life is already very dirty and has a lot to be desired. Some human rights violations and denial of basic personal and political freedoms already make a long list, among these:

(1)   While the regime talked of a cease-fire, the Army has run amok in Wau. In four days from 21/7/89 to 25/7/89, 350 innocent citizens were killed in cold blood in Wau. These killings took place in Grinti, Zogolona and Airport Sectors of Wau Town. These killings are continuing to this day. Many citizens have fled from Wau Town to SPLA administered areas and have reported these atrocities. A list of civilians killed in Wau since the Junta took power is being compiled and this will be made available to the public, to the Sudanese Human Rights Commission and to International Human Rights Groups.

(2)   In Southern Kordofan villages are being bombarded and innocent citizens killed by the Army. On 26 July, the Army bombarded Kurung Abdhalla and Katch villages. Again on 27 July the Army bombarded Umsardubo, Umdorin and Acharon villages, all in the Nuba mountains. In these incidents innocent villagers were killed and many huts set on fire. There is no SPLA in these villages. The Army very well knows the location of SPLA camps in the Nuba mountains. This is just reckless and wanton slaughter of innocent citizens, and worse still at a time when the Junta says they are observing a cease-fire.

(3)   In Khartoum you have heard of the arrest of a University of Khartoum Professor, Dr. Ushari Mahmoud. The reason for

his arrest is that he and his colleague Dr. Baldo wrote a book in 1987 exposing the existence of slavery in the Sudan and the atrocities of the Diéin massacre. Instead of investigating these atrocities and accusations about the reappearance of slavery in Sudan, the junta arrested the author instead of praising him for exposing the atrocities. The arrest of this professor of course raises lots of questions about the junta's respect for, or commitment to, Human Rights. If the junta has not released Professor Ushari yet we call on them to do this forthwith.

(4)   Regarding basic political freedoms, you have heard of the junta locking up many politicians, dismissing over 1000 officers from the Army and Police, dissolving all Trade Unions and shutting down the Press. In connection with these arrests, Brig. El Bashir recently assured his interviewer over the BBC that the arrests were only for corruption, not for political reasons. One would understand that those who held constitutional or ministerial posts could have engaged in corruption, since they had the resources and power of the state at their command. On this basis one would understand the arrest of members of the state Council and of Sadiq al Mahdi and his Ministers, but what about the others? What about Sayed Mohamed Osman al Mirghani? Although patron of the DUP, he held no constitutional position. The same holds for Mohamed Ibrahim Nugud, Eliaba Surur and many others; on what corruption charges are these citizens being held behind bars? These citizens must also be released.

(5)   Similarly with the banning of the Trade Unions. This is unprecedented. On what grounds are the Trade Unions banned? This is simply illegal, and the ban on Trade Unions must be lifted.

42   The issue of respect for human rights and human dignity cannot be taken lightly, it is part of the situation that led to the war, and Brig. El Bashir cannot possibly expect to reach a peace settlement with the SPLM/A when he has so much tarnished his human rights record in only 40 days. If El Bashir is serious about peace he must clean up his human rights record as this is part of peace. Indeed the international community must exercise its moral responsibility to speak out on human rights violations in the Sudan, and, except for humanitarian assistance, withhold all other

financial and material assistance to the Sudan until democracy, the rule of law, human rights and basic personal and political freedoms are restored.

No, to Military or Sectarian Dictatorship

43   I felt it necessary to explore the Junta's views and positions on the vital issues of our time, and to present the Movement's views and positions on these issues. It is your right to be fully briefed and informed. I end my address to you by summarizing the SPLM/A position on the recent military coup and I present to you a general outline of the Movement's programme to bring about peace under the conditions created by the *coup d'état*.

44   From what I had said today, which is what we have said over the last six years, it should be abundantly clear that the SPLM/A can neither support a *coup d'état* nor a military dictatorship that results from it. We did not fight for the last six years, suffered and sacrificed so much in order, at the end of the day, to endorse and entrench a military dictatorship. That would be very unnatural, indeed it would be criminal and politically irresponsible were the SPLM/A to help in the entrenchment of the present or any other military dictatorship. We are convinced, as we have always been, of the correctness of our vision. We took up arms in order to bring about the creation of a United New Sudan of democracy, justice, opportunity, prosperity, and equality for all citizens irrespective of the colour of their skins, tribe, religion or sex. I have shown that the attainment of the New Sudan is possible, and that indeed we have been moving in that direction over the last six years. The process of creating a New Sudan and establishing a Great Democracy of freedom and prosperity is a historical necessity and is irreversible. The recent events of 30 June were precipitated, as I have shown, not by the bravado of a few officers, but by the dynamics of the interplay of the Sudanese political forces, and are a part of the process of the socio-political mutation that is underway and that will inevitably culminate in the formation of a new socio-political entity, in the United New Sudan. Our position is therefore clear and irrevocable. We stand solidly, as we have always done with the Sudanese people in their just struggle for the establishment of Democracy and a United New Sudan; indeed that is the essence of our Movement, the SPLM/A is a Movement for the establishment of Democracy and a United New

Sudan. Obviously we are opposed to any form of dictatorship and nobody should expect us to be otherwise with respect to the present junta. In the Sudan we have known two types of dictatorship over the last 33 years of our independence, military dictatorship and sectarian dictatorship. Both have failed the Sudanese people and have been the cause of wars, instability and enormous suffering to our people. *Both military dictatorship and sectarian dictatorship stand condemned* and there is no reason that the latest military dictatorship that has installed itself in Khartoum can be an exception. The only salvation for the Sudan lies in the establishment of democracy, national renaissance and independence of decision-making in all our economic, political and foreign affairs.

Basis for Dialogue with the Junta

45 With respect to whether the Movement will talk with the New Military Junta in Khartoum, the answer is yes; we certainly will talk with them. They are *de facto* government in Khartoum and our policy has always been to talk with anyone who claims to be in power in Khartoum. Besides they are Sudanese citizens and part of the Sudanese political forces that have a potential to contribute to the formation of the New Sudan. Yes, I have said we do not believe in any form of dictatorship, but that does not mean we should not talk with the junta. The Government of Swar al Dahab was a military dictatorship while the Government of Sadiq el Mahdi was a sectarian dictatorship masquerading in the name of liberal democracy, yet we talked with these governments. We cannot shut our eyes to reality. So, we have agreed and we are prepared to talk with Brigadier Omer el Bashir's Military Junta. Shall we talk without preconditions as the junta demands? Yes, certainly. As I said no one needs to place pre-conditions to talk to another, this would be unnatural. All that is needed is acceptance by both sides to talk, and possibly an agenda. We have already notified the junta through President Mengistu Haile Mariam of Ethiopia of our willingness and readiness to talk with them. We have even suggested dates and we are waiting for the junta to respond.

46 Regarding the agenda of the meeting, the junta will have to brief the Movement as to why they took over power in Khartoum, and presumably they will present to the Movement their peace and other programmes regarding how they plan to bring about

National Salvation. The Movement in turn will listen. However, we will not listen passively, we will present to the junta and to the Sudanese people the Movement's peace programme within the context of the establishment of democracy and the United New Sudan. Essentially the SPLM/A will demand an immediate return to democracy. The return to or establishment of democracy will of course be a process, and we envisage it as involving the following steps:

(a)   Establishment of an Interim Broad-based Government of National Unity free of the various sectarianisms (racial, religious, tribal or any other politicized localism) that have plagued and bled our country for the last 33 years of our formal independence. We see the forces forming such an Interim Government as including the two armies (the SPLA and the regular Sudanese Army), political parties that believe in democracy and the New Sudan, the Trade and Professional Unions and other non-sectarian mass organizations such as the Women's and students' Movements and peasants or small farmers associations. Only such a broad-based government of national consensus can in the short term rescue the economy, ameliorate the suffering of the people and implement the remaining steps towards democracy. This step of course demands the release of all political prisoners who have not committed any corruption crimes and the lifting of the ban on Trade/Professional Unions and political parties that believe in democracy, so that these forces participate effectively in the formation of the broad-based Interim Government and in the subsequent steps towards democracy and a United New Sudan. It also certainly means replacement of the present military Junta by the suggested broad-based Interim Government, and it will be up to the Army to discuss and agree as to how they would be represented in this government, since the Army will be one of the elements constituting the broad-based Interim Government.

(b)   The second step, almost simultaneous with the first step, is the establishment of a national, non-sectarian, non-regional Army from both the SPLA and the regular Army so that the new national army is consistent with the particularity of the emerging New United Sudan and so that such an army is capable of restoring internal stability, defending democracy and safe-guarding our country's independence and territorial integrity.

(c)   The third step is the convening of the National Consti-tutional Conference by the Interim Government of National Unity to resolve the country's fundamental problems based on the Koka Dam Agreement and the Sudanese Peace Initiative and any other agreements that may be reached at the National Constitutional Conference, whose purpose of course shall be the drafting of a permanent Constitution that shall be ratified by the Constituent Assembly or Parliament.

(d)   The fourth and last step is the preparation by the Interim Government of National Unity for free elections, the holding of those elections, the subsequent ratification of the Consti-tution by the Constituent Assembly and the establishment of a democracy-based government.

47   The four steps I have just outlined are a minimum programme to restore Democracy and save the country from tyranny and disintegration. This is a programme that should be acceptable to all peace-loving Sudanese and I believe that it will be endorsed by all the forces of democracy, peace and justice. The programme will be implemented in one of two ways:

(a)   The military junta can agree to sit down with the SPLM/A and other forces for the establishment of democracy and a United New Sudan to discuss and effect the peaceful implemen-tation of the programme, and thereby play a positive construc-tive role, avoiding more suffering and bloodshed. I advise the junta to consider this option seriously and I appeal to each member of the junta to sit down in his own room and give it serious individual private thought.

(b)   The second case is if the junta is intransigent and rejects the programme then the SPLM/A acting in the name of the forces for the establishment of democracy and a United New Sudan, will have no other choice but to call a general strike and a popular mass uprising to remove the junta and have the programme implemented by the forces of the uprising and the SPLM/A.

In the second case the SPLM/A will participate in the popular uprising also in the military aspect, making its full military contribution in the capital itself, and this in full coordination with the democratic and patriotic elements within the Regular Sudanese Army and the other organized forces. Whether the programme is implemented by peaceful means through dialogue with the junta, or through a popular uprising in the event of the junta's intransigence, in either case, I want to underline that the time has come, now is the time, for the historic convergence between the rural-based revolutionary armed struggle waged by the SPLM/A and the urban political struggle in the form of mass action. In this connection I ask the forces of the popular uprising in the capital and other cities to start organizing for this convergence, to be vigilant, to be on full alert and to be on standby waiting for coordinated action.

Postscript

Since this work has gone to press, some important events have taken place in Sudan and within the SPLM/SPLA. Most important among those events was the split in the ranks of the Movement following a rebellion by three of the SPLA commanders against the Commander-in-Chief, Dr Garang. In an announcement issued at Nasir (Upper Nile region) on 28 August 1991 Commanders Riek Mashar, Lam Akol and Gordon Koang Chol alleged the "removal" of Garang from the leadership, announcing themselves as the Movement's interim leadership. The other SPLA commanders, the announcement said, were in accord with that "rebellion". In that announcement Garang was also accused by the self-appointed leadership of being a "dictatorial" and "autocratic" leader who has "humiliated and degraded people and turned a popular struggle into warlordism and a reign of terror". As for their agenda, the self-appointed leadership called for democratization of the Movement since the Movement "cannot remain behind when the winds of democracy are blowing all over Africa". They also demanded "strict adherence to the respect of human rights and the rule of law" and a peaceful settlement to the present Sudan conflict. In this respect they maintained that all options that lead to "permanent peace" should be kept open. However, this shapeless statement was soon explained by the Nasir group to mean the secession of the South.

While this was going on Dr Garang remained firmly at the helm, and ten out of the thirteen commanders of the SPLM/SPLA declared their commitment to the unity of the Movement and allegiance to its leader. Coincidentally the SPLM/SPLA High Command was then meeting in Torit to review the situation following developments in Ethiopia. That meeting, to which all commanders were invited, was scheduled a month before, and of the thirteen SPLA commanders nine were present. The three at Nasir excused themselves from attending, giving the bizarre excuse that they had 350 bodyguards to move with them were they to attend. The thirteenth member, Cdr Yusaf Kwa, could not make it to Torit having been engaged in operations in the distant Nuba Mountains. The nine commanders allegedly in support of the Nasir rebellion issued a signed statement denouncing the action. Kwa wired his support; the Commander from the Nuba Mountains would have been the last person to be amused by the call for secession.

The way the three commanders behaved clearly indicated that their so-called coup was not hatched overnight. Indeed, a few months before the Nasir announcement a document entitled *Why Garang Must Go* was being circulated in Europe to Sudanese and non-Sudanese alike. That statement found its way into the hands of some journalists, one of whom was Stefan Klein of the *Suddeutsche Zeitung* who wrote in that paper on 3 September 1991, drumming up the calumnious accusations levelled against Garang by his detractors and adding that Macar and Akol "wanted to take account of the changed political situation in the world and bring the SPLA on a social democratic course". Clearly the Nasir group was endeavouring to ride on the crest of a popular wave in the West. Their incessant references to democracy, human rights, popular participation and respect for private property were, to be sure, addressed to Westerners – hence the bombardment of Western media and NGO's with statements to this effect. The libertarian attitudes of the group are too thin to be given credence, coming, as they did, from those who often took pride within the Movement in posturing as the leftists of the band and including some who posed as firebrand Marxists. Little wonder that at no time in their media campaign did those "radicals" who metamorphosed into libertarians seek to address Sudanese public opinion on their new political agenda for the nation.

As to democracy, however, at no time did John Garang portray himself as a democratic leader chosen by the people. Rather, he viewed himself as a revolutionary leader who established his ascendancy through the political platform he has espoused and the victories he has scored in a liberation struggle. Precisely because of those victories commanders Riek and Lam, two university engineers – as well as others – left their jobs to flock to Garang's support. No combatant has ever joined the SPLM/SPLA because of the rewards it offers; sweat, blood and personal insecurity are no reward. Nor had commanders Riek and Lam been elevated to the highests ranks within the Movement through democratic processes, either by election by grass-root constituencies or selection by their peers. True to this "undemocratic" tradition the Nasir group, rather than using the existing structures of the Movement to resolve the issue of leadership, chose to "relieve" Dr Garang and two other commanders (William Nyoun and Salva Kiir) and appoint themselves as the new leadership over the heads of seven other commanders; this skew arithmetic of "democratic" politics does no honour to the scholarship of the two "engineers".

On the other hand the SPLM/SPLA, being as it is both a political and a military organization, cannot be subject to universally accepted democratic standards in the day-to-day management of its affairs. The lines of distinction between civilian and military discipline are often blurred. In this respect there is no denial that, in some attempts to mete out punishments on presumed offenders, excesses may have occurred. Bad as this may sound to genuinely concerned human rights groups (Amnesty International and Africa Watch, for example, have in a few instances expressed concern as to the fate of some SPLM/SPLA prisoners) the wailing of the two commanders over the fate of "Garang's victims" is only crocodile's tears. The issue of human rights abuses by the Movement was even raised in some instances by the Khartoum government in order to rebut similar accusations levelled at them by the SPLM/SPLA. In one such instance the accusation was coupled with a list of people who have been allegedly treated unjustly by the Movement.

Curiously, the Movement's spokesman in defence of these alleged acts of violence has been Dr Lam. In the course of the peace negotiations between the government and the Movement, in Nairobi December 1989, Brigadier Hassan Dahawi presented, on behalf of the government delegation, a list of SPLA officers whom he claimed were either incarcerated or condemned to death by the Movement. Dahawi's intention was to embarass the SPLM and ease the pressure against the government. Both the umpire of the meeting (President Jimmy Carter) and the SPLM delegation were debating the issue of human rights in the Sudan. To that accusation, Dr Lam responded, "Yes, we have imprisoned some and killed others and we will kill many more because we are a liberation movement who would not take risks." Those can hardly be the words of the same person who came to say at Nasir, less than two years later: "a number of members of the Movement are under detention for many years for no reason other than differing with John Garang." Garang is no saint; as a man he suffers from the frailties of all men and as a leader of an armed struggle he can hardly be expected to take chances.

However, what did the newly-born democrats of Nasir do in order to restore respect for human rights within the ranks of the Movement? Their record only two months after the alleged coup is by no means creditable in this regard. The Nasir "rebels", as to be expected, were not received with open arms by all the combatants under their command. Some officers challenged their action. Rather than resolving this difference "democratically" and with due respect to the human rights principles so dear to them, they went ahead and killed by firing squad 7 officers (A/Commander Peter Panom Thanyplneu, A/Commander Joseph Mabil Ruot, Captain Winor Jok Abid, 1st Lt Dan Akoc Jurcuk, 1st Lt Martin Malren Gumwel, 2nd Lt Wuor Marial and 2nd Lt Mangar). In addition 26 officers in Nasir, 3 in Akobo and 3 in Liir were subjected to severe torture, including Captain Kuol Deng Kuol (a brother of Dr Francis Deng) who was roasted alive in an empty barrel. (See Appendix 1.) The barbaric "mullahs" of Khartoum no longer need to go to Teheran in order to improve on their methods of torture, "technical assistance" is now closer by.

Having exposed the flimsiness of their "democratic" protestations one may ask what then is the hidden agenda of the Nasir group and what prompted them to act at this point in time. In this regard one may venture to say that the real intent of the group is surrender spurred by a sense of frustration and blind ambition. The frustration is evident in the call for secession of the South since, according to them, the creation of a united secular Sudan is well-nigh impossible. All the Northern political establishment, they claimed, adhered to a *Sharia*-based state. However, this is the very same old Sudanese establishment which the Movement has fought against and vowed to reconstruct; that thesis was not only reflected in the Movement's manifesto and the public utterances of John Garang, it was also ably defended by Dr Lam Akol in the Khartoum journal *Heritage* in 1987 when he wrote under the title "Why the SPLM Must Fight for Unity". The Unity of Sudan was indeed the cardinal theme in all peace agreements with the Khartoum political forces and all SPLM policy papers for peace negotiations. The chief negotiator and signatory to all those documents, on behalf of the SPLM/SPLA, was the very same Dr Lam Akol. And if thousands of Sudanese from outside the geographical South had joined the ranks of the SPLA fighters it was only because of this principled and revolutionary stance. Consequently, for the first time in the political history of Sudan, a Southern-based movement has come to the centre of attention in the North, particularly among those disenchanted with the way national politics was conceived and managed in Khartoum.

The rebels at Nasir may have thought, however, that in light of the long-time suffering of the Southern people and the bloody strife of the SPLA to liberate the country without any tangibly commensurate support from their brethren in the North, it was time to make a break and be contented with what had been achieved up to now, the liberation of the South. Admittedly normal life cannot endure revolutionary altitudes for long. However, the way the Nasir group has set about achieving this end gave rise to a lot of doubt about their political judgement if not credibility. Shortly after the events in Nasir, Khartoum despatched one of its Ministers of State (Ali al Haj) to meet with Dr Lam in Nairobi. For a group that claims in its initial declaration that the "SPLA shall be reorganized in order to prosecute the armed struggle more effectively", the meeting with the very people against whom that struggle is waged was suspect. Dr Lam sought to explain away that meeting first by claiming that as a politician he had the right to meet with all Sudanese forces and later by maintaining that he was the SPLM's officer in charge of peace negotiations. However, what has transpired out of that meeting substantiated the suspicions; al Haj (an NIF leader) offered financial support to the group. This was accepted by them and the NIF government began air-dropping ammunition at the sites occupied by the group.

The NIF was, evidently, true to its political agenda, for while they continued fussing in Khartoum about commitment to the unity of the Sudan, they said in private that they were ready to condone secession of the South so long as the South continued to be an impediment to the Islamicization of the Sudan. The NIF is well aware that the existence of a Southern-based armed movement capable of frustrating the NIF's policies will continue to embolden secularist elements in the North who are bent on the creation of a non-religious state (the same "unattainable" objective in the thinking of the Nasir group). Effectively the dissident group has become part and parcel of the stratagem of the NIF; their role now was to neutralize this menacing force, the SPLM/ SPLA. It is with this understanding that the dissident group commenced hostilities against SPLA-held areas such as Akobo, Waat, Ayod, Kongor, Bor, etc. For a group that has claimed the support of the rank and file of the Movement and that of the majority of its commanders those attacks were incomprehensible. More incomprehensible, indeed reprehensible, was the way in which those battles were fought, pitching one tribe against another. This was a portent of what would happen in the new republic of the South under this leadership. Indeed one of Garang's greatest achievements was the exorcizing of tribalism within the SPLM/ SPLA; without that, no political locomotive in the world could have pulled that heterogeneous mass in one direction.

There is no way in the world to explain those attacks except as a rear-guard action beneficial to the NIF government. The objective of those attacks was nothing but the undermining of the on-going offensive on Juba, the capital of the new Southern republic the Nasir group wants to establish. Charitably one may assume that the Nasir group thought that by frustrating the attack on Juba they would prevent Garang from capturing that prize and thus establishing his ascendancy further. The dissidents, in this instance, were virtually cutting off their nose to spite their face.

On the other hand by counting on the NIF's support to capture the South the dissidents have failed to realize that the only reason why the NIF is amenable to acquiescence to secession is because of the indomitable challenge posed by the SPLM/SPLA both to the NIF's short- and long-term strategies. By weakening that Movement the South would no longer jeopardize those strategies and there would, therefore, be no reason for them to give in a single iota of the South to the "secularists" – otherwise known, in the common NIF parlance, as the infidels. Furthermore the

NIF's agenda for an islamicization of their image does not stop at Khartoum; Sudan's "Islamicization" *à la* NIF is but the first step towards a larger "Jihad" to spread Islam elsewhere in Africa. If the NIF has already extended its tentacles into Algeria and Tunisia and begun dabbling with Egypt and Uganda, it would be foolhardy to assume that an independent South would be immune to their "Jihad". The Nasir group's agenda is, therefore, at best myopic and ill-considered, and at its worst, wrong-headed and treacherous.

Alongside the Nasir events the High Command of the SPLM/ SPLA met in Torit between 6–12 September 1991 to discuss several issues. That meeting had been conceived long before the events at Nasir. The main reason for the convocation of the Torit meeting was developments in Ethiopia and their implication on the Movement. The Ethiopian situation, following the demise of President Mengistu, had serious spillover effects on the SPLM, not least of which was at the human level when half a million refugees gravitated from Ethiopia towards SPLM/SPLA-controlled territory. Current peace initiatives, relations with the National Democratic Alliance, military operations and relief assistance were also among the issues featuring on the agenda of that meeting. Another important reason for the meeting was the administrative problems resulting from the SPLM/SPLA's victories in terms of the vast areas that are now to be managed; that includes not only areas in Upper Nile south of the Sobat and Eastern Equatoria but also Western Equatoria and some parts of Bahr el Ghazal. Those successes have brought all Sudan's borders with Kenya, Uganda, Zaire and Central African Republic under the control of the SPLA, a matter that poses its own administrative problems.

Additionally, the revolutionary changes that have gripped the world with a direct impact on ideologies necessitated a reflection by the Movement on its Manifesto and basic philosophies. In this respect, SPLM/SPLA, under the chairmanship of Dr Garang, had always sought meticulously to maintain a balance between different ideological groups within the Movement, shunning any attempts to apply ideological labels to the group as a whole. Whenever he was asked about the ideology of the Movement, Dr Garang resorted to using a nebulous definition. "If I have to choose an "ism", Garang said, "it would be 'Sudanism'." Garang was obviously wary of opening Pandora's box. The Torit resolutions emanating from that meeting have progressed a long way in setting the stage for a new era in the evolution of SPLM/SPLA. (See Appendix 2.)

The Torit resolutions triggered off some combustible issues, particularly that of self-determination, confederation or union of sovereign states as an ultimate goal for the Movement. The reaction to that was one of consternation in the North, particularly among the ranks of the National Democratic Alliance. Regrettably the text of the resolution was read out of context; references to confederation, union of sovereign states or self-determination have come within the framework of the discussion of current peace processes. In this connection the Torit meeting affirmed the Movement's unyielding adherence to the idea of a united Sudan under a secular constitution; failing that a wide range of options was offered to those Sudanese who do not support a religious-based constitution. Nowhere in the reference to self-determination did the word "South" appear. Self-determination was meant to be exercised by each and every group or region in the Sudan who do not wish to submit to the policies of a theocracy.

Evidently the issue of secession has raised its head once again and the SPLM/SPLA could not be silent on it. The Nasir group raised it, and so did a group of concerned eminent Southern Sudanese who assembled at Adare, Ireland, between 3 and 8 September 1991. The Adare group asserted what many Southerners believe, including those in the SPLM/SPLA; that the only way for Sudan to remain united is through adherence to the principles of democracy, secularism and a pluralistic constitution. But the Adare group went on to say that, failing to achieve that end, secession of the South should be considered as a viable option. That contention was rebutted there and then by some participants in the meeting; among those were supporters of the SPLM/SPLA as well as others who had gone through the secessionist phase in the 1960s and concluded that its days were now over, e.g. Mr Gordon Mortat.

The Adare meeting, however, brought uneasiness and a sense of apprehension among political forces in the North, and while the uneasiness may be understandable any apprehension as to what some Southerners were up to could not be justified. Indeed since the overthrow of Nimeiri, many elements within the Northern political establishment, rather than addressing the main issue of unity in the Sudan on the basis of the thesis postulated by the SPLM/SPLA (the only Southern-originated Movement in the Sudan to declare from the outset its national vocation), spent their energies debating the legitimacy of that Movement's "national" credentials and hence its vision for Sudan's unity.

In a sense the Torit resolutions have turned the tables. By presenting the issue in the way it did Torit conveyed more than one message. In the first place it addressed those who called for immediate secession and arrogated to themselves the right to decide *a priori* what Southerners would want in the event that a secular Sudan was not possible. Whether or not secession ought to be the next step should be a matter to be decided by the people themselves through self-determination. The second message was addressed to other groups and regions in the Sudan who share the Movement's vision. They too now have an option: self-determination, confederation or establishing their own sovereign states. The most important message, however, is the one sent to the political forces in the North. The choice before those forces is between unity of the Sudan under the umbrella of a secular constitution, where people can live in harmony irrespective of race, ethnic origin, sex and religion, or, if they feel so strongly bound to *Sharia*, then foregoing unity, except probably in the form of a confederation of sovereign states. The political establishment in Khartoum has, therefore, to confront these issues seriously; gone are the days of soft options.

Peace efforts on which this work has deliberated abundantly were also on the agenda of the Torit meeting. The mediation attempts by a number of African and non-African leaders continued unabated. The last of those efforts was the one undertaken by the current Chairman of the Organization for African Unity, General Ibrahim Babangida of Nigeria. The Nigerian President has been in close contact with both the government and the SPLM since January 1991 with a view to organizing a meeting between the two parties in Abuja, Nigeria. Several dates for that meeting have been set and subsequently cancelled in view of lack of agreement between the two parties on the agenda of the meeting. Khartoum insisted on basing the agenda on its own plans for peace, i.e. a brand of federalism which allows the South to opt out of *Sharia* while laws for the rest of Sudan and the federal government remain *Sharia*-based. The SPLM, on the other hand, wished to address the issue of the future of a united Sudan, which necessarily entails deliberation on the nature of the federal laws governing all citizens in the united Sudan (specifically, universally applied laws), the nature of the state itself, system of rule, etc. In this respect the NIF was uncompromising on the issue of multi-partism (the only way to reflect politically the cultural multiplicity of the country), hence their opposition to the inclusion of the issue of multiparty democracy on the agenda. In essence the NIF wants to talk the SPLM into accepting a religious apartheid that does not speak its name.

The peace process took a new turn following the Nasir events. The government immediately changed its tone and proclaimed itself a spokesman for the Nasir group; there shall be no peace talks without the participation of the Nasir rebels, they told the Nigerian President. In response to that contention, the SPLM stated that either the Nasir group is merely a splinter group of the SPLM and thus the issue is to be dealt with by the Movement internally, or that they are an independent force and consequently they must identify themselves and state their purpose. Since that group is ostensibly not inimical to Khartoum and since their per-spectives on peace (secession) coincide with the medium-term objectives of the NIF, the SPLM does not oppose their partici-pation in the negotiations as a part of the government delegation. However, the SPLM also maintained that, in such an eventuality, the talks should include other Sudanese political forces and par-ticularly that the questions at issue before the meeting shall no longer be ones focusing on peace between two combatting armies but also that of the future of the Sudan. This dodging by the NIF government goes a long way to show that Khartoum has never had any peace policy, only peace politics.

In effect, the callousness of the NIF government in their exploitation of the Nasir group for their own ends did not end there. The government has seriously impeded various relief efforts. In a meeting between a high-powered Sudanese govern-ment delegation and the SRRA representatives, with Mr James Jona, United Nations Secretary-General, the Khartoum dele-gation insisted once again that the Nasir group should be part and parcel to any agreement on relief; their goal was to use the United Nations as an instrument of legitimization of that splinter group. The SPLM adamantly opposed that ruse, so did the UN.

However it did not take long to expose the Nasir secessionist group for what they sadly are; a group of elitists driven by blind ambition that would stop at nothing to achieve its earthly objectives. Early in June Khartoum mounted the biggest military offensive ever on the South, its armada (armed and equipped by Iran and Libya) was made up of twenty thousand men and included armoured battalions, gunboats and newly acquired bombers and air fighters. The offensive, dubbed "Khatimat al-mataf" i.e. the end of the road, was meant to deal a final blow on the SPLA before the onset of the rainy season in April-May. The Sudanese Army's Chief of Staff declared at the beginning of the offensive that he "shall pray in Torit's mosque" by the end of January 1992. The NIF government was certainly emboldened by two factors, the Nasir secession and political changes in Ethiopia. In effect, they may have misread the implications of both incidents on the SPLM/SPLA, a movement that controls two thirds of the territory of the South. This is hardly a force that can be wished away, the NIF and its allies in Nasir have wishfully construed an adversity as a terminal illness.

Nonetheless, the new Ethiopian authorities (despite assurances to the contrary made to third parties) have allowed the Sudanese army to intrude, through their territory, into SPLA backlines (in Pochala). The Nasir group, on the other hand, assured the invading army free passage through the territory under their control in Upper Nile. To put the final touches on that collusion, however, a meeting was held in Frankfurt, Germany on 23–25 January 1992 between Ali El Haj of the NIF and Lam Akol. That meeting was the last in a series of meetings. The outcome of the meeting was an agreement signed by the two parties (Appendix 3), though later denied by Lam. To his chagrin the agreement was announced and denounced by two of his supporters in the Nasir group who later regained their positions within the ranks of the SPLM/SPLA. Dr Machar, on the other side, attempted to distance himself from the Frankfurt deal and declared it null and void, that was just hot air, the unsuspecting Machar was now a hostage of the government, and there was nothing he could do to match words with deeds. The ditherings of Lam and the secrecy in which he wished to shroud the agreement revealed that there was more than meets the eye in that agreement. In effect the government got from the Nasir Quisling what it wanted, collaboration in the areas under the control of the Nasir Group so that the government's army can march freely to the SPLA-held areas.

Appendix 1

The following are officers known to have been fire-squaded by the Nasir Group as from 28 August 1991

1	A/Cdr	Peter Panom Thanypieny
2	A/Cdr	Joseph Mabil Ruot
3	Capt	Wuor Jok Abiei
4	1st Lt	Dau Akoi Jurkuc
5	1st Lt	Martin Matien Gumwel
6	2nd Lt	Wuor Marial
7	3rd Lt	Mangar

Officers and men known to have been detained and are being subjected to severe torturing by Nasir Group

(a)   *Nasir*

1	A/Cdr	Elijah Maduk Yuang
2	A/Cdr	Akim Aluong Kang
3	A/Cdr	James Lem Kuany
4	A/Cdr	Maguet Dhaal
5	A/Cdr	Ruben Abiel Chan
6	A/Cdr	Kuereng Akoi Jurkuc
7	A/Cdr	Nyang Chol
8	Capt.	Kezekia Ruet Puot
9	Capt.	Makuol
10	Capt.	Kuol Deng Kuol
11	Capt.	Malual Aguer Ding
12	Capt.	Garang Maluac
13	Capt.	Michael Manyuon Anyang
14	Capt.	Geneons George
15	Capt.	Aguer Bior Duot
16	Capt.	Ajak Aruai
17	Capt.	Magot Piok
18	Capt.	Monykuer Mayen
19	1st Lt	Thon Makor Guoy
20	2nd Lt	Atem Madhier
21	2nd Lt	Chol Manyuon Aney
22	2nd Lt	Majok Dhuor Awuol
23	2nd Lt	Abraham Madit Aler
24	2nd Lt	Abraham Mayol Ayual

25	S/M	Awan Lual Jok
26	Sgt	Akec Aguto

(b)	*Akobo*	
1	2nd Lt	Deng William Nyuon
2	2nd Lt	Andrew Bul Deu
3	Sgt	Kuol Piok

(c)	*Leer*	
1	A/Cdr	Kuol Ajak Deng
2	A/Cdr	Chol Riak
3	Cpt	Bior Pageer

Appendix 2

The SPLM/SPLA Torit Resolutions, 1991

Contents

Attendance

The meeting was attended by 9 (nine) of the 13 (thirteen) Members of the High Command, that is 70 per cent attendance. Cdr Yusaf Kuo Mekki could not attend because of distance and military operations in southern Kordofan, but he sent a radio message endorsing whatever resolutions the High Command passes. Three members, Cdrs Riak Machar, Lam Akol Ajawin and Gordon Kong Chol, refused to come to the meeting and instead declared on 28/8/1991 that they had overthrown the historical and legitimate Leadership of the SPLM/SPLA and appointed themselves with Riak as President and Lam his deputy. They hoped that the SPLA rank and file would rise in their support, but this did not and could not happen. The nine members who attended the meeting are: (1) Cdr John Garang de Mabior, (2) Cdr William Nyoun Bany, (3) Cdr Salva Kiir Mayardit, (4) Cdr James Wani Igga, (5) Cdr Daniel Awet Akot, (6) Cdr Kuol Manyang Juuk, (7) Cdr Martin Manyiel Ayuel, (8) Cdr Lual Diing Wol and (9) Cdr Galerio Modi Hurnyang.

The SPLM/SPLA Torit resolutions, 1991

The SPLM/SPLA Politico Military High Command (PMHC) conducted its series of meetings from 6/9/1991 to 12/9/1991. The High Command meetings ended by adopting the following resolutions:

Resolution No. 1 The Riak/Lam theoretical coup of 28/8/1991
In its first session held on 6/9/1991, the PMHC resolved that:

1.1 The Riak/Lam theoretical coup is denounced and condemned in the strongest of terms as devisive and destructive; only the enemy can benefit from it.
1.2 The Nasir coup situation will be approached peacefully and an amicable solution sought and reached, so as to maintain the cohesiveness and unity of the struggle and of our people.

Resolution No. 2 The Ethiopian situation
In its first session held on 6/9/1991, the PMHC, resolved that:

2.1 The SPLM/SPLA shall seek to improve relations with the new Ethiopian Government. Friendly countries shall be requested to assist.
2.2 The SPLM/SPLA shall seek to establish and maintain good and special relations with the population and authorities of Gambella Region in Ethiopia, as part of improved relations with the Ethiopian Government.
2.3 It is clear that keeping the refugee returnees in the inaccessible areas of Nasir, Pachalla, Akobo and Pakok is untenable. The resolution therefore recommends that the returnees be afforded and facilitated the following four choices:
   2.3.1 Voluntary resettlement in their villages in the Sudan.
   2.3.2 Voluntary return to refugee camps in Ethiopia.
   2.3.3 Voluntary resettlement in refugee camps in Kenya.
   2.3.4 Voluntary resettlement in camps for displaced people in easily accessible and peaceful places in SPLM/SPLA liberated and administered areas.

Resolution No. 3 Current peace initiatives
In its second session held on 7/9/1991, the PMHC resolves that:

3.1 Since the inception of the Movement in 1983, the SPLM/SPLA has been committed to peaceful resolution of the conflict through dialogue. Hence, in March, 1985 the Movement called for convening a

National Congress; in 1986 the Movement concluded the Koka Dam Declaration, which called for a National Constitutional Conference; in 1987 the Movement reached peace agreements with the Sudan African Parties (SAP); in November 1988 the Movement signed the DUP-SPLM Sudan Peace Initiative; and in 1989 the Movement entered into peace talks twice with the present Military Junta. In this spirit, the SPLM/SPLA shall continue to actively seek peaceful resolution to the conflict with the Government of the day in Khartoum and other political forces.

3.2 A centralized system of Government in the Sudan based on Arabism and Islam with local autonomies or federal states granted to the South (or other Regions) has been tried, failed and discredited, and thus the country has oscillated between war and peace since independence with 25 years of war out of 36 years of independence. In any future peace initiatives and talks, the position of the SPLM/SPLA on the system of Government shall be based on resolving the war through a united secular democratic Sudan, confederation, association of sovereign states or self-determination.

Resolution No. 4 The National Democratic Alliance (NDA)
In its second session held on 7/9/1991, the PMHC resolved that:

The SPLM/SPLA shall continue to be a member of the NDA and will actively seek ways and means to strengthen the NDA, so that it plays its full potential role in bringing about peace within the context of a united secular democratic Sudan.

Resolution No. 5 Military operations
(Withheld, not for public consumption, for obvious reasons.)

Resolution No. 6 Military administration
(Withheld, not for public consumption, for obvious reasons.)

Resolution No. 7 Civil administration
In its third session held on 8/9/1991, the PMHC resolved that:

7.1 With liberation of vast territories there is basic and urgent need to establish, develop and improve effective civil administration at the grass-roots, as has been done in East and West Bank of Equatoria and in former Jonglei province. The basic autonomous local government unit of administration shall be the *COUNTY*. A county shall be sub-divided into *PAYAM* councils, and the Payam into villages.

7.2 At the COUNTY level, where there are no active military operations, civil administration shall be separated from the army, and, where there are active military operations the form of administration shall be decided by the Front Commander, subject to approval of the Chairman/C-in-C.

7.3 The population of a County shall be at least 50,000 and may not exceed 150,000.

7.4 At the Payam and Village levels administration shall be civil and separated from the army in all cases. However, the Front Commander may impose military administration on any Payam or village should it be necessary.

7.5 The theatre of war shall be organized into *FRONTS*, and all countries within a Front shall fall under the Front Commander assisted by his staff and the county administrations.

7.6 In order to enhance effective civil administration and socio-economic development, the SPLM/SPLA opens its doors to Sudanese civilians supporters inside and outside the country who are willing to participate in the development of the Liberated Areas. Military training shall not be required for membership in the Movement.

7.7 The current civil administrative set-up of COUNTIES and PAYAMS shall form the basis of the New Sudan systems of Public Administration, and shall be developed as more areas get liberated and more experience gained in the already liberated areas.

7.8 A Commission to Organize and Develop Public Administration (CODPA) shall be formed under a High Command Member, and will present its work to the next meeting of the PMHC for discussion and adoption.

7.9 Competent former police, prisons, wild-life and public administration officer, NCOS and men shall be screened out and assigned to their respective departments. Other suitable officers shall be trained and appointed into these departments as well as into other civil departments such as education, agriculture, health, etc.

7.10 The Chairman/C-in-C shall appoint committees for selection of candidates into the various colleges (Military, Police, Prison, Wild-Life, Public Administrations, Institute for Legal Affairs, etc.). The committees shall forward their recommendations to CODPA for further screening and subsequently to the Chairman/C-in-C for final approval.

7.11 It is to be reiterated that the SPLM/SPLA is at war, and its primary task remains the destruction of the enemy combat capabilities. Hence, the separation of civil administration from the army must not adversely affect the army's combat effectiveness, but rather should enhance it.

Resolution No. 8 The economy
In its third session held on 8/9/1991, the PMHC resolved that:

8.1 The Sudan is bountifully endowed with vast amounts of natural resources, most of which are untapped. In agriculture we have a base potential of more than 200 million acres of arable land of which less than 10 per cent is utilized. There are good investment opportunities in the commercial production of Coffee, Cotton, Tea, Sesame, Lulu, Groundnuts, Sunflowers, Sorghum, Maize, Rice, Wheat, Sugar, Fruits, Forestry products, etc. In the area of animal husbandry, there are good investment opportunities in ranching and dairy. In fisheries, there are millions and millions of tons of freshwater fish in the many rivers, lakes and lagoons, especially in Southern Sudan. In addition to fisheries, the many rivers are potential source of hydro-electric power, which can be produced through giant or micro-plants. In the field of mining, the country is very rich in oil, gold, copper, uranium, cement, iron, etc. Finally, the vast and exotic wild-life and natural features provide excellent opportunities for investment in tourism and hotels. Other investment opportunities exist in the areas of banking, river transport and in road, rail, airfields and housing construction. The PMHC resolved that it is not necessary to wait for the end of the war to exploit these resources. Hence, the SPLM/SPLA calls upon international and domestic private businesses to start investing now in the SPLM/SPLA administered areas. Pre-investment in feasibility studies, etc. is also possible and recommended to international business.

8.2 The SPLM/SPLA shall devise policies and modalities to expedite the efficient exploitation of the above resources to raise the standard of living of our people to benefit humankind in general. In this connection, the SPLM/SPLA shall adopt the policy of *"mixed economy"* based on a composite of freely competitive private, cooperative and public sectors, and on equity in the distribution of income, wealth and development opportunities in the regions. The SPLM/SPLA shall encourage local and foreign business to invest in any of the three sectors including joint-ventures. Appropriate laws shall be promulgated to enable foreign businesses to repatriate profits without undue hindrances.

8.3 The National Economic Commission (NEC) shall be the advisory organ to the PMHC on economic policy. It shall encourage local and foreign private business to invest in the liberated areas, and formulate supervisory regulations governing their activities. Such laws shall be approved by the Chairman/C-in-C.

8.4 Local and foreign private business are allowed and encouraged to take up export and import trade and wholesale and retail trade in the liberated areas, in order to provide basic commodities and services to the population in these areas.

8.5 Sudanese currency and currencies of the neighbouring countries shall be legal tender in the liberated areas until such time the New Sudan develops its own currency. The NEC shall advise on exchange rates and effect transactions within its capacity. Barter shall be permitted.

Resolution No. 9 Foreign policy and SPLM/SPLA offices abroad
In its fourth session on 9/9/1991, the PMHC resolved that:

9.1 The SPLM/SPLA shall seek friendship, mutual understanding, co-operation and mutual benefit with all countries and international organizations that are sympathetic with the objectives of the Movement and the just cause of our people.

9.2 Special emphasis shall be given to establishment of good relations with the neighbouring countries and the countries of our Region and Continent. In this connection, the SPLM/SPLA shall seek to restore and improve the historical and special relationship with Ethiopia, Egypt and East Africa.

9.3 The PMHC encourages and calls upon supporters of the Movement abroad to declare their membership of the SPLM/SPLA, so that they are organized into chapters of the Movement in the countries where they work or reside, and thereby contribute fully, to the liberation and development of our people. Membership cards will be made to this effect, and members will be required to pay membership fees as well as contributions according to their abilities.

9.4 Foreign nationals shall, on recommendations of an SPLM/SPLA chapter abroad and approval by the Chairman/C-in-C, be granted Honourary Membership of the Movement, and such may be, if desired, converted into citizenship in the future New Sudan.

Resolution No. 10 Relief assistance
In its fourth session held on 9/9/1991, the PMHC resolve that:

10.1 The SPLM/SPLA considers relief assistance to innocent civilians caught up in the war situation and natural disasters as a human right, and the Movement shall facilitate passage of relief assistance

to the areas of need in both SPLM/SPLA and Government administered areas.

10.2 In this connection, the SPLM/SPLA appeals to all Governments,
the United Nations and Non-Governmental humanitarian organizations to increase their efforts in relief, resettlement, rehabilitation
and development assistance to SPLM/SPLA administered areas.
Whereas relief assistance will still remain central and vital as long
as the war continues, the Movement urges that rehabilitation and
development be emphasized more and more. Hitherto, development
in the Sudan has moved, if at all, from North to South. The Movement visualizes a need to develop a situation where development
moves from South to North as crucial factor in the peace process
and subsequently in maintaining unity and stability in the Sudan,
and such development must begin now under relief, rehabilitation
and development assistance to SPLM/SPLA administered areas.

10.3 All international and local relief, rehabilitation and development
assistance and efforts shall be organized and processed through the
Sudan Relief and Rehabilitation Association (SRRA), which shall
remain an autonomous humanitarian organization for the SPLM/
SPLA administered areas as well as contested areas, such as Southern Kordofan, Southern Blue Nile and Southern Darfur in War
Zone II.

10.4 There is sufficient documented evidence that individuals within the
NOG relief community were deeply and actively involved in the
recent Nasir theoretical abortive coup by Commander Riak and
Commander Lam. Relief planes, relief radios and foreign relief
personnel were the main agents used in the abortive coup. The
Movement strongly condemns the use of relief as a political weapon.

10.5 The SPLM/SPLA shall declare *persona non grata* and expel any
individual relief personnel who involves in activities incompatible
with his or her relief status. The expulsion shall affect only the
individuals involved but not the organizations to which they belong
or for which they work, unless, or course the organization itself is
so involved.

Resolution No. 11 Acquisition of war equipment
(Withheld, not for public consumption, for obvious reasons.)

Resolution No. 12 Judiciary
In its fourth session held on 9/9/1991, the PMHC resolved that:

12.1 With the liberation and administration of vast territories, the establishment of the rule of law and independence judicial organs is imperative and a priority for the Movement. Judicial organs, where not existing, shall be established at all levels from Payam to the Front and at the Movement's General Headquarters.

12.2 There shall be separation of civil and military laws. A panel of judges, former army, police and other suitable officers shall be informed to draft amendments to the existing laws, as well as draft new laws for approval by the PMHC.

12.3 As the Movement lacks trained judges, a New Sudan Institute for Legal Affairs (NSILA) shall established to give crash training to Members of the Movement including chiefs to act as judges at various levels.

Resolution No. 13 Ideology and political work
In its fourth session held on 9/9/1991, the PMHC resolved that:

13.1 The ideology of liberations movement is the political philosophy on which its principles and objectives are based and which guides its policies, programmes and action. The Manifesto of the SPLM, issued on 31/7/1983, has served the Movement for the last 8 years. However, the internal and international situation has been changing and evolving and there is, therefore, definite need to review and revise that Manifesto. The SPLM Manifesto of 31/7/1983 shall be reviewed and revised, and the PMHC here forms a committee from among its members to make the necessary review and revisions, incorporating and reflecting the necessary internal and international changes so that the revised Manifesto better serves the Movement.

13.2 Political work among the people and within the army shall be based on the forthcoming revised Manifesto. In the meantime the relevant portions of the Manifesto shall be suspended forthwith, that is, political work shall be based on the old Manifesto as modified by the eighteen resolutions of this PMHC meeting.

13.3 The committee to review and revise the Manifesto shall present its draft revised Manifesto to the next meeting of the High Command for discussion and adoption.

Resolution No. 14 High Command powers, rules and code of conduct
In this fourth session on 9/9/1991, the PMHC resolved that:

14.1 A committee of the High Command shall be formed to draft the powers, procedures, rules and code of conduct governing the Politico Military High Command and lower organizational echelons of the Movement to the Payam level.

14.2 The Committee shall present its draft work to the next meeting of the High Command for discussion and approval.

Resolution No. 15 Human rights and civil liberties
In its fifth session held on 11/9/1991, the PMHC resolved that:

15.1 The SPLM/SPLA is a liberation movement fighting for justice, equality, freedom, democracy, prosperity and human dignity. The SPLM/SPLA shall adhere to internationally accepted norms and standards on human rights and shall protect and respect the rights and civil liberties of all persons resident in areas under its administration without prejudice on race, tribe, religion or sex.

15.2 The SPLM/SPLA shall guarantee freedom of worship and proselytization to all religions or beliefs without favour or prejudice to any one of them. It is on this principle that the Movement has encouraged formation of the New Sudan Council of Churches (NSCC) and recently of the New Sudan Islamic Council (NSIC).

15.3 Consistent with the Movement's policy on human rights, the SPLM/SPLA believes that the object of combat is to render the opponent non-combative, and, hence, whenever an enemy soldier is disarmed or unarmed his or her life will be spared, protected and respected as a prisoner of war (POW) under the Geneva conventions.

Resolution No. 16 Women's rights and participation
In its fifth session on 11/9/1991, the PMHC resolved that:

16.1 In any country Women constitute more than 50 per cent of the population and suffer all manner of discrimination in the social, economic and political fields simply because they are Women. In the Sudan the plight of Women is further exacerbated by underdevelopment, poverty, the Sharia Laws and a host of other archaic customs and traditions. The SPLM/SPLA affirms the equality of Women with Men and shall do everything possible to open up opportunities for Women in all fields of social, economic and political activity.

16.2 Because women have been historically discriminated against and oppressed, the SPLM/SPLA shall adopt affirmative action in favour of women, and shall encourage women to organize on their own to take advantage of the Movement's positive policies and struggle to realize their rights and dignity.

Resolution No. 17 Wild-life and the environment
In its fifth session held on 11/9/1991, the PMHC resolved that:

17.1 Previous Sudanese Governments paid little attention and abused our wild-life and natural environment to the extent that Government officials actively participated in poaching. Animals such as Elephant, Rhinoceros and Buffalo were hunted down using army helicopters! This greatly reduced our wild-life and forced mass migration of animals to the neighbouring countries. In addition the 8 years of war has created a situation where a big number of automatic guns are in the hands of unauthorized persons, thus making our wild-life further vulnerable. The SPLM/SPLA shall do everything to halt the destruction of our wild-life resources and to protect and develop them for us and for posterity.

17.2 As came in the SPLM/SPLA Punitive and Disciplinary Laws, 1983 concerning the preservation of wild-life, and with the establishment of civil administration and the rule of law in the liberated areas, the SPLM/SPLA is now better able to implement its laws on the preservation and protection of wild-life and the environment. Protection of wild-life and the environment is the duty of all citizens, not just the Departments of Wild-life and Conservation, and the PMHC all citizens and organs of the Movement to respect and protect our wild-life and environment, and for the empowered authorities to implement the law and severely punish culprits.

17.3 New laws shall be promulgated to reinforce existing ones for the preservation and protection of the environment and appeals made to world environmental groups and other organizations to assist SPLM/SPLA programmes to protect and enhance the environment in areas such as afforestation, prevention of forest fires and prevention of soil erosion.

Resolution No. 18 Reference to the above resolutions
In its sixth and last session held on 12/9/1991, the PMHC ended the historic High Command meeting and resolved that:

18.1 The 18 resolutions passed by the SPLM/SPLA Political Military High Command in its meetings from September 6, 1991 to September 12, 1991 in the historical city of Torit shall be referred to as the *"Torit Resolutions, 1991"*.

The SPLM Political Military High Command,
Torit, Sudan: September 12, 1991

Appendix 3

Joint Statement

During the period from 23 to 25 January 1992, two delegations representing the government of the Sudan and the Interim National Executive Committee of the SPLM/A (Nasir Faction) have met in Frankfurt City, Germany, to discuss and negotiate the peace process in the Sudan.

The government delegation was chaired by Dr Ali El Haj Mohamed, the SPLM/A was headed by Dr Lam Akol Ajawin. Among the issues broadly discussed about the peace process in the Sudan, the following points were agreed upon.

1   There shall be a transitional period (to be agreed upon) from the day of signing an agreement between the Sudan government and the SPLM/A, during which Southern Sudan shall enjoy a special Constitutional and Political Status within the united Sudan after which period the people of the South shall exercise their right to freely choose the political and constitutional status that accords with their national aspirations without ruling out any option.

B   To avoid resort to armed confrontation in the future between the people of the south and the central government as a way of resolving constitutional, political and other differences, elaborate legal and constitutional procedures shall be worked out and agreed upon, for the ascertainment through a plebiscite of the views of the former with respect to their political and constitutional status after the transitional period.

2   The two sides have agreed to attend the Abuja proposed peace talks at the earliest possible time.

3   The two sides have discussed the issues of the system of government during the interim period particularly on the power sharing, resources, security arrangements, relief, rehabilitation, resettlement and reconstruction and agreed to subject them to further negotiations.

4   In order to provide an atmosphere conducive for peaceful dialogue and negotiations, Abuja peace talks shall be preceded by a declaration of cease-fire throughout the South and other affected areas in the Northern Sudan.

Signatories,

Dr Ali El Haj Mohamed   Dr Lam Akol Ajawin

Frankfurt, 25/1/1992